An Ocean Away

AN OCEAN AWAY

by

Dave Clarke

with

John Holloway

Small boat: Big dream

BLUE DOLPHIN
BOOKS

Contents

List of Illustrations

Facing page 110

Facing page 174

Charts

For Elaine

Acknowledgements

THREE YEARS LATER AND several thousand e-mails with plenty of face-to-face meetings, John and I finally signed off *An Ocean Away*.

Without John's assistance, passion and skill with the written word in turning some of my jumbled ramblings into legible text along with the great belief that this was a story worth telling, I would never have completed this book. I will be forever in a dept of gratitude that I could never attempt to repay with a few simple words but it is with sincere thanks for all your effort and hard work. Thank you John.

I also want to thank my family. Elaine for her patience and my two boys Bradley and Joel, also known as Shaky Harry and Polar Bear for their understanding when "Daddy" was always on the computer. Sorry!

There are many friends and colleagues I would like to mention for their help and support in completing this book, to many to list here but you all know who you are. A special thanks does however go to Chris, the only guy mad enough to set sail with me across Biscay. Simon for his excellent cooking on what could only be described as a pleasure cruise from Madeira to Tenerife. Jane for managing the process and reminding me that good things come to those who wait!

But most of all I thank the people and characters I have met and befriended along the way. They are the real story; I am just the teller of tales…

.

Introduction

ALL OVER THE WORLD there are people who like to mess about in boats; and I'm one of them.

Kids with Pooh sticks and boats in the bath, earnest model-makers, day skippers and trawler men, ferry captains, admirals of the fleet, rowers, paddlers and punters, dedicated race yachtsmen and women. We all seem to cling to a primeval instinct that sees us drawn back to tracts of water in the same way as lemmings go to cliffs.

With children it's understandable. Water is messy, strange, fun. Playing with boats is part of growing up. But as you grow up life drags in other priorities, like sex, pubs and mortgages. You'd be forgiven for thinking that boats and water would be way down the pecking order, but for many the passion doesn't go away. Playing and working with boats has a peculiar mix of ingredients: contentment, excitement, fear, obsession, with a huge dollop of freedom and an even bigger dollop of madness. Often it's a recipe for days spent being tossed about, often wet, freezing and miserable. No sane, rational adult human being would ever get involved with boats. Ever!

But we do. I reckon most people can't stand by a river, lake or ocean without feeling some sort of mysterious affinity with water, while some go further. The mad, crazy ones who for some unfathomable reason decide that since the human body consists of seventy per cent water they might as well spend their lives on it or immersed in it. I'm a Northern lad, born as far from the sea as is possible. As a young child I never had boats for toys; I rarely played in rivers. My earliest memories of water involved soap and the rough hand of parents who thought that the way to fame, fortune or high office was to ensure that the backs of my ears were constantly clean.

So what made me take the decision to sail single-handed across the Atlantic, a decision that gave me the adventure of a lifetime? Why was I drawn to boats and to sailing in particular? How did the simple act of sitting in a boat for the first time give me a craving that has lasted all my life? Who and what shaped my passion for adventure in the natural world?

The sea has been an indefinable catalyst that led me to my biggest adventure and most testing life challenge. I never deliberately set out to sail across the Atlantic. There is no tradition or bloodline I can trace back to Raleigh or Nelson. Like most people, opportunities and events conspired to give me the life I have. The idea of a solo ocean adventure gradually crept into my brain and stubbornly refused to go away. As I set foot on my boat on that first day I felt elated, driven and a bit apprehensive. It was as if I was joining an elite band of people who'd overcome adversity, setbacks and moments of real doubt; a sort of inclusive club open to anyone but not *for* everyone. A club where membership was determined by one's own resolve and self-belief; where forces of danger and uncertainty have to be faced; where, in order to gain what you seek, something has to be sacrificed. I write these words after my adventure and with time for reflection. At the moment of launch I had no such articulation; I just wanted to get started and see what happened, but nevertheless, the fact that I'd made it to my own start line did feel like some kind of rite of passage.

This book is not a technical manual of sailing expertise. I'm no Robin Knox-Johnston or Bernard Moitessier but I've shared the mysterious seduction of the sea and the intense roller-coaster ride of emotions when tested against the most powerful element on the planet. Sailing has scared the wits out of me and brought me a joy that has had me sobbing my heart out, but I still class myself as an ordinary man. I guess all my sailing heroes think of themselves as ordinary, and while I'm not in awe of them I am in awe of their exploits, if only because they have dedicated their lives to the sea. They have taken their dreams to an elite level that is exceptional but at least I share a common beginning; I dared to dream, and then nurtured that dream into a life-changing reality.

I could not have undertaken my Atlantic journey without a basic competence and understanding of sailing, weather forecasting, reading charts of the wind or the sea, because it would have been irresponsible to do so. I'm from the North of England so I don't suppose I have the niceties found in many a sailing club. Where I come from nautical terms such as 'lee ho' and 'coming about' are translated into 'Duck, you pillock, we're turning!' And much of the sailing fraternity don't like single-handed sailors. They think we're dangerous and a menace to others. On long-haul voyages single-handers can't sleep, eat, tack, plot and manage the boat all at once, all the time, can they? They put the lives of rescuers at risk, don't they? Theoretically we'd never make it, would we?

Try telling that to Tony Bullimore.

If the criteria for being a single-handed sailor are a streak of selfish independence, stubbornness and general insanity, then I'm well qualified. My philosophy on life is that if you wait until you're ready and fully prepared then you'll never do anything. I've met dozens and dozens of people throughout my life who all dream of finding an escape from a routine existence. They're still dreaming because they're 'not quite ready yet'. I learnt early on the difference between taking unnecessary risks and those of an instinctive or calculated kind. I wasn't certain I was ready to sail the Atlantic, I couldn't afford the best essential equipment, but I lived my dream and found my escape.

I'm an ordinary bloke who undertook an extraordinary journey, a voyage that brought adversity, humour, high drama and ultimately a focus and understanding to my life. I had an adventure, the memories and impact of which will last me all my days.

This is my story; some of it could well be yours.

CHAPTER ONE

Sharky's Reincarnation

The spray, the wind rush, the sheer thrill of being alive.

SHIP'S LOG, 14.15 HOURS, Tuesday 21st July 1992, Falmouth. The first words I ever wrote on my transatlantic voyage were:

> 'Cast off! Well, here goes. Absolutely unsure of what's ahead.
> Self-steering is not working very well. Dinner time!'

Looking back, it's good to know I had my priorities right. I couldn't do much about the trip ahead but I was damned if I was going to do it on an empty stomach. Imagine the embarrassment of a worst-case scenario and the post-mortem declaration: 'Stomach contents – none.'

I'd been sailing for a few years by now and, somehow, at the age of twenty-eight, I'd gradually talked myself into sailing across the Atlantic. Now here I was, on the threshold of a great adventure that I hadn't really planned to do. It just seemed to have happened, just like that! I'd spent the few days before departure in a state of excitement and anxiety, checking and stowing gear and food, then re-checking and re-stowing. I wanted to start, with part of me not wanting to leave. Looking out at the sea swell beyond the harbour wall I didn't quite believe that in a few hours' time where I was now would be out of sight. I'd be at the mercy of the elements and thrust on my own skill and resources, or possibly a lack of. Mentally I recalled the cold facts and figures about the Atlantic. The second largest ocean, slightly more than six times the size of the USA with a total area of 76,000,000 square kilometres. Seventy-six million! Oh, and deep – down to eight and half thousand metres. Perhaps this was not the time to make an unfavourable comparison with statistics closer to home. Dave Clarke, 1.9 metres tall in a sloop ominously called *Sharky*, 5.5 metres long. It didn't seem like a fair fight to me but I'd never been in a fair fight in my life.

It was odd, I thought, that at that moment, and that point of departure, the hundreds of people milling around Falmouth harbour had absolutely no idea what I was about to do. For all they cared, if they cared at all, I was just another seafarer about to cast off on a trip around the bay. I liked that sense of anonymity as I was never one for publicity or the big occasion. I was happy to be there for me, because this was my adventure and I didn't want any emotional farewells. I relished that sense of obscurity. I relished the sound of 'seafarer' even more. It rolled around my tongue and tasted of history. I was about to undertake a huge adventure and I required an appropriate name – 'sailing' was for inland and coastal waters. In the supreme arrogance of the moment, I pompously declared myself a seafarer.

I'd caught the sailing bug in dribs and drabs as I'd been growing up. There hadn't been a single flash of insight, no instant jolt of enlightenment, no sense of life ambition. As a youngster born in the steel town of Sheffield, then growing up around the hills of Buxton, I'd been more into moorland and rolling hills than boats, but bit by bit, as my life evolved, I found myself in their company. I think much of my fascination had come from reading. Despite struggling through my school years – and later diagnosed as dyslexic – I found an escape in books as I grew into my late teens and beyond. Reading helped improve my use of language and stimulated my imagination. Books became just more than pages and print; they became accessible kingdoms where dreams were realisable and nothing seemed impossible. I was drawn more to travel and factual adventure books than fiction and avidly sought out stories of exotic wanderings, from Mark Shand's travel with an Indian elephant to Ranulph Fiennes' Arctic treks. I even tackled the Bible, the Koran and Aldous Huxley. Imperturbably, I began to include books about sailing exploits. Without realising it, I was challenging unsettling life experiences, and my random interaction with boats, as a child and later a teenager, began to coalesce. Two authors in particular stand out in my mind from those days. Bernard Moitessier, an unassuming Frenchman, had penned an account (*The Long Way*) of his entry into the 1968 *Sunday Times* non-stop solo round-the-world challenge. Out on the Pacific Ocean he had had a life-changing experience when competitive sailing no longer held any meaning for him. Literally, in mid-stream and in a winning position, he changed course, disengaged himself from the race and sailed off to find his own sunset in Tahiti. I remember being deeply affected by his story, trying to understand the man behind such an amazing decision. It was one I realised I could identify with but wondered whether I would ever have or want the same resolve.

The other book that gripped me intensely was *Shrimpy* by a little-known guy called Shane Acton. In 1972 he'd bought a small eighteen-foot Caprice-class sloop and for the next eight years circumnavigated the world, mainly on his own; he still holds the record for this trip using the smallest boat. What appealed to me was that Acton was not a professional sailor, he had extremely limited funds, and he seemed to be just an ordinary guy who wanted control of his destiny. Both men were sea gypsies, independent thinkers who went their own way in life against the odds and convention. I read both books many times, drinking in the atmosphere and finding something that went deeper than just a good read. The strength of their self-belief had struck a chord within me. The chord had yet to find a tune but my love of the outdoors, of nature and travel, had been given a new and different impetus. It's true to say that these accounts created a pleasant but unsettling ache in me. I was beginning to experience what comedians would call a long-felt want. Still unfocused and ill-defined as these thoughts were, I began to wonder whether I should consider buying a boat. Then in my mid-twenties and heavily involved in a retail business, I was far from plans to sail the Atlantic, let alone do it on my own, but through the magic of reading I began to harbour wistful and impossible thoughts about the notion of a great ocean journey. A tiny seed had been planted and was plucking up courage to germinate.

I remember the date well. The 29th October 1988; the date I fell in love with a flirty temptress from Chesterfield. A wreck turned sea mistress that would turn my life upside down. The more I thought about the idea of owning a boat, the more convinced I became that it was imperative. My retail business was a confectionery, tobacco and newsagent's shop in Buxton. This meant I could regularly order a number of sailing magazines and scan them to see what was available, particularly something that would fit my bank account, which seemed to hover permanently and stubbornly just above red. I hadn't done much in the way of deciding what sort of craft I wanted though the notion of a Caprice – the small boat used by Shane Acton – kept recurring. Whether I had mentally stepped into his shoes I'm not certain but my eye was always drawn to the pages where a Caprice was for sale. All I had to do was find one that was up to the task.

After a few months of scanning papers and trade journals a phone call led me to a Chesterfield boatyard, an improbable, landlocked gravel-patched couple of acres sandwiched between the A61 and an industrial estate. The owner assured me he had 'just the thing'. Boatyards are strange places, where the term 'fish out of water' neatly applies to boats out of their natural environment. Chesterfield, being on the edge of the Peak District, is not exactly the centre of maritime activity, the nearest decent stretch of water being at least thirty miles away. As I entered the yard I was greeted by a forlorn showing of distressed little boats, perched on their cradles, all seemingly longing to be back in the water again. The place felt like a Dr Barnardo's for orphaned vessels.

The 'just the thing' was a pitiful, despondent wreck unceremoniously jammed in between two quite decent yachts, making her look even more miserable, and, as so often happens, I took to her straight away. I had found my sailing companion. The technical description confirmed she was an eighteen-foot yacht, built in the 1970s of fibreglass and wood with two steel-and-timber keels and a beam (width) of around seven feet at her widest point. She had a single cabin, a self-draining open cockpit aft of the cabin, and a single twenty-foot mast. The non-technical description, about which I could bore for Britain, was that she was gorgeous – in an extremely beat-up sort of way – painted in filthy white on the topsides and deck, with acres of dried weed and ancient anti-fouling paint below the waterline. The cabin was – well, I suppose 'cramped' would be generous. Imagine less room than the inside of a Ford Fiesta with a working height of about four feet. It felt claustrophobic but I put that down to the dark paintwork, and, while there wasn't much stowage, I reckoned I could cope. The top deck was coming away from the hull, the rigging was useless, the boom was a piece of rough wood and there were no sails, otherwise she was perfect! Mentally claiming her there and then I decided to call her *Sharky*, a nickname given to me a few years earlier when I was grubbing for money through hard-nosed deals. *Sharky* needed some work. Actually she wanted a *lot* of work, but by then I had been smitten, blinded to her condition, captured by her potential. I wanted her as badly as a teenager wants his first real kiss.

I must have spent over two hours crawling over her superstructure, examining her hull, planning the cabin layout, just lovingly rubbing my hands over every inch, all the while convincing myself I had the skills to restore her to her glory days and kit her out for the worst weather conditions I could imagine. If she'd been a car I would have walked away without a backward glance; but she wasn't. She was affordable (just), she was available and she represented a challenging opportunity that threw any ounce of reason out of the window. I was convinced I had the practical skills to spruce her up and I had the arrogance to assume that learning to sail would be simple. I spent the inspection time wisely, carefully appraising the work I needed to do, pretending that I would be objective in my final decision, but the illusion was skin-deep. *Sharky* had got her teeth into me and wasn't about to let another suitor stand her up. I was the master of the moment but she was the mistress of my future and so, at last,

I wandered over to the boatyard office and did the deal. On a date forever etched in my memory I parted with an ill-affordable £950 of hard-earned money, but gained a key to the gates of freedom. I trailered *Sharky* back home to Buxton and parked her by the side of our shop, where, living in the flat above, I could keep an eye out for her. I formally registered her as mine and eagerly bought a red ensign flag, proof of owning the most cared-for boat in existence. I was in love.

Having now bought *Sharky*, I was in a state of fevered enthusiasm to get her shipshape and perfect. I would look out of my landing window each time I went up the stairs, the mast looming up to the pitch of the roof, and I could never pass by with a momentary glance down to the boat. It was more a bonding action than a security check; a fond peek at what I'd bought and a pensive distraction from the business to hand. Sometimes I'd just rest my hands on the windowsill, look down wistfully and imagine myself riding the ocean waves, a free spirit with few cares. It was soppy, puppy-love stuff but I relished the bitter-sweet feelings within me.

To the rear of the shop were the garage and stock rooms, soon to become *Sharky's* workshop, the makeover department that would turn the ugly duckling into a fine swan. Customers to the shop must have wondered why a boat was beached in the middle of a Derbyshire town. My mum and step-dad Norman had a general understanding of my interest in sailing, but only I knew the level of determination I had to master this new pursuit. Within a month of buying *Sharky* I'd enrolled for a five-day beginner's sailing course down in Warsash, a little place near Southampton widely regarded as the gateway to the Solent. This was no fit of initial enthusiasm. I approached my new interest with all the focus and intensity of a surgeon in an operating theatre, and I was determined to absorb as much technical knowledge and competence as I could. The problem was time and money. The shop took most of my waking hours and most of my spare cash as well. It had been bought between my mum and me, as we'd had previous experience in the trade. It gave her something to get her teeth into while Norman was at work, and it gave me the chance of settling down to a steady job. Small shops though require a large investment of time and while we employed some staff it was still taking up a lot of my hours, which I would rather have spent on my boat. I was beginning to despair that I would never get *Sharky* in the water.

Working on her moved at a snail's pace. I soon realised that just cleaning off the weeds, barnacles and other detritus from her hull was a major operation, and I was in no mood to compromise. Despite my urgency to get her afloat I was not going to cut corners and I lovingly tended to her as a parent does a child. Much of the superstructure was unsound and going to require many hours of fibreglassing, much of the external woodwork was rotten to the point of replacement and chips and cracks to her hull needed serious attention. The pint-sized cabin and cockpit lacked charm and cosiness and I was going to need all of my design and woodworking skills to manufacture new wooden storage lockers. Slowly, slowly over that winter, I bought *Sharky* back to something approaching her former glory. Fresh paint added a glow to her features and new wood, brass and stainless-steel fittings completed her restoration. Most of the work I did myself, calling in favours from skilled mates when required. I fully owned her when I made an elegant sticker of her name and lovingly eased it onto the stern. *Sharky*. From waif-like beginnings to a christened child she had become a part of my family. The eight-month travail, long on frustration, had finally been worth the wait: she was ready for the water.

Two months into my project, however, the practical repair skills were set aside for more cerebral ones as I took a precious week off work and motored down to Warsash to attend my Competent Crew course; five days of intensive study, with four other novices, that would inculcate me into the mysterious world of sailing. I approached the course with a mixture of anticipation and apprehension. I fretted a bit about mastering the theory part but felt I might not fare too badly with the sailing. As a boy I'd grown up in the United Arab Emirates when the family followed my dad's job, so I'd been exposed to the delights of sailing in the Arabian Gulf. However, Warsash was different. Warsash demanded discipline, technical understanding, adroitness in the reading of charts, currents and positioning. Warsash demanded I have a damn good time – so I did. Four other people and I went aboard our thirty-six foot sailing yacht on the Monday morning and nervously awaited our skipper, Adrian Donavan, a world-class competitive yachtsman. The first thing that struck me was the incomprehensibility of the thousands of feet of rope, some of which wasn't called rope, and the seemingly awkward way it all jumbled together to make something happen. It was as though a spaghetti producer had teamed up with Heath Robinson and chosen the most intricate and most complex way of moving sails about. Although I'd read about the fundamentals of sailing and generally thought I could understand the principles, I was totally unprepared for the aesthetic design and grace of this yacht. As I stepped on board for the first time, my apprehension disappeared, to be replaced by an almost uncontainable excitement. The course had cost me a king's ransom but I knew the experience was going to be worth every penny. I bubbled inside at the prospect of five days in a new element but outwardly I was careful not to appear overly ignorant. Whenever I had some spare few minutes to myself, I would quietly walk the deck and marvel at the sleek lines, the symmetry and elegance of her design. The simple act of running my hand softly across a deck rail, part of the gunwale or folded sail as I gazed out on a watery horizon, stirred inner feelings, a lust to sail as much as I could. The simple pleasure of rising before dawn, to stand on deck as the pastel colours of a new day stealthily conquered the night, and to hear the gentle slap of water against the hull, had a profound impact on me. I would stare into new horizons in my mind's eye, and so in that crucible of awareness began my resolve to sail the oceans.

Sailing is a mixture of passion and brass tacks. I had sentiment aplenty but needed all my concentration to assimilate the seamanship, navigation, meteorology, safety, manoeuvring, crewing and skippering that we were bombarded with. I learnt how vital teamwork was and as we slewed through the Solent quietly wondered whether I would ever be able to sail *Sharky* on my own. I did a lot of listening to others and asked questions I hoped didn't sound foolish. The highlight of the course was inevitably the thrill of each day's sailing. To be part of, and partly in control of a living entity that responded to wind and sinew was like being a kid with unlimited ice cream. The spray, the wind rush, the sheer thrill of being alive – I wanted to whoop out loud and scream my joy at the top of my lungs. But I didn't. I battened down that primeval urge and focused on being a competent crew member, but resolved that the first time I sailed *Sharky* on my own that was what I was going to do – shout the top of my bloody head off!

Towards the end of the course I was having my second pint of Guinness with the skipper. I was light-headedly waiting for dinner and he casually asked me what my plans were after the course. I explained that I'd just bought a small boat and, without any sense of intention, I blurted out, 'I quite fancy sailing solo across the Atlantic.'

I remember him looking at me with serious eyes. 'I once took a crew in a thirty-footer down to Madeira,' he said. 'The weather turned bad and we nearly didn't make it.'

Suddenly I felt foolish and awkward. I grinned and laughed it off. 'Yeah, well, just a crazy idea, y' know.'

I lay in my bunk that night, the short conversation running over and over in my head. Why had I said I wanted to sail the Atlantic? Where on earth had that thought come from? Was I being given a friendly warning to keep off the big stage? I suppose the whole exchange had taken less than two minutes but I couldn't let it go. I had only the rudiments of sailing, I'd bought a second-hand boat in a state of disrepair, I'd last been in a boat as a fourteen-year-old lad and now I'd made a stupid remark to a seasoned yachtsman that I intended sailing across the Atlantic. As the boat creaked and settled around me I thought about the line between ignorant blockheadedness and self-belief. I'd become independent, stubborn and decisive as I'd grown up but this course was raising new questions. I was beginning to understand just how dangerous the sea could be. Did self-belief have a thin line that hovered as an epitaph for the irresponsible? Did I truly think I was capable of sailing one of the world's great oceans? I drifted off to sleep with a single thought in my head: why not?

Returning from Warsash with my first seamanship certificate and a lasting determination to learn more, I immediately signed up for a yachtmaster correspondence course. I was impatient to get *Sharky* onto water, and at long last, in mid-June the following year, I hitched her to the car and towed her a dozen or so miles down to Rudyard Lake. Rudyard is a two-hundred-year-old, two-and-a-half-mile-long narrow reservoir built to hold water for the canal system, and lies majestically in a steeply wooded valley in the Staffordshire moor land. On a beautifully sunny afternoon, surrounded by sparkling water, trees and abundant wildlife, I eased my boat onto the public slipway by the dam wall and into the water; my first boat and my proudest possession. She shot into the water as if eager to return, then, held by the ropes, bobbed gently, looking tiny and a bit overawed in the immensity of the lake. Having been tarmac-bound for months, and hemmed in by the confines of grey stone houses, now that she was unencumbered from those closeted conditions I couldn't help thinking that she was indeed quite diminutive. Nevertheless, here she was, here I was; it was time to get nautically acquainted. Clambering onto the deck I began to recall the training I'd received at Warsash, which seemed ages and ages ago. There was a light wind blowing and I fumbled awkwardly with the sails, messing up the cast-off and hoping no one was taking too much notice. At last I headed into the water and turned *Sharky* into the wind. I was nervous, exhilarated and uncertain but overall I felt great. A huge grin spread over my face and I picked up confidence, noticing especially how quiet and peaceful my surroundings were. I eased back against the gunwale and draped my elbow against the coaming. Tension and anxiety dropped like heavy weights as I felt the wind, felt my boat ride the water's motion and felt near contentment. At the back of my mind still lurked the fear that I was now alone. The shoreline was all around but I was now solo in a boat for the first time in my life, and I needed to tack. As the shore side rapidly approached I rehearsed the drill mentally, apprehension rising, a sensation I felt in my mouth. Grabbing the tiller and spreading my feet, I half-stood, pulled the sail in, ducked under the boom and stumbled to the other side of the stern. *Sharky* responded as a seasoned horse to an apprentice jockey – I'll go along with your instructions but don't expect me to like it. I couldn't get the hang of pulling the mainsail in and releasing the jib at quite the same time, so the boat lurched rather than turned smoothly. I felt clumsy in my movements but I had done it! Achieved my first solo tack, not perfectly but competently, and I knew I would get better with practice. Confidence restored, I spent all afternoon putting in more tacks and gradually improving my technique with the sails and tiller. I felt like a fledgling bird leaving the nest for the first time, awkward and gawky but gradually I was rewarded for my efforts as *Sharky* began to turn more smoothly in the water. I now needed to fulfil a promise I had made to myself some eight months before down in Warsash. Self-consciously I looked about but there was no one in the vicinity. Drawing in a deep breath I let out a great whoop and screamed my bloody head off!

The next day I was back at Rudyard, eager to recapture the thrill. This time I brought along my mate Ian, a complete landlubber but someone I thought might be useful on the helm while I tried out routines with the sails. I was in a rush to learn quickly and get in as much practice as I could. I'd wangled a couple more afternoons off from work and so wanted to maximise my learning. With a crew aboard I had a bit more time to check *Sharky* out and was delighted to discover that she was as responsive, sturdy and reliable as she had been that first day. Best of all there were no leaks and the winter repairs seemed to have been effective.

An unconventional upbringing had taught me self-reliance and an ability to be a quick learner. Over the next few months, whenever I could grab a rare afternoon, I'd get myself ready for the short twenty-five-minute drive to the lake, eager to release *Sharky* from her mooring. I'd impatiently race through the paperwork, sort out the staff then dash off quickly before any problems arose. Each time it was as though I'd been released from a stifling prison – time out for good behaviour, even if only for a few, short precious hours. It was dawning on me that the art of sailing was more in the 'feel' than the technical expertise. Rudyard was a good and sometimes harsh teacher, a place where the wind was unpredictable, where a blow would spring up with a suddenness that would catch me unawares – on one occasion a near knockdown submerged the port cabin window and flooded the cockpit – giving me salutary lessons in over-complacency.

But what I learnt I absorbed. I got to know every inch of *Sharky*, who continued to delight. I began to understand and sense the wind. I could feel the water through the rudder. I practised routines for raising, dropping and reefing the mainsail and changing the jibs every few minutes until I could do them without thinking, then tried them single-handed. I sailed late into the evening to experience the sensation in the dark. Sometimes I sailed on my own, sometimes with one of a few like-minded friends; once I bought my new girlfriend Elaine for a romantic afternoon. For all of us they were fun days with some hairy moments, but for me there was an additional factor. Deep, deep down in my mind the little ocean sail seed was growing, pushing at my psyche as a flower bulb pushes the earth. As I continued to gain love, respect and knowledge for this wondrous new environment, so my thoughts were turning ever more ambitious. Already after just a few sailing hours, Rudyard was beginning to impose its restrictions and I found pottering around the reservoir a tad boring. I'd listen out for weather forecasts announcing strong winds or gales, then dash down to Rudyard to test myself and *Sharky*. Impatient as ever, I wanted to break free of the landlocked boundaries and measure *Sharky* and myself against a greater force. I was sensible enough to know that more work was needed and more money would have to be spent on my boat, but determined enough to know that was what I wanted to do. These thoughts I kept to myself but the trap had been baited with salt spray and I was willingly walking into it. When someone called me a 'puddle sailor' for the first time it was as though the trap had been sprung. Rudyard had been my nursery, now I wanted my sea legs.

Chapter Two

Learning the Ropes

As I wrestled with the helm I was constantly analysing
my decision to set sail.

ONE OF THE REASONS I began to think I was ready for a greater
challenge was a difference I noticed between me and the friends
who occasionally sailed with me. They were all willing crew members,
all with a total lack of sailing experience. I really wanted an extra
pair of hands on the boat as I literally learnt the ropes, and while
my mates were all keen, they weren't committed to the same extent.
Afternoons at Rudyard were great fun but there the similarity died.
I enjoyed them as much as my friends but I wanted to learn, while
they were content to sail and enjoy a controlled exhilaration. I wanted
to test my boat, the conditions and myself. I constantly changed sail
patterns, I sailed the lake looking for gusts, I practised casting off
and mooring up. If we arrived at the slipway with the weather turning
cold or skittish, I wanted to get out on the water against the reluctance
of my sailing companion. It might have been the fact that *Sharky*
was my boat but I was always the one with more passion, the one
who would take more considered risks. Out once with Ian, we hit
strong gusty conditions, pretty choppy and spray flying everywhere.
I put a reef in the mainsail and hoisted the storm jib with waves

splashing onto the deck, but there was still too much sail out. Still relative novices, the conditions were a little frightening for us, made more so as we continued to pick up speed. As the wind increased I took in the jib, but it made little difference, we were still speeding along and heeling severely in the gusts, and Ian thought we should head back into the mooring. As I gybed, the boom whipped across the front of my face and snapped clean in half with a doomed cracking sound. We finally made it back to the mooring but I noticed Ian was not looking at all happy, his pasty complexion revealing how shaken he'd been. 'Wow,' he said, 'that was a bit close.' And that was the difference. He thought it had been close; I thought it had been close but I'd revelled in the challenge. That challenge cost me £92 for a new boom but I couldn't help thinking how spine-tingling that would have been on the open sea.

By New Year 1990 I'd made my mind up that I was going to try a sail across the Channel to France, and had persuaded another friend, Chris, to act as crew for me. The ocean sailing bug was now firmly in the bloodstream and I spent many hours speculating whether I could actually sail across to the Caribbean, whether I might have a future as a charter skipper, whether I should trade *Sharky* in for a bigger boat, perhaps a thirty-footer. I spent a lot of that winter dreaming until I realised that was all I was doing; I needed a plan and a target to aim for, something to spur me on and a goal that would test my mettle. I ditched the idea of a bigger boat simply because I couldn't see any way of affording it; besides which, there was no way I was going to ditch *Sharky* either. We'd become a pair, a team of equals, and having spent many hours together I felt real affection and affinity. To my mates she was just a form of transport, something to be enjoyed when a thrill was needed, and, while I never shared my innermost thoughts with them, I did get some ribbing.

'Your trouble, Dave,' remarked Ian one time, 'is that you've fallen in love with a damn boat.'

He was joking and I grinned but he never realised how close to the truth he'd been. *Sharky* was going to be my transport of delight, the means to my fulfilment, and that was something my friends didn't understand. I wasn't completely anthropomorphic but *Sharky* was certainly a lot more than just a damn boat. She would want a lot of work doing to get her fit for hazardous conditions and she wasn't the only one who needed improvements. My Competent Crew course had got me started but I was going to have to study a lot more, something that didn't come naturally or easily to me.

And the goal? The target that this apprentice, wet-behind-the-ears, would-be sailor was aiming for? In the cosy warmth of my flat on a chilly winter's night, surrounded by charts, books and manuals, I set myself the biggest challenge of my life – one that would stretch me physically, mentally and financially; a challenge that might mean severing the security of work, home and close relationships. The more I thought about it the more I realised I didn't want to think about it. I wanted to do it. I was going to sail solo across the Atlantic as soon as was humanly possible.

The dream was cast, the gauntlet thrown down; a lot of work was involved, requiring even more of my time and money, and so began my life of lists, something that has probably been added to my genetic code for future generations of Clarkes. I became obsessed with writing down everything that needed to be done. I wrote lists on anything that came to hand and at any time of the day or night – I even wrote a list of lists. I carefully crossed off each task completed and worried that, for everything I had crossed off, I needed to add another three. I found it an extremely useful exercise, which disciplined my mind and taught me the value of time management. Lists enabled me to compartmentalise aspects of my life and to focus on the job in hand – so long as I had a piece of paper and a pen I could cope. There was just one thing I daren't put on a list and that was time set aside to see Elaine, someone I was beginning to think might be a bit special; plus if she'd found out she was on a 'to do' list I would be in no physical shape to get on a boat let alone sail the oceans!

In July I lifted *Sharky* from Rudyard and towed her to Warsash. Chris was still keen to accompany me, everyone else believing we were mad. Ian wanted to know what flowers I wanted at my funeral. Jason just shook his head, but my determination was greater than any self-doubt; this was my first sea adventure and I was raring to go. I was impatient now to try sea conditions and despite my lack of experience I was confident, in a scary sort of way, that I could handle them. Rudyard had given me the 'feel' I wanted and soon I would have the testing environment it couldn't provide: stronger winds, tides, currents and navigation. Most exciting was the fact that once launched I really would be on my own with no immediacy of a safe shore or a buoy to moor to. Now I would truly be in charge of my destiny.

We launched her with half a bottle of champagne at five o'clock in the afternoon. *Sharky* flew down the slip like a rocket and took all of ten yards of rope before she stopped. Once on board Chris began to wash her down and promptly fell overboard, thus necessitating an earlier-than-planned man-overboard drill. This was not an auspicious start so we celebrated his survival with a pot noodle each before going for a quick sail. Warsash is nicely protected from extremes and I found it an ideal place to become comfortable with sea conditions. We pottered about for a few days and again I revelled in the freedom and joy that being on a small boat can bring. Memories of sailing on the course yacht the previous year flooded back, and each morning I couldn't wait to cast off and enjoy the sea, pitting my wits against its mood swings, not fighting it as in battle, not attempting to master it, but accepting its challenge. You cannot beat me, it seemed to say, but you can become an occasional sparring partner.

After five days I decided we were ready for the Channel crossing to Cherbourg, and I psyched Chris up for the attempt. I'd studied the charts and reckoned that my navigation skills were good enough. At the moorings we'd befriended a guy and his wife who had a large yacht, and I casually mentioned to them that we were going across to Cherbourg.

'Bloody 'ell,' he said. 'When are you going?'

'Tonight, about seven o'clock,' I replied.

He went very quiet, then 'In that?' pointing at *Sharky*.

I nodded.

'Bloody 'ell,' he repeated. 'Our boat's a thirty-four-footer and we wouldn't risk it.'

'Oh, it'll be a great sail,' I said, with as much conviction as I could muster.

'You're mad,' he replied. 'Bloody mad.'

We left to the waves and good luck cries of our newfound friends in a perfect wind, moderate waves popping occasional white crests. I put up the mainsail expecting to have to reef; then settled down at the helm. We smiled and waved back but a small doubt in my mind wouldn't go away. Was I really confident and competent? Elaine had worried before I left home that I was running before I could walk, and her concerns could not be dismissed. Was I just mad to the point of recklessness or did I really have a dogged belief that I was born to do this? Too late; I was committed; to glory or disaster would now be up to me.

I'd calculated the crossing at sixty nautical miles and at a steady speed of three to four knots I'd expected to land at Cherbourg the following lunchtime. The Channel was busy, extremely busy, and while I was certain of my position there was constant need to watch out for shipping moving at far greater speeds than *Sharky*. I had read that the tactic to adopt was to aim for the back of a ship and cross its stern as it goes by. Doing this meant that we were able to spot the next ship looming over the horizon and plan accordingly. I loved being busy like this, the adrenalin coursing through every part of my being, the mind calculating the relative speeds and distances, the body sensing the boat's motion. This was what being alive meant. The weather was part cloudy and the moon favoured us for companionship as we beetled along. I say 'we'. It was soon apparent that Chris was very tired and kept dozing off, which I regarded as dangerous. I sent him below to sleep and found that I didn't really miss his company. I had a lot to do; I was alert and thoroughly enjoying what I was doing. Fear and excitement competed for priority, yet I knew I had made the right decision to sail. Mad? Probably. Reckless? I didn't think so. I'd planned meticulously and read extensively. Sufficiently skilled? No, but where was I supposed to gain the skill? The testing ground was out here. There were no safe simulator substitutes. An unbidden thought flashed into my head; I can do this because I believe I can. In my own small way I'm doing what Acton and Moitessier and all the others did. They believed they could. To my astonishment and embarrassment my eyes watered as a mixture of pride and humility swept over me. 'C'm' on, you prat,' I said wiping my eyes, 'there's a long way to go yet.'

By seven o'clock the next morning, dead tired and in worsening weather, my mind was trying to convince me I might be lost. Three hours earlier I'd been certain of our location, using the calculations from the chart, compass and boat speed, and even now still intuitively felt we were on the right heading. I was pretty certain we'd hit France somewhere – after all, there was a lot of it to hit – but I was after the right bit, the peninsula that was Cherbourg, which required me to calculate the tidal stream correctly. A grip of doubt tormented my guts and I re-checked the calculations once more, half my mind doing the maths, the other trying to handle the boat. A low mist hung over the horizon and in the half-light everything was featureless. I had no option than to trust in myself. The thought thrust itself into my mind again – I can because I believe I can. Well, we'd soon see if that were true.

The wind had swung round to west sou'west and strengthened, gusting to near gale force with the sea heaping up, viciously spilling white foam as breaking waves blew around in streaks. I was glad I'd fully reefed the mainsail and changed to a storm jib; with several big waves sweeping over the boat I had little choice but to close-haul, staying as near to the wind as was possible to keep the boat on the right heading. This was indeed a baptism of fire. I'd never been in conditions like this, never encountered a near gale and never before been around a busy shipping lane. What I didn't want was to be lost at sea; I think the posthumous headline humiliation of 'Inexperienced sailor drowned with crew in Channel' was something that spurred me to succeed, but in truth I had little time for esoteric musings or wondering whether I was in fact completely mad. I was too busy with survival and protecting my boat. I was scared, certainly, but still there existed an underlying belief that we would pull through. Wishful thinking, intuition, superstition or obstinacy, I couldn't tell for sure but I'd have bet on obstinacy. What really confused me were two totally different mysteries. Why, despite being exhausted, totally sodden and raw with salt spray in these awful conditions – why was I thoroughly enjoying myself? Secondly, how the heck could Chris sleep through what should have been the most invigorating night of his life?

At midday, after a five-hour battering and a lot of praying, to my huge relief I spotted the outer sea defences of Cherbourg, exactly where they should have been. Once rounded, they offered a calming protection as I headed towards the pontoons to tie up, pulling alongside a thirty-five-footer. An open-mouthed, bemused owner named Colin greeted us.

After telling him where we'd come from he shook his head. 'You are fuckin' mad,' he said. 'I'm going to buy you the best steak in town.' And he did. That evening the three of us tucked into rare rib-eye washed down with endless bottles of beer. Chris retired early but I chatted with Colin over several malt whiskies until the early hours, exchanging life stories and the earnest philosophies to right the world that are so obvious when alcohol brings a clarity to global problems. I clambered into my bunk hazy from the drink but feeling utterly satisfied with myself. I'd fulfilled the first phase in my Atlantic conquest and felt I had joined a loose band of brothers at sea. I was becoming a comrade to be recognised and respected wherever in the world I chose to sail, an equal among madmen. I was now a madman too and thoroughly delighted to be so. This was a part to sailing that no course could ever teach. In my woozy state I grinned and giggled like a smug idiot in the darkness of the cabin. I'd actually bought a boat, learnt to sail and taken it across the Channel at night. Now all I had to do was sail back again.

After a couple of days we slipped away, back to the UK and the Needles, leaving late afternoon in light-ish winds. With one exception it was an uneventful return. Some time around two in the morning, Chris again tucked up asleep, we were nearly run down by a cargo ship steaming up at around twenty-five knots on the blind side. I hadn't seen it because of the way the sails were set. Panic filled my mind and nearly my trousers; I had never been so scared. I hove to and within seconds it flew past just thirty metres or so from us. The sound of the engines was deafening as the horizon filled with dark sheet metal. There was nothing to do but hang on for grim death as the wake pummelled *Sharky* mercilessly, pitching us every which way. Chris slept throughout it all, which, rather irrationally, angered me. We moored up at Lymington in the late morning and headed into town for a liquid celebration of our safe return and my first real sailing achievement.

Later, and in more reflective mood, I wrote in my log, 'Something happened to me today that made me realise the Atlantic would have to be crossed alone.' To this day I'm not certain what I meant. I may have not wanted the responsibility of a crew member but I think it may have been more fundamental. I'd known for a good many years that I was comfortable in my own company. Not a loner but someone who understood the difference between being alone and being lonely. I think I sensed that I didn't want to share the journey, not through simple selfishness, though I recognised that trait in myself, but because I wanted something akin to a religious experience, a oneness with nature that I'd felt since I was a young lad. A solo trip of such magnitude would give me the opportunity to see if I could achieve that condition.

In a quiet but euphoric state, I returned to Buxton and working life, leaving *Sharky* at Warsash. The yachtmaster offshore correspondence course I'd signed up for had not been going well and the intricacies of chart work, tidal calculations, pilotage, advanced meteorology, rules and signals, radio procedures and so forth taxed my brain incessantly. With little time other than when I was dog-tired and with no natural inclination to study, the course nearly broke my will. With limited practical experience, I relied heavily on my assignment tutor, frequently despairing at my slow progress and the fear of a dream disappearing under the mass of theory. Eventually I sent off the last assignment and won my certificate two years after starting. It had been without doubt the hardest part of any learning I had undertaken. With relief and confidence I enrolled on a weeklong day skipper practical course back at Warsash.

Re-motivated and with the success of the day skipper course behind me, I needed another stint on *Sharky*. My mate Chris was keen to tag along again though I was beginning to have some doubts about his commitment to hard work and sharing the load. He seemed to regard sailing as a nine-to-five activity after which he felt he could clock off and go to sleep. Nevertheless, he was a good mate and the only one I could persuade to crew with me. In late September we took *Sharky* to Yarmouth on the Isle of Wight, then set a course for another Channel crossing for a couple of days' sailing. The weather forecast had predicted a west-sou'westerly, force four to five, with occasional gusts to six, so I took the decision to go. By 5.30 in the afternoon we had passed the Needles, then all hell let loose. Once in open water, the sea became horrendously choppy, throwing us indiscriminately around while pouring water over the deck. The wind picked up from the west to a good force six, necessitating a reefing of the mainsail and hoisting of the storm jib. All trace of light from the sky was rapidly disappearing, leaving just the screech of the wind in the rigging and the continuous slap-slap of the sea against the hull. By eight o'clock Chris had lost all spirit. Wan-faced and clutching his stomach, he retired to the cabin, later vomiting over my sleeping bag and gear, retching so loudly I could hear him from the helm. Within a couple of hours the wind veered to south sou'west and strengthened yet again. Conditions now were really bad, waves were swamping the boat and flooding into the cockpit; I decided to abandon the trip and head for home, altering course for Portsmouth, as I judged the Needles would be even more atrocious. By midnight, in sheeting rain, I was lost, totally clueless as to where we were and trying to throttle down a sense of fear-ridden panic. *Sharky* was now surfing the crests of the waves at about eight to ten knots and I had no idea whether she was capable of holding together. I was now seriously scared – for our safety, for Chris's condition, and as to whether I had the competence to get us back. As I wrestled the helm I was constantly analysing my decision to set sail. I had checked the forecast but the wind had blown up more than had been expected. Had I set too much faith by it? Was I just an incompetent and reckless sailor putting lives at risk? Was I sufficiently knowledgeable about the weather? Ultimately, was it my fault we were out here?

By three o'clock in the morning I'd gained a rough idea of where I was and managed to coax Chris out of the stinking cabin, now with several inches of rancid water slewing around it. I clipped Chris's harness to one of the fixing points and told him to grab the helm while I snatched a quick drink, realising just how parched I was from fear. A quick look at the chart confirmed the light from Nab Tower Lighthouse at the entrance to the Solent and I dashed back to the helm desperate not to lose sight of it as I took a fix. With one hand on the tiller, one arm around Chris, and as terrified, exhausted and cold as I had ever been, I fought a building sea and the recurring thought that I might have to tell Chris's mum I had caused his death, assuming I would still be alive to make it to shore. Clinging desperately to retain some semblance of control we shivered into the entrance to Portsmouth harbour followed by a police launch, which was holding back the Isle of Wight ferry for us. The swells were ferocious, throwing the ferry lane marker buoys and us around like toys. A sudden gust of wind flattened us and we broached, momentarily losing all control and scaring Chris witless. Broaching can be enormously scary; the wind gusts into the sail, the boat heels over alarmingly and just as you think the sails will slap the water, the boat slews into the wind and pops up again. On a lovely sunny day broaching can be great fun. On a wild running sea with a big ferry up your arse it's not so great. As we righted, I threw in a quick tack to wrestle control then gybed back on course. One moment the police vessel was behind us, struggling into view between the surging crests, the next heading straight for us. Both vessels were heaving and clawing for position and I spotted the serious concern etched on the face of the pilot. Clearly we couldn't take much more of this.

Past caring, soaked through and completely knackered, we turned into the shelter of the harbour and all went still. I dropped the mainsail, feeling in control for the first time in many hours. In my exhaustion I had turned into the naval harbour by mistake but hadn't the energy to seek out the correct moorings. I tied up near a couple of submarines, thinking bugger to national security, crawled into the tiny cabin and slept, with the sight and smell of Chris's vomit everywhere, along with the debris of our sodden supplies. And yet... . And yet deep down I was content. Despite the real fear, I felt I had again coped well and learnt extensively from the experience. My inner resolve to succeed had not been dented. I had survived a severe gale gusting to over forty knots and I had found my way back home. Fear, I now understood, was an essential part of sailing. It acted as a counter to complacency and arrogance and as long as it could be held in check I felt I had a chance to achieve my ultimate ambition. I also understood that in a perverse way I had enjoyed fighting the fear. I had met it head-on and had not turned away. I had relished the challenge and believed I had the mental strength to master it. In the foul, reeking stench of *Sharky*'s cabin I knew I was capable of an ocean voyage.

It's odd how a good night's sleep, a decent shower and a full stomach can alter your perspective on life. Within a couple of days of our harrowing experience, Chris and I were both back to our usual spirits, Chris in particular chirpy and chatty now that the sickness had left him. With his flippant, dismissive humour he had begun to convince himself that he'd heroically fought the elements and had the adventure of a lifetime against all odds. We cleaned up the cabin and with the weather improving set out for another sail up the coast pottering about between different harbours. The weather for once had been good. A strong southwesterly was filling the sails and we were zinging along, laughing and joking; just two mates in the heaven of no immediate responsibility, other than to each other, past terrors forgotten. Life is sometimes like that. A freedom calls, your spirit soars, the soul is unfettered from reality and for a few glorious minutes, hours even, you are at one with the universe and all is well. A feeling like that doesn't need alcohol or other stimulants. Circumstances conspire to bring a sense of total fulfilment and contentment and you know that life is good – just really, really good.

It was in this heady state that I turned to Chris and determined my future. 'Chris,' I enthused, 'I'm thinking of sailing across the Atlantic, do you want to come?'

Chris was the only bloke who'd stuck with me in sailing so it seemed on that giddy day quite fitting that I should offer him my insane proposal. Looking back now it really was an insane proposal. Chris was slim, dark-haired and good looking, the sort of lad who was handy by your side for getting the attention of women but whom you later resented for stealing the best of them. He was energetic, a dreamer and a great one for exaggeration. In other words he was absolutely ideal for responding with an immediate 'Absolutely!' to my Atlantic aspirations.

'Great,' I shouted back, 'but you're gonna have to do your share, it's not going to be a pleasure cruise.'

I remember being struck by powerful conflicting thoughts the moment Chris agreed. That had suddenly crystallised my dream. I had come to a crossroads in my life and committed myself to a course of action I would not retract from. More worrying, I felt an overwhelming, irrational surge of intense resentment and irritation towards Chris. I didn't actually want him, or anyone for that matter, to share my adventure. Too late I recalled the earlier entry in my log, the recorded instinctive feeling that I needed to sail alone. As we sailed back to Warsash I couldn't shake off this feeling of selfishness. He'd helped me to sail, he was a good mate but in the last few days he hadn't shown an aptitude for hard work and trying conditions. Why in a rash moment had I invited him to sail the Atlantic with me? I instantly regretted my offer and hated him for agreeing. Not for the first time I looked inwards and questioned my own character. Despite the bravado, perhaps I really didn't want to spend a long time locked in my own company. I fell a bit quiet for the rest of the day, feeling something had been lost, and I remained irritated with Chris, who had now fancifully adopted the invitation, much to my resentment. With our leisure time spent and the weather closing in again, we moored *Sharky* securely and returned home.

An autumn melancholy drifted over me in November and long hours at the shop were taking their toll. I couldn't get *Sharky* out of my mind, wondering whether she was safe and whether I should bring her back. In the end I told my mum I just needed to get away from the business, packed a bag, hitched the trailer and returned to Warsash on my own. The weather was rough; cold driving rain, scudding clouds and the dismal chill of a grey-green sea churning under an opaque horizon. *Sharky* was stale and damp. A pencil I'd left on the chart table had turned mouldy and bent by twenty degrees in the clammy air. I felt alone and lonely, questioning why I had come down, feeling lost and at a loose end. I went to a local pub and felt even more miserable. There is no worse place to accentuate reclusive solitude than to be on your own in a quiet pub. In the end I went back to my boat and attempted to define loneliness. I didn't feel depressed, just somehow misplaced. I'd committed myself to the Atlantic crossing but I was still unsure about taking Chris: would good company be a sufficient persuasion against the uncertainty of his mettle? I needed the positive solitude of a sail to clear my head and buck me up, so I resolved to sail each day no matter what. And for a week I did. I meandered about and got used to my boat, practising sail changes and noting how she handled in different conditions. Busy and alone, focused on enjoyment and improvement, trying to imagine how different an open ocean would be to the relative confines of the Solent and Channel. The weather remained rough but did not bother me. I sailed, read books and went to the pub in a better frame of mind to chat to locals. Making good a small repair on *Sharky*, I inadvertently stuck a bradawl through the middle of my finger, pushing it clear through to the other side. It hurt like hell as I pulled it out, as the bone scraped against the metal. I padded it with kitchen roll, stuck a plaster over it, wrapped my finger in insulation tape and took a couple of tablets, all the time thinking that if this sort of accident or worse were to happen on a long voyage, this was the kind of first aid I would have to administer. I also realised that I'd injured myself through carelessness and lack of concentration. That fact alone concentrated my mind. On my own in an open sea when I was likely to be fatigued I'd have to stay alert to avoid even the simplest of misadventures; there was a very fine line between inattention and its possible consequences.

By the end of the week I was in good shape again both physically and mentally. The week had been another test of personal survival and I had passed. I drove home happily, this time with *Sharky* in tow and a firm plan in my mind. We would spend the winter together preparing ourselves for a major ocean journey in the summer. The Atlantic call was becoming louder and the lists were going to get a lot, lot longer.

CHAPTER THREE

Falmouth at Last

Some trepidation certainly but always a quickening of the pulse and a glimpse of freedom; always a glimpse of freedom.

BECAUSE OF WORK COMMITMENTS and severe cash restrictions – and the reluctant acknowledgment of my relative lack of sailing experience – I knew that a single voyage across the Atlantic could be impractical and would be foolhardy; it just wasn't going to happen in the heroic way I'd envisaged, though I spent hours trying to discover an ideal solution. In the end I resigned myself to the fact that however idyllic I wanted it to be, I couldn't just sail off into the deep blue yonder and leave all my responsibilities behind. Running the shop was still exacting a toll on my energies so I agreed with my mum I'd take five weeks off work in the forthcoming summer. At least now I had a clear goal. I set about planning where I might sail to, without abandoning the challenge of ocean sailing. Even so I couldn't fully dismiss the concerns that everyone held. I was pretty positive about my ability to handle *Sharky* from the difficult open-water conditions I'd previously encountered, but it was clear that a five-week haul would be a major undertaking. Nevertheless I was determined to do it despite the obvious worries from others about being sufficiently ready. I made the decision. I would sail from

Falmouth to Northern Spain or even Southern Portugal and see how it went; I would make no further plans than that. Exciting though that prospect was, it was still a bit frustrating. I couldn't rid myself of making a Moitessier-style, momentous decision, which would see me 'just go'. I agonised whether I had the guts to do it; I even made a list of what I would gain and what I would lose, but rationality held me back. I did have responsibilities I couldn't ditch. I told myself this was sensible and level-headed. Patience would have to be a virtue, but oh how I still lingered with the notion 'just go!' I was also mindful of the fact that although I quite fancied a solo crossing I had sort of made a commitment with Chris, and it was probably the more responsible thing to do. With two of us a system of 'watches' would ensure one of us could get some sleep while the other took the helm, so it pleased my family and Elaine that I was being 'sensible'.

Snatched hours found me in the workshop tackling the considerable strengthening that *Sharky* needed. I also used the time to scour the papers and boatyards to buy additional equipment including an outboard, global positioning system (GPS), better foul-weather gear, and a radio – the GPS alone setting me back nearly a thousand pounds (it was nothing special at that, just the model that nowadays I could purchase for under a hundred). At the time I reasoned that although the technology was expensive, I would at least have an alternative to the sextant.

Working on the boat was an opportunity to hone the reasonable practical skills I'd acquired as I'd been growing up. These skills could well determine whether I survived on open water, so there was no way I was going to bodge the work. I strengthened the windows with quarter-plate stainless-steel frames and toughened Perspex, though the curved shape of the boat made this a difficult task. There are few straight lines on a small boat and thick metal plate and Perspex do not easily lend themselves to leak-proof bending. Similarly the bow hatch leaked so I replaced that with new marine ply, bolting and fibreglassing it into place. I also strengthened the main hatch but chose to fix it in place with screws. This was an important decision. Once below deck my only escape was through this hatch. In the case of serious trouble, such as it jamming or being trapped by rigging,

I needed to be able to get out by lying on my back and kicking the hatch through with my feet.

As spring gave way to summer I felt schizophrenic and increasingly claustrophobic. My mind was torn between business efficiency and the ocean journey. As the deadline loomed I was still working to rig out *Sharky* to my satisfaction, studying the charts, listing provisions and the thousand and one other things I needed to do. The shop consumed my body; *Sharky* consumed my mind. Steadily, space in my flat diminished as piles of stores, clothes and marine equipment invaded any available surface, my home rapidly assuming the trappings of a well-equipped chandler's.

In the late evening of 16th July every nerve in my body tingled with expectation. I was done and ready for the off. I'd persuaded Maurice, a friend of mine, to drive Chris and me down to Falmouth and return with the car and a now very rusty trailer. The prospect of adventure hung in the air as we piled the car high and fussed around *Sharky*. I was a bundle of nervous energy yet still confused in my own emotions. I was grateful for the help and support from my friends but still, ungenerously, I wanted to savour the experience for myself alone. What really surprised me was the calmness of my parents. They knew that I'd been planning the trip for a long time; they'd heard my bravado tales of previous sailing jaunts, so perhaps they just thought I'd be okay. What they really knew of course was what I'd chosen to tell them. I had carefully selected the positive aspects to my sport and selectively forgotten to inform them about the bits that had gone wrong; the minor disasters, the near misses and the general cock-ups I thought might distress them. Too late now, I rationalised, so, discretion being the better part of cowardice, I just gave them a wave and left them on the street. Ignorance is bliss; especially when it's someone else's bliss.

At two o'clock in the morning, somewhere on the M5, a loud bang accompanied by some serious slewing across the road indicated a tyre burst on the trailer. 'Bugger it!' I shouted in some frustration. I'd tried to find a spare tyre and wheel before setting out but couldn't get a wheel to fit the trailer hub. Leaving without any spares at all and trusting to Lady Luck, we realised that sod's law had intervened instead, leaving us stranded on the hard shoulder. I was ranting and raving, Chris found it all mildly amusing; Maurice calmly sat in contemplation and awaited the hand of fate.

The hand of fate arrived ten minutes later dressed in the uniform of the motorway police. I could imagine their first reactions: three men of unconvincing appearance in the early hours, crammed in an old car and towing a boat on a barely legal trailer.

'Morning, officers. Erm, we've had a puncture,' uttered Chris, thereby gaining maximum points for a statement of the blinking obvious.

The two police officers did what they all do best. A seemingly casual look round the vehicle, a sideways glance at the tax disc, a not so subtle look at the registration plate and then a 'So where are you lads off to then?'

It was overwhelmingly tempting to reply, 'Across the Atlantic, officer', and watch the reaction, but sense overrode self-importance for once and an honest 'Falmouth' was the rejoinder. The police directed us to an all-night garage about seven miles back in the direction from where we'd just come then left us with a quick 'Good luck, lads'. Maurice and I unhitched the trailer, jacked it up, then realised we hadn't got a socket set to remove the wheel. Leaving Chris in charge of *Sharky*, we shot off to the garage where the somewhat bemused owner lent us one.

We returned to find Chris quietly dozing so maliciously we woke him up and got him to unscrew the wheelnuts. He'd just got to the last one when the socket split apart.

'Bugger it!' I shouted again. Using sheer brute force we somehow managed to free the offending nut, slung the wheel in the boot and Maurice and I sped off to the garage again. Sod's law was still in full swing. The mechanic informed us the tyre was irreparable and he had no others of the same size in stock. Pointing us in the direction of another garage fifteen miles south of where we'd broken down we shot off again like some manic team of cross-country treasure hunters. Arriving at five o'clock we discovered the garage didn't open until eight that morning so we cooled our heels for three hours trying desperately not to glance at our watches every ten minutes. We didn't even spare a thought for Chris.

To our great relief, the owner had the tyre we needed and, noting the joy on our faces, promptly overcharged us. We were past caring. Hurtling back to Chris and the M5, we fitted the replacement and resumed our journey. Stopping at a motorway café for lunch it occurred to me that I'd forgotten to pack any cutlery for the boat. The obvious solution was to leave the café with our coat sleeves stuffed with knives, forks, spoons and cruets. I wouldn't have been surprised if we'd been nicked for theft but we arrived in Falmouth without further ado. Nevertheless, the incidents did cause me to ponder the future trip. If the journey to Falmouth had been blighted because of poor planning, how would we fare when we were truly on our own? There would be no instantly available emergency services where we were heading. I needed to use the couple of harbour days wisely before we set sail.

Safely in Falmouth, Chris and I stood on the harbour side after having floated *Sharky* from the trailer. Although there was much to do I stood gazing down at her. A beautiful but fragile life-support system, if we were lucky. She had loomed large on the trailer down from Derbyshire but now seemed somehow forlorn and lost in the damp, drizzly conditions; like a bewildered puppy adrift from the comfort of its home. Maurice joined us where we stood; a rare fellow about fifteen years older than I was, with whom I'd become firm friends over many years. He was one of life's unique individuals, tall, powerfully built with a well-trimmed beard and an almost mystical, intense presence. An ex-policeman with some agonising experiences, Maurice had turned his back on the normal trappings of life and had become a loner inclined to a philosophical and spiritual way of life. He was a strange outpost of a man but I had enjoyed his company over the years and he understood the passions that were driving me.

'Thanks, Maurice,' I said. It was somehow sad to leave him behind. He'd been as excited as us about the trip and assured us he would be with us in spirit. Wishing us God's speed, he gave me a Buddhist scarf that had been blessed for safe travel by a senior lama. This was a poignant moment for me but Maurice understood my nod and pat on the back. In an earlier moment of inspiration I'd decided to name our self-steering gear after him and had commissioned a small sticker, which I'd fixed to the wind vane. Feeling slightly embarrassed, I showed him what I'd done and knew from his quick nod of joy that it had been the right thing. He left Falmouth with an empty heart and empty trailer. The latter he ditched somewhere on the route home after the A-frame snapped. In my mind's eye I can see him pulling off the road, removing the number plate and, without a backwards glance or care, go on his way. I would not have expected anything less.

The next day I awoke with the realisation that my dream of an ocean sail was about to become a reality. All the effort of the past year was coming to fruition and I was glad I'd spent that time preparing *Sharky* for the worst. The Bay of Biscay has a fearsome reputation and I had no intention of leaving anything to chance. I spent the morning endlessly tweaking the rigging, knowing I'd still be doing it as we cast off. A lot of the bottle screws were second-hand, a few had locking nuts missing and I ran extra five-millimetre rope through to the rigging wires in case the screws gave way. Chris helped to get the fresh supplies in, we found a new paddle wheel for the log, and after a long day of running about we retired to the pub for some well-earned beers. The forecast was looking good for a Monday cast-off and we both needed time to unwind.

I can be incredibly self-centred, to the point where I just forget about other people, focusing instead on my own problems and the task in hand. I had barely noticed Chris over the past couple of days but was gradually becoming aware that he was getting edgy, so a few beers was a good opportunity to see if he really wanted to make the trip or bow out gracefully. It turned out he was really scared about crossing the Bay of Biscay. Having been ill on previous sailing journeys, he was in a quandary about the adventure and the month off work and the thought of serious seasickness.

'Let's just hurry up and set off,' he said. Poor old Chris; torn between adventure, friendship and self-preservation. Could he manage all three?

A further day's delay due to weather conditions, a final fretful argument with Chris, a brief glance towards Falmouth, and we made the transition from landlubbers to salty dogs. Once aboard *Sharky*, I busied myself with the essential tasks prior to cast-off. A last look at the charts and yet another peek to see if everything was stowed; it's amazing how inanimate objects can defy the best efforts to keep them securely fastened. The tiny space, creatively called a cabin to give the notion of luxury, was about the size of two adjacent coffins, but this area was now crammed with two five-gallon water drums lashed to the vertical mast support, food and provisions, luggage, cooking pots, an anchor, chains, ropes, fenders, sails, charts, books, radio – oh, and two large blokes who would literally have to rub shoulders with each other. To the rear of this space on the starboard side sat two gas-cooking rings on gimbals to help maintain a level plane when at sea. Stretching forwards from the cooker, a narrow seat curved into the bow, but this was being used to accommodate other stores and the chart table, which I'd fixed to the edge of the cooker unit and the mast support. To the port side, a longer, equally narrow seat accommodated the length of a sleeping bag, with just enough room at the end for the second person to sit with his head shrunk into his shoulders to avoid hitting the roof. Beneath both seats was limited storage space into which much of the food and clothing, all sealed in plastic bags, was stuffed. I'd generously allowed Chris the full-length bunk, meaning I would have to sleep in a sitting position by his feet or, if I moved the chart table, go for a squeezed foetal position last encountered nearly three decades earlier. Small portholes and an even smaller light bulb completed the 'sardines in a tin' effect. We'd been sailing in small boats for some time so there was no sense of claustrophobia – but boy was it tight! It looked comfy in the false security of Falmouth harbour; I just wondered how we'd fare in open waters. It was time to find out.

Although the harbour temperature was a reasonable thirteen degrees centigrade, I nevertheless pulled on an extra sweater and thicker trousers as experience had taught me that even benign sea breezes can quickly chill to the bone. Essential drinks and biscuits were placed within immediate snatching range and finally I donned my 'Musto', a one-piece waterproof that I hoped would keep the Atlantic in its place and where I wanted it to be. As usual I removed my socks and irreverently chucked them in the cabin. My bare feet felt more comfortable in my old tatty trainers. I could wait no longer.

'Come on, Chris,' I said. 'Let's go.'

At last I was ready to be off; away and free.

Tuesday 21st July, 14.15 p.m., the exact time when my sailing ambition began. Not quite solo, nor a single dash, but the adventure had started and I was grateful just to have cast off and got on with it. The sky was cloudy with a westerly edging wind as we untied the moorings. Chris slipped the outboard into reverse and slowly backed up, dropped the revs and slid it into forward gear. Just prior to leaving, I'd nipped ashore to make last-minute phone calls and to issue reassurances to my family. My mum acted as though I was just going for a quick jaunt around the bay rather than a five-week haul!

We sailed down to the harbour entrance at a steady four knots, both of us snapping away with our cameras at Falmouth town; the neat grey and white buildings steeping down to the waterfront, partially hidden by a veritable forest of clanking yacht masts bobbing on the tide. The town front was busy with tourists ambling and relaxing. As we drew further away, they began to merge into a grey amorphous snake winding along the seafront, a world already distant and irrelevant. As we sailed through the gap between Rosemullion Head and Pendennis Point, we spotted a basking seal on Black Rock and convinced ourselves it was a lucky omen. We were like two characters from a schoolboy's Ripping Yarns book; excited, hyped-up, chattering away, the fear and anxiety gradually disappearing with every wave crossed. I have always experienced this heightening of emotions whenever I have started an adventurous pursuit. The anxiety of inactivity gives way to the euphoria of challenge. Potential dangers are minimised, fear is suppressed in the heady mix of the moment and a surge of pure freedom blossoms. It's a transient feeling but at the time the soul is released from care. I have spoken to many friends and am certain it is a common emotion at any level of adventure. Whether sailing a boat, scaling a mountain or something as mundane as a holiday break, there is a sense of new beginnings, some trepidation certainly but always a quickening of the pulse and a glimpse of freedom; always a glimpse of freedom.

Out of the harbour we steered a heading of 180 degrees. The wind had lightened and veered westerly so I kept the engine running as we raised the sails. It was a fine, cool afternoon and we spotted more seals as I set the full mainsail and working jib. I'd had some problems with the outboard and rationalised that since the thing was seemingly chugging away quite contentedly I'd leave it to settle in. Secretly however I was going to try and sell it once we got to Spain, as I was pretty sure it was more trouble than it was worth. With hindsight I'd forgotten *Sharky*'s First Law. Outboard motors are unreliable characters, have sensitive souls and are able to read minds.

With the harbour protection behind us I could feel the first Atlantic surges power their way around *Sharky*. Once beyond Lizard Point, Chris put the kettle on while I figured out the self-steering, which kept slewing off course. I'd spent quite some time in my workshop designing the equipment, essentially a simple vane gear connecting horizontal and vertical pulley lines through to the tiller. Fix the vane into the wind on the desired course and theoretically the boat stays on that course. The open sea, however, does not hold with theory and I began to realise that self-steering might actually mean steering it by myself. Perhaps I shouldn't have called it Maurice, as it seemed to be adopting some of its namesake's idiosyncrasies. We would have to wait and see.

With the euphoria of the start still coursing through my body I turned my mind to the important matter of getting from A to B in as straight a line as possible. On my yachtmaster course it had been drilled into me that it was pointless to over-plan a route as perverse variables such as weather and sea conditions will rapidly render it useless. Better to have a simple plan but also back-up ready to be put into action. With this in mind I'd decided to head off from Falmouth on a west southwest heading, making sure I sailed far enough west in case a severe southwesterly blew me back in again. Unusual at that time of the year but I wanted to take all precautions as I now had the additional responsibility of Chris as my crew. Many people cross the Bay of Biscay by sailing to Brest, where they await favourable weather patterns before dashing off towards Finistère but, as ever, I wanted to do things differently, so other than reading pilots and looking at charts, thus my plan was formulated.

Pilots are interesting books, a sort of atlas of the sea written by all sorts of people, including naval personnel or just sailors who have been there and done it. They range from personal perspectives to highly technical and specialised information concerning tides, probable weather conditions, wind strength and so on. They also provide some of the best knowledge you can get as well as being extremely interesting to read; a roadmap of the sea might best describe them.

With nautical matters now well in hand, our thoughts turned to matters gastronomic; time for a late-lunch-cum-early-tea. We hadn't really planned menus as such. It was a matter of identifying anything and everything we liked and stuffing it on board, so our first meal consisted of all the goodies we could find. In the first few miles from the harbour I'd already demolished two packets of Jammy Dodgers from a secret supply well hidden from Chris. He was an obsessive biscuit-muncher, as I'd discovered on an earlier trip when he'd taken the helm while I grabbed an hour's sleep. I'd given him my last packet of Garibaldi biscuits and asked him to save me some for later. I'd relieved him from his watch and had asked him where the biscuits were.

'Just over there, mate,' had come the confident reply as he'd disappeared below deck. I'd looked 'over there' to no avail. By then it had become pitch dark, there'd been a strengthening storm, the sails had been flapping like crazy and serious waves had come crashing over the deck. As the boat had twisted and turned beneath my feet I'd feverishly scanned around with my torch while trying to hold the boat together.

'Chris,' I'd screamed into the night, 'where are the damned biscuits?'

Back had come the faint response: 'If they're not there they've been washed overboard.'

I learnt two things that night. Despite the potential hazards of sailing in atrocious weather, my stomach takes priority, and secondly Chris was a liar of epic proportions when it came to biscuits. Months later, he'd confessed to eating the whole packet.

As our first evening fell, we headed south on a sou'westerly wind. It was a cool night with an intermittent then increasing cloud base. The blue-grey Atlantic looked vast from deck level and the only noises were the lapping of waves, the wind in the rigging and a quiet whistling from Chris. We were tiny specks adrift on a new adventure and it was a time forever etched in my memory. So many things in my life had conspired to bring me to this point. In my deepest thoughts I still hankered after the desire to be there alone but for now I was at peace. I was on my way.

Edging into the wind at three or four knots, my mind was off in different directions. Subconsciously it was focused, handling the boat, feeling her response to the sea and the wind. That part of my mind was on task and clear. The rest was having a field day of jumbled-up thoughts and emotions racing in, then disappearing before I'd had a chance to wonder where they'd come from. I didn't feel worry or anxiety, just a tremendous release of these emotions; my world had shrunk to simple survival on distant horizons; work, family, finances were no longer immediate priorities. They'd dip in and out of my thoughts unbidden but, in the best possible sense, they were now on the edges of my new universe. I'd waited a long time for this opportunity and I was determined to look forward not back.

Odd then that two of the first thoughts that rammed into my head were from my earliest childhood. In happier times, before my mother and father had separated, we'd lived in a flat above the Fine Fare supermarket in Wye Street, Buxton, where my father was manager. My mum used to describe to me how I would sit in my baby walker on our enclosed backyard, pick up the frame so the wheels were off the ground then run as fast as I could, return the wheels to the ground, pick up my feet and bash into the far wall. 'You were daft,' she'd say. 'Determined and daft; always used to be doing it.' Not daft because I did it – daft because I kept on doing it. A couple of years older and I'd stand and watch my father carefully load the van (a Ford Escort I think) with boxes of orders, neatly stacking them in the correct order, in much the same way as I imagined Father Christmas did with presents on his sleigh. A final check of his list then he'd scoop me up with a 'Come on, young 'un' and wedge me in the back surrounded by the pungent, mixed smells of fruits, vegetables, cheeses and meats. It's a memory that floods back every time I go near a market or greengrocer – the faintly musty odour of root vegetables pervading all else.

The weekly trip out, however, was not in itself the main thrill. Wedged in the back, I'd hear my dad grind the gears, then stop at frequent intervals, slam his door, open the rear, give me a quick grin then disappear with one more box. I'd hear the muted sounds of conversation, an endless succession of cheerios, then the door would slam, the engine catch, the gears grind and off we'd go again. Each time we'd stop, the space around me in the van would increase and I'd sense a bit more freedom; and then the moment I'd been waiting for would arrive. Dad would poke his head in the back and with a bigger than ever grin would produce an empty box and stick me in it.

'Time to be a Fine Fare driver,' he'd call out. Back in the cab I'm sure he increased his speed a little and took the corners just that bit sharper. Snuggled in my box the sensation of whizzing and sliding around the confines of the van, not knowing where I'd hurtle next, was the most exciting experience of my young life and definitely the highlight of the week. Today's kids stuck in their safety-conscious seats, with seatbelts and in-car entertainment, have no idea of the fervent joy that can be had from a freewheeling cardboard box and a dad who could distinguish irresponsible recklessness from intensely simple pleasures. The whole of Buxton must have heard my unfettered screams of delight and wondered what on earth was so exciting about deliveries from Fine Fare!

So Wye Street became the first crucible that helped mould the person I've become. Determination, stubbornness and a sense of adventure that I have had all my life; these traits probably came as much from a baby walker and a Fine Fare van as from my parents. Did I develop some measure of independence and fearlessness because of the simple acts of sliding around a van and running fearlessly into walls, or did I do those things because the traits were already within me? Mum would typically have told me to stop contemplating and just get on with things.

Chapter Four

The Off

There was much to do that day but I deliberately took time to look around, with nothing and no one in sight, and tried to absorb and appreciate the wonders that nature can create.

ON THE SECOND DAY out of Falmouth I awoke early and took a GPS fix before breakfast. Five o'clock in the morning is often a grim affair and on that occasion the sea was running a steady swell under a porridge-grey sky. Everything looked cold and uninviting. I was tired, unshaven, damp and my back ached. I think I still hadn't fully tuned into what I had started and it took a moment or two to comprehend where I was and what I was doing. For a brief moment I entertained thoughts of a snug, soft bed and a hot shower but a quick pee over the side of the bobbing boat swiftly returned me to reality. I did the calculations; we'd logged fifty-two miles, with which I was quite content.

Just as I was going below to wake Chris, the wind began to die away and we gradually became becalmed, always an odd feeling and more so in the early light of a streaky yellow grey dawn. It's a strange experience because the normal situation in a boat is one of forward or lateral movement provided by the wind. Remove that force and you're left with just an up-and-down movement, which, while pleasant and relaxing for a while, eventually instils a sense of uneasy restlessness. A doubt forms in the mind as to whether the wind will ever pick up again; like waiting for a train that's late and wondering if it will ever arrive.

A bedraggled Chris grumbled up on deck, looking distinctly horrible and unattractive. He mumbled an unenthusiastic 'Morning' and glanced around. I could have read his thoughts – what the hell am I doing here? He looked as rough as I felt and there was a grim humour in our situation; two bleary-eyed casualties of life stumbling around at first light trying to wake up and renew our enthusiasm for sailing. Nevertheless, we enjoyed the peace and took breakfast while keeping an eye out for nearby shipping.

It seemed as though the wind had also breakfasted. An hour later it picked up again from the south so I headed west trying to pinch as much southerly direction as possible. I began to play around with the pulleys on the self-steering system and it seemed to work better in the stronger wind. Taking the noon fix, I was reasonably pleased with our progress, considering the weight of the boat. We were low in the water and it dawned on me I had heavily over-provisioned, perhaps subconsciously thinking I was doing the whole Atlantic in one go. Still, I reasoned, at least we weren't short of biscuits.

For most of the afternoon the wind stayed just west of south and we could only make a heading of 270 degrees at best. At this rate we were going to finish up in America and not Spain. The mood on board remained subdued and my feelings were in conflict. The highly charged emotions of the first day seemed a lifetime ago and we were beginning to experience the reality of life aboard a damp, cramped small boat. We had both slept fitfully and were cold and tired. Chris was certainly more restrained than the day before and the still, small voices of uncertainty that had been banished began to creep imperceptibly into my consciousness; nothing too startling but a gradual gnawing away of the over-blown early confidence. For no definable reason I felt I had to keep an eye on Chris.

About six o'clock that night I noticed a slight increase in the wind. This was fine as we'd spotted a large tanker on the horizon. One of my constant nightmares had been the thought of becoming becalmed in an area noted for heavy shipping; stray into the path of one of those behemoths and we'd have been swatted like an unseen fly. With the increase in wind, the sea was also picking up and we were getting a lot of white caps and cold spray breaking over us. It was important to get some hot food down and while I took a watch on deck Chris struggled in the galley.

The difficulties we'd experienced on previous sails in the Channel had hardened me to uncomfortable conditions, but at that moment I felt they were containable and nothing out of the ordinary. 'Worse things happen at sea, eh Chris?' I smiled, but was rewarded with nothing more than a wan, tight-lipped grimace. The day passed without much event or conversation, as we were both in something of a trance. We sailed mechanically, each lost in his own thoughts for much of the time.

Eight o'clock that night was notable in that it was the first time Chris was sick since leaving Falmouth. He'd been feeling poorly for most of the day and the combined effect of tiredness, the cold and the severe motion of the boat had triggered the inevitable. The boat was rocking badly in the swell and heavy seas were splashing on deck. There is nothing pleasant about being sick anywhere but on a small boat it's magnified tenfold. Add the fact that there is no respite in the shape of nearby land, a soft bed or dry clothing and everything can seem desperate. Chris had had enough and was physically exhausted so I sent him below to bed. I suspected it was going to be a rough night and I was going to have enough to do running the boat. I sent him down not because I was worried about his health but because he would have been a hindrance up on deck. I took the decision without hesitation, but why I had weighed the priorities as I had did cross my mind as I battened down *Sharky* for what might turn out to be an interesting night. Was I being selfish again or just decisive?

The southwest wind increased as whitecaps appeared on the larger waves; I harnessed myself on to ease the mainsail and moved forward to change the working jib to a smaller and stronger storm jib. *Sharky* was bucking wildly and the freezing sea spray cut into my hands and face. I quickly slipped open the hatch to check on Chris. In the comparative smelly warmth of the cabin he lay sleeping, mouth open and snoring, completely oblivious to the bucking motion around him, his sleeping bag tightly jammed into the available bunk space. Conditions worsened as I returned to the cockpit and twice I had to put a reef in the mainsail. Reefing is the way of reducing the amount of exposed sail – a sort of balancing act between harnessing the power of the wind while not allowing it to overcome the boat. I'd had a particularly heavy sail made for me in Warsash. It had lots of extra reefing lines and strengthened holes set laterally into the fabric at intervals down the length, which enabled it to be bundled up neatly to the boom and put safely out of the way. Being able to reef gave me more control in worsening seas, though at times I wondered just exactly what control I did have!

The endless practice of reefing I'd done at Rudyard Lake had now become second nature. I kept to a set of procedures that I could do with my eyes closed, in the dark and with one hand and my front teeth. I was well aware of the constant dangers aboard a small craft and reasoned that if I had broken or deeply cut my arm then being able to reef this way just might save my life, especially when sailing solo. A Caprice class boat has a mainsail that can be worked on from the main hatchway. I'd practised hauling the topping lift by stretching over from the hatchway, loosening the halyard and pulling down the mainsail to the reef line to tie off. I'd then tighten the halyard, tie up the rest of the mainsail and release the topping lift to reset the sail. This worked well when I could lie on my back near the open hatch cover with one leg drooped inside for stability, but in the heavy seas we were now beginning to encounter I had to close the hatch, which meant a lot of crawling around on the cabin roof like a drunken caterpillar on a fairground ride.

Compared to the mainsail, however, the jib was in another league entirely. Taking in the jib meant negotiating a trip to the bow, fully harnessed and scared witless. As the wind increased in ferocity I needed to stash the jib. So, with heart in mouth, I crawled forward as best I could and clung on to the bow railing for dear life. The roar of the wind and the sea was deafening. Each time *Sharky* buried herself in the bow waves my whole body became submerged as I took the full brunt of the force. I was already completely soaked but this was another massive drenching. Aching in my whole being, I eventually tied the sail down and crawled back to the relative lee of the cockpit. I was glad I had practised the routine physically and mentally many times. I prided myself on my ability to sail with 'feel'. I got to a point where I could feel the tension and slack in the sails, I could feel the wind, feel the boat, feel the sea. Each time I reach this point I become a true sailor, at one with my environment, in harmony with nature and the elements. It is one of the greatest experiences I have ever encountered. It is not about conquering the sea; it's about being part of it.

My log for one o'clock that Thursday morning read: 'Just missed two ships, double reefed the main; very bruised, severe case of arse twitching!!!' I was sailing in pitch-dark conditions in a heavy swell with driving rain and a strengthening, gusting wind. I say sailing, really more a case of hanging on. I was in a busy sea lane, tired, scared, cold and hungry. My mate was next to useless at that time; and yet I loved it! For the first time in twenty-four hours I'd come alive. For me there is exhilaration in adversity. There is a point where the body thinks it has had enough yet the mind steadfastly refuses to give in. There's a sort of 'sod it, don't give a damn' attitude, which in my case, when the pressure's on, makes me laugh out loud. Athletes talk of 'hitting the wall' when the body wants to give in; the good ones go through the wall and I think I understand what they mean. It's a spiritual act of defiance that heightens the awareness, intensifies the senses and somehow brings out a perverse sense of enjoyment. Put people in extraordinary situations and they do extraordinary things.

As the seas became increasingly fearsome, the waves assumed proportions I found unbelievable. Pitching and rolling in the troughs, the boat was being flung around in an erratic swell that had no rhythm or direction – a bit like the agitator in the old twin-tub washing machine. We were in a short sea situation typical of the Bay of Biscay. We were still on the continental shelf and the huge mass of sea being funnelled north and into the Channel was making the distance between troughs short and volatile. A Biscay sea is a real bitch and with the wind against the tide it was a horrible, horrible place to be. It was like being on an endless roller-coaster ride. But this was no safety-controlled attraction. This was a roaring, stomach-churning, deafening reality in a tiny boat to which we were entrusting our lives.

As *Sharky* slithered down the peaks, the rain drove constantly and horizontally into my face. There was no pattern to the seas – just unpredictable heaving and lurching in all directions. I was sodden and stinging from constant drenching in ice-cold salt water. The main was stretched in tortured agony, the rigging was creaking and moaning, and I feared for the self-steering gear as it flailed helplessly out of the wave crests before crashing back into the sea and finding the wind again. This really was Dante's Inferno in the raw. I was shit-scared, on my own (Chris forgotten) and still glad to be there, frantically busy in appalling conditions, under the illusion of having some control over the uncontrollable, yet revelling in the challenge. Somehow I sailed throughout the night living on adrenalin, grabbing a snatched five minutes of sleep with occasional snacks and drinks. Good old biscuits, you can't beat a Jammy Dodger in a crisis. In a sea that had remained angry and confused we had logged sixty-three nautical miles, a total from The Lizard of ninety-two miles.

I awoke with a start after what felt like several hours and glanced at my watch. Eight o'clock. In reality I'd snatched another few minutes' sleep. I felt really dreadful after taking quite a battering throughout the night and although it had stopped raining we were still running a heavy swell on more or less a west sou'westerly heading. I was desperate for a westerly wind to get us back in a more southerly direction. I opened the cabin door and hit a foul, rancid stench of stale air, sweat and vomit that almost had me gagging. The cabin was a mess with wet clothing and items that hadn't been stowed securely. In the midst of this chaos lay Chris, ashen-faced and lolling like a rag doll in his sleeping bag, which was stained with sick. He'd been crying through fear and depression and I realised that for him this trip was already over. He'd simply had enough. He was a social animal who needed bright lights and the comfort of people around him. The bravado of a big adventure had appealed to his ego but the reality of distance sailing had destroyed his will to continue. I tried to reassure him but I felt uncomfortable in doing so. He drank a cup of sweetened hot water and said he was sorry for letting me down but reckoned he'd be better soon, now that the big storm was over. I left him snuggling back into his sleeping bag and hadn't the heart to tell him that, while the 'blow' had been bad, it hadn't really been a storm. It was quite possible we were going to experience a whole lot worse. I daren't tell him I'd actually found the whole thing exhilarating. Also re-surfacing was the thought that perhaps a solo journey might after all be the best option.

Back on deck I spent my time sailing *Sharky* and thinking about things in general. Sailing gives you a lot of time to think and there's a melancholy pleasure of enjoying being alone while also wanting to share the feeling with someone close to you. I was already missing Elaine and began to ponder about what the future would hold for us as we'd been together for about four years. I was getting extremely fond of her and we felt good about each other. Blokes aren't very good at the romantic stuff yet out there in that vast ocean of emptiness I let my heart fill with thoughts of love and my eyes filled with tears. I must have looked pathetic. A dishevelled, soggy scrap of humanity wiping tears away, pretending they were sea spray. In that moment I didn't know whether I was happy or sad, content or forlorn. Or yes I did. Within the jumble of conflicting emotions I knew, just knew that I wouldn't have wanted to be anywhere else. I also, rather selfishly, thought that if I'd been given the choice of a quick cuddle with Elaine or a bag of hot, crunchy chips, right then I'd have gone for the chips.

By early afternoon a lot of cumulous cloud had bubbled up and I sensed rain. I glanced in at Chris who was still feeling very ill and guilty. I opened up the hatch to get some fresh air in and was rewarded by a crashing wave that pitched water everywhere. We were still trapped in the wretched Biscay short seas. Chris panicked and began to cry; he was absolutely petrified he was going to drown. There was much to do in a short time. I banged the hatch shut, shouted to Chris that he was going to be okay and leapt back to the helm. For an hour the rain lashed incessantly as a vicious squall blew waves of increasing length, white foam breaking from the crests. Visibility dropped to a gloomy few yards and I began to ache and become very tired. In the murk I heard the deep-throated sound of a nearby engine, but where was it and where was it heading?

As if in answer to my prayers, the mist lifted briefly to reveal a fishing boat moving slowly to port. He was trailing a net and was really being tossed about but at least he was warm and dry in his cabin. I put in a tack to show I had seen him. He waved a response and within seconds visibility had reduced to yards as the squall reasserted itself.

By nine o'clock that Thursday night the wind took pity on us, swung into the west and calmed down. I set the self-steering gear, hoisted a working jib and took a reef out of the mainsail. Adrenalin had kept me going for nearly two days of relentless weather but now that the crisis was over I suddenly felt the tiredness and cold and badly needed some dry clothes. Down below Chris was still in his sleeping bag, still badly shaken by the squalls and ocean swells. If we'd been sailing in a forty-footer the conditions would have been merely uncomfortable, but in a tiny craft like *Sharky* all sensations and effects were intensely magnified. The bad weather we'd experienced on Channel trips, while rough, had not felt as severe as this and, unlike the Channel, there was no prospect of finding land within twenty to thirty miles. Out here in open seas lying helpless in a bunk must have been worse than helming; at least I'd been occupied and able to respond to the situation. The cabin remained an absolute stinking mess with water and debris sloshing everywhere, but overall I was too tired and tense to care. My hips and legs were sore, my back ached and I just wanted some respite. I changed into Chris's dry waterproofs, brewed us some tea and settled down for a few hours' sleep. We barely exchanged a dozen words. I didn't go to bed; I just slept where I was, totally exhausted but sensing, with quiet satisfaction, that I had gone through a baptism, and passed a test. Throughout the night the wind blew steadily, making two-metre waves, but by dawn it had started to drop.

Friday 24th July. I awoke at six and went on deck to a transformation. I am always amazed at how the sea can alter its mood, and that morning was no exception. The intensity and drama of the previous night had given way to a beautiful rich red dawn, and while the waves were still a little on the choppy side it was as though we were witnessing our very own dawn of creation. There was much to do that day but I deliberately took time to look around, with nothing and no one in sight, and tried to absorb and appreciate the wonders that nature can create. I knew I was privileged to be there, at wave height, trying to drink in the sky's colours, the sea patterns, the noises of the boat and rigging. For that one moment alone the trials of the previous nights had been worth it.

Sitting low in the water, I felt my little boat skim comfortably in her environment. She had done well under extreme duress and I felt proud of her. It was as though she was showing her appreciation for all the work and time I had bestowed on her. *Sharky* and I had become close partners and I knew that I was becoming attuned to my adventure and to my surroundings. I felt truly happy. The beauty of it all made me ache inside but it was a pleasant ache. Again I felt the need to sail on my own; at some stage a discussion with Chris was unavoidable.

I could have spent hours in quiet contemplation but my stomach was having none of it. I'd fed my mind, now the body demanded its dues. A celebratory breakfast was in order and I rustled up a gourmet meal of beans on toast, even managing to tempt Chris with a small mouthful. I suspected he'd been silently crying again during the night but in my deep sleep I'd been oblivious to him. Rinsing the plates after our meal, I heard a commotion and turned to investigate. Dolphins! About six or seven sleek, slate-grey animals cavorting around and across the bows and the first ones I'd seen in the wild.

'Chris,' I screamed, arms waving like a dervish. 'Dolphins, quick or you'll miss them!'

For the first time in two days Chris came up on deck and savoured the fresh, salty air. The dolphins, often called friends of the fishermen, played around the boat skipping and diving. It was as though they were saying hello and I found myself trying to make contact with their jet-black eyes, shining like tiny buttons above their grinning mouths, as if to return the greeting. Then they were gone, a final flip of tails and we were alone again, but a brief encounter that lifted my already high spirits a notch higher.

'It means good luck, Chris,' I said, trying to instil some of my enthusiasm. 'We're going to be fine now.'

The experience and the change of air seemed to do him some good and after a bit of gentle persuasion he agreed he was well enough to help clean up the cabin. We had a strip wash and began to tackle the chaos that was our home.

At about noon I took the midday fix, which gave us a day's run of 53 nautical miles, a total from Lizard of 148. *Sharky* still seemed overloaded in the light wind, and in these conditions Maurice, the self-steering gear, was not at its best. I was expecting to drop off the continental shelf later in the afternoon and I thought it merited a bit of a celebration. I was also pleased that we'd had a light day's sailing. The prospect of having 4,000 metres of water beneath us rather than the shelf's 200 would have seemed more daunting in testing conditions.

As expected, we 'dropped off' about 3.30 in the afternoon and celebrated with a huge mishmash of a tea. Chris ate a reasonable amount but decided to return to his bunk. Left alone again, I knew our sailing days together were now a thing of the past. He clearly hadn't got the sailing spirit and was continuously oscillating between wariness and being downright terrified. An unexpected shudder or dip of the boat would make him cast around fearfully like a cornered animal. The sea had become an alien environment for him and while I felt some compassion my thoughts remained clouded by feelings of resentment. He was no longer a crew member, and I was carrying a passenger I didn't want or need. The confined and cramped living conditions had created some tense moments between us and we had exchanged some harsh words at times. I could sympathise with his condition but I couldn't empathise. I was enjoying the challenge, he was not. Yet again my selfishness rose to the fore. This was my journey and now I didn't want him as part of it. I felt ashamed of my feelings and began to harbour thoughts of frustration and animosity. I'd warned Chris before we set off of what he could expect and now he was admitting defeat. I was angry with myself and took some of that anger out on him. With time to myself as I helmed into a sunset tinged with orange hues, the serenity of the moment took some of that anger away, but it didn't fully prevent me from feeling a bit of a bastard.

As the sunset deepened on that quiet evening, the wind died away, so I took in all the sail and by nine o'clock I'd clambered under my sleeping bag, fully clothed as usual in case I needed to extricate myself in a hurry. I settled down with a hot chocolate and glanced over to Chris who had been asleep for a few hours. I preferred not to analyse the events of recent days and just let my mind wander wherever it took me. It was strangely quiet, virtually no noise from outside the cabin and just the odd sleepy sniff from my cabin companion. It still felt unreal being so far from land, the farthest I had ever been in a small boat, and I briefly wondered what the rest of the world was up to – not that I really cared. My family, my friends and my boat were all that really mattered; that and the fact that I was running out of fags. Then there was the increasingly disgusting odour emanating from a damp cabin and its contents, the constant possibility of being run down by a ship... . Enough! I drained my drink and settled down to sleep.

But I couldn't. Not for more than an hour or so. Some instinct kept waking me to peek outside for a quick check on things. Glancing around the cabin, I realised it wasn't just damp and smelly, it was untidy. Chris had formed a habit of dumping not stowing things and it was bugging me more than I'd thought. In fact Chris being ill was thoroughly irritating and while a small part of me understood he wasn't being deliberately sick, I think deep down I just wanted rid of him. Confused thoughts kept me awake; if he was ill he was out of the way, which I liked, but being ill meant he was a burden and I wished he'd get better – though if he were better I'd lose my solitude. Irritation, selfishness, concern and conscience battered at my brain, so I needed a distraction. At 3.30 in the morning I went on deck and discovered a slight breeze picking up. It was a westerly and quite light but at least it was wind, so I put up sail. There was a damp clamminess in the air that was beginning to chill me. I quickly made a brew and miraculously found a new packet of Jammy Dodgers, and thus a cause for celebration. I spent an hour or so just sitting by myself until the chill eventually forced me back under my sleeping bag. Chris was still in slumber, oblivious to the world, and yet I wouldn't have traded places with him. I had enjoyed the tranquillity of the darkness, just sitting listening to nothing in particular, my mind drifting with the boat, content on my own; alone yet not lonely.

By seven o'clock I was up again tending to Maurice, the self-steering gear. Once set for our course, I made myself some breakfast but with the wind steadily dying away again I was reduced to hand steering by mid-morning. Maurice was still struggling in the lightish winds, a fact giving rise to a rich vein of earthy, northern vernacular. It made not a scrap of difference and I was left to do the helming without the benefit of mechanical devices. The only sign of movement all day, apart from Chris eventually rising mid-morning, was the shape of a whale fin about a hundred yards to port; a quick snap of the camera later producing a fuzzy outline of it against a steel-blue sea. By the time I took the midday fix I calculated we were 165 miles from The Lizard with another 300 left to Cabo de Finisterre. The now light southerly winds were not helping our progress and we really needed a swing to a more north-westerly direction to make up time. Already desperately short on cigarettes, short on patience with Chris and long on praying for more wind, I realised that at this rate we were still days away from safe harbour.

CHAPTER FIVE

Biscay's Lesson

*A powerful unseen dynamic scooped up our tiny craft
and hurled it skywards.*

I NEVER TIRE OF looking at the sea, whether I'm on it or by it. A soulless person would probably regard it as just wet, salty stuff. Okay, it changes colour and a Caribbean deep blue is preferable to a North Sea grey but once you've seen it, you've seen it.

What utter nonsense! I'd go out on a limb – or should that be a yardarm? – and declare that the sea has its own personality; a powerhouse of life that sucks you in and transforms your own personality. Touch the sea and you touch your soul. I have lost count of the times when I have sat on a shoreline and felt myself drawn by its power. Within minutes of sitting down, gazing from the foreshore to the horizon and watching the ebb and flow, a hypnotic energy works its spell. Elements and senses combine. Noise, be it gentle lapping or storm crashing, the primeval force of current and tide, and size, the sheer vastness of water all coalesce into a single description. Endless. I defy anyone to sit by the sea and not wonder at its immensity or marvel at its infinity. The sea has been surging for all time, its song unheard for most of its existence. Today we hear what prehistoric people heard millions of years ago. I cannot believe that, on seeing the sea for the first time, they would not have been drawn by its majesty nor been fearful of its power. To sit by the sea is to reflect on your innermost thoughts. Where is more evocative to ponder the meaning of your life – at whatever level you choose to do so?

If sitting by the sea is sensuous, consider the impact of sitting on it. Not on a floating gin palace far removed from nature but down where you meet the sea on its own terms; where the tides, wind and spray provide the adrenalin rush and the certainty of not being fully in control. There are similar feelings of insignificance when journeying through remote landscapes but the sea is different. The sea is unpredictable. It moves. The feeling of your insignificance is heightened by additional uncertainty. It's not an element we can control to any great extent. To be on the sea is exhilarating but we are never fully sure.

I think it was a small chink in my own self-belief that drew me to sailing; a bit of insecurity behind the mask of confidence. In a way I enjoyed pitting myself against the odds because I felt the need to prove that I could conquer fears. I inherited a northern stubbornness to fight my own way in life and developed a maturing belief in my own cerebral and practical skills. Others would probably just call me an awkward bugger. Get my teeth into something and I wouldn't let go.

So sailing became something I didn't want to let go of and a journey across the Atlantic became my Holy Grail of determination. Four days into the first leg and despite severe bad weather, little sleep and a sick crewmate, I had lost none of my will to succeed. It hadn't been the best of starts and while Chris and I were still communicating I knew we had lost that essential spark of unity towards a common goal. He'd had enough of sailing. I wanted more of it. It came down to nothing simpler than that. I felt as though we'd been nautically divorced.

That Saturday Chris felt able to take the helm for a few hours. He was confident he had recovered from his bout of seasickness and rapidly approached his usual cheery self. I was still distrustful of this return to good humour but said nothing. There was something in his eyes that didn't gel with the smile on his face. It was good however to enjoy his company and banter again, and I pushed my guilty feelings of the previous night behind me. We talked of shared past experiences; of parties, girls and lost loves. It was silly inconsequential stuff but it seemed to restore a link between us. To celebrate his return to the land of the living, we conjured up an exotic dish of chicken and rice, piping hot and just what we needed. The sun was warm and everything conspired to put some colour back into Chris's cheeks. He soaked up the fresh air at the helm while I practised my astronavigation. Deliberately, I steered clear of any conversation relating to ending this part of the journey and it became an unwritten and unspoken agreement between us.

At ten o'clock that evening the stars were beginning to pinprick their way through a velvet-black sky, and I sat sipping hot chocolate, trying to identify constellations. Again I was drawn to the huge mysteries of the universe and, like millions before me, trying to get my brain to accept there was no end to it, no big sign that said 'The End'. One bloke sipping hot chocolate in an evening swell was not going to unravel that mystery, but I wasn't concerned with that. The wonderment of it all was sufficient. Actually, the ability to wonder at it was what I appreciated. I hadn't lost my childhood feelings of love for the natural world and I still revelled in the opportunity to marvel at things that were beyond my understanding. The feeling came upon me again – I enjoyed my own company but it wanted a special person for the times I needed someone to be with me. I thought of Elaine and momentarily my heart stabbed at the unforced separation. I thought of my family but not of Chris; still alone, still not lonely but somewhere inside me there lodged a small dull ache, an ache of something I couldn't fully understand or express. I felt almost at one with the sea and stars but didn't feel I yet truly belonged.

Staring at the stars dragged my thoughts back to the time I lived in Ajman, a small dusty town in the United Arab Emirates. Norman, who'd recently married my mum, worked as a plant and machinery fitter for Tarmac and his expertise was needed to teach the indigenous and foreign workforce the finer points of fixing and maintaining equipment. This was an exciting opportunity for him and he accepted the posting on the understanding that the whole family would be able to move out as well. At the age of eleven I left Kents Bank school in Buxton with no regrets, and encountered a fascinating country of permanent sunshine and a totally different culture. I grew up fast in a land where fair-skinned boys were objects of desire but rapidly asserted my independence and made genuine friendships with Arabs and Asians alike. Apart from the delights of being in my new world, it was also comforting to have all my family still around me. When Norman and my mum first got together and we lived at Peak Dale, near Buxton, he and I had quickly established a rapport and mutual respect. While I still saw my real father from time to time, Norman became my day-to-day 'dad', and it became very natural to call him that. He taught me many lessons; about life and sticking up for myself, as well as valuable practical skills with wood, metal and engines. Moving to Ajman gave me the best of all worlds, independence and freedom from the strictures of a UK education and the excitement of new ventures, all combining with the continuity of a stable and loving family. I had the life every schoolboy could dream of.

Living by the Gulf, with its sparkling azure sea, was certainly the stuff of dreams, but something that awed me on first sighting, and continues to awe me, was the vast expanse of the starry universe that rolled out its galaxies to greet me every evening. I'd seen the night sky at home many times but cloud or haze frequently obscured its immensity. A few minutes' walk from what few lights there were in Ajman would bring me to a night-dark deserted beach, lit only from the white crests of wavelets on the sand. I'd lie down, the tumbling of surf close to my ears, put my arms behind my head and marvel at the sublime infinity stretching above me. Thousands and thousands of tiny specks of light would wink down at me; stars and planets in their wondrous setting, occasional tracer lines of meteors on their doomed journeys and, reaching through it all like a hazy ribbon, the Milky Way. At that time I had no real knowledge of constellations, content to draw my own pictures, a giant dot-to-dot that was mine for the taking. Since those childhood times I've always been drawn to the heavens, my mind freefalling at the impossibility of it all. Now on my own boat, arms stretched behind my head mirroring those times on Ajman beach, I reflected that while I'd changed in just a few short years those most distant of galaxies roofed above me had a comforting permanence; so very far away; so close to my heart.

An hour later and the wind had become breezy with a small but noticeable increase in the swell. I spotted the lights of a yacht as I put a reef in the mainsail, far over on the port bow, but it grew smaller and we had the sea to ourselves again. Back in the cabin, now tidier at my insistence, I drifted into a deep relaxing sleep, waking in panic at seven o'clock the next morning. I'd slept for seven solid hours without any sixth sense waking me – proof of how exhausted I'd been. During the night the wind had veered southerly and we were drifting off course towards Bordeaux. I altered course, grabbed a coffee and helmed until the midday fix. The distance to Cabo de Finisterre had reduced to 260 nautical miles and I felt superbly refreshed. Naively I felt we'd come through the worst that Biscay could offer us; we now just had a straight run through to the Spanish-Portuguese coastline.

Sunday was by and large a great day for sailing and we made good progress. I tuned into the shipping forecast, which reported a strengthening wind to the west of Finisterre, anything from a gale to a storm, and before long the swells seemed unusually large and rhythmic. At about five o'clock in the afternoon Chris plucked up the courage to ask what I knew he had been thinking for most of the day.

'Dave,' he said hesitantly, 'have you got any idea how this weather is going to turn out?'

The wind was moderately lively but clearly immediate past experiences were returning to haunt him. I reassured him but perhaps a little too bluntly, perhaps because I was concentrating on rigging up Maurice, perhaps because this was hardly bad weather.

'Look, Chris,' I replied, 'we're on a perfect heading going south, the sea's running well, we're not being tossed about, are we? Why don't you tidy up, then make us some tea. We're not going to die.'

Instantly I felt I'd dismissed him and I knew he felt hurt by it. He was trying to gather some mental strength to fight his fears and I'd patronised him.

'Sorry, mate,' I mumbled, 'we'll be fine.'

He shrugged feeble acceptance and did my bidding. I felt ashamed. I'd been focused on an important task and hadn't had the sensitivity to pick up his anxieties. I tried to make amends over dinner and during the evening and to an extent we were okay again. We retired to bed early and both slept well through the night.

Monday 27th July. I awoke at half past six and couldn't place the humming in my head. Momentarily displaced I couldn't figure out the source. I closed my eyes in sleep then shot bolt upright, banging my head on the cabin roof.

'Chris,' I screamed, 'get up now!' Flinging the hatch cover aside I stuck my head out of the opening and looked aft. Less than half a mile away to port and on course to overtake us loomed a huge cargo ship, its foaming bow waves clearly visible; to starboard another vessel steamed roughly in our direction about five miles away. Looking ahead I could just spot the faint outline of a ship's wash leading in to the distance. Chris awoke with panic-stricken eyes, fearing the worst. Both ships aft appeared to have spotted us, the nearest sounding an angry klaxon, but I'd already begun a tack to get us out of immediate danger, a cold sweat breaking over my body at the thought of the potential for disaster. At that distance and at a possible twenty-five knots any large ship on our course would have run us down in little over a minute. What would have happened if I'd slept on for that extra minute?

As the huge leviathan safely passed us, the immediate horizon obliterated by its massive, grim rusty hull, we were still at the mercy of its wake and the extensive swell; being thrown around seemed to be the punishment for my poor seamanship. We had drifted into a shipping lane that wasn't marked on my full Atlantic chart. Searching out my small-scale chart it was clearly evident in black and white, and I suffered the embarrassment of my incompetence, feeling like a total prat and lucky not to be a dead total prat. Noticing Chris's edginess, I resisted the temptation to lighten the moment with black humour, so, keeping a careful lookout for our new neighbours, I made a brew and handed out the remaining Jammy Dodgers. The wind was swinging north of west, with a westerly swell that was perfect for us. As the morning progressed the seas began to pick up, the wind breezy with occasional stronger gusts. Chris briefly took the helm as I reefed the mainsail and put up the smaller jib. This seemed to trim *Sharky*, putting less strain on her so we continued apace. With noon approaching, the sea again became erratic with cross swells of ice-cold green water thrusting up into pyramids. Maurice was getting confused with the swell changes and the yawing, so returning the helm to Chris once more, I went below to make some drinks and prepare food. I'd been at the helm from half past seven that morning. I was soaked with spray and my arm ached badly, so any break was welcome. I took the opportunity to change my clothes, stowed away all loose gear and fastened down the five-gallon water carriers. Sensing there was going to be a lot more of this already long day, I battened down the hatches in anticipation of bad weather. The noon fix put us some 200 miles from Finisterre. Throughout the morning I'd been in a quandary again with Chris. Whether at the helm or in the cockpit, he was becoming increasingly nervous as the seas picked up. We'd been in worse conditions on day sails on and around the south coast but the last few days, the near miss of that morning, and his frequently expressed wish to 'just get beamed up off this damn boat' was bringing all his anxieties to the surface again. I just didn't know what to do. I was thoroughly enjoying the challenge of handling *Sharky*, which made the gulf widen between us. I resented his references to 'this damned boat', which I took as a personal affront. Selfishly I wanted him out of the way, but he was still a mate and I owed him loyalty. I decided to break my vow of silence and face the unspoken barrier between us.

'Chris, we need to get this clear between us,' I stumbled. 'The best I can do is get us to land as soon as I can so you can bugger off home, but you've got to pull your weight. We've been in bad seas before and we've been okay. We'll be okay this time, yeah?'

To his credit he nodded and I think he was pleased I'd said something. The mere fact that going home and getting off the boat had been mentioned had boosted his morale but already the grey-green tinge of more seasickness was beginning to cross his face. He took the helm once more and it kept his mind off the deteriorating conditions. He even began to enjoy it a little until lack of concentration and a particularly rough patch of water swamped the boat and he gybed, a situation that occurs when the wind is coming from behind the boat and the boom whips across it, taking the sail with it. Being in the way offers the serious chance of being killed or knocked overboard, which, in the conditions we were in, would have amounted to the same thing. As it happened we'd done the sensible thing and, as was the norm, had harnessed ourselves on. Chris corrected the gybe, got us back on course and I congratulated him on his efforts; for once I'd done the right thing.

As the day progressed the wind intensified and the sea grew ever more turbulent. We were frequently thrown from wave crest to trough, sliding down big green walls of liquid noise. I reduced the sail again, down to a fully reefed mainsail and small jib. I glanced back to Chris at the helm and couldn't believe my eyes, he was laughing! The sheer force of the conditions, perhaps the fact that I had promised him safe passage, had torn the fear from him, despite the knocking we were receiving. Within seconds we gybed again and lost momentum, a crest of water flooding knee-deep into the boat and swamping the cockpit. *Sharky* lay heavy in the seas and was becoming difficult to control. I decided to take the helming from Chris. Exhilarated, I turned and shouted above the din, 'This is the life, eh Chris? Fantastic!' Never have I seen a mood change so rapidly. The last time I'd looked at him he was on a high, literally riding the waves. Now he was ashen and visibly weakening.

'Can't do it, mate,' he said, 'just too tired.'

For the second time I sent him below to bed. I couldn't be angry with him, he'd tried to regain a sense of being part of a team but plain old-fashioned fatigue and lack of nourishment had done him in. At least he tried, I told myself. At least he tried.

For what seemed like forever I wrestled the boat and the weather. Being spray-lashed and soaked was now the norm. The wind was fierce but the main problem was the erratic nature of the sea.

Churning, twisting and turning like a corkscrew, we were thrown in every direction. I ached not from just the helming but having to brace my body constantly against unexpected bone-crunching jolts. We were the plaything of the wind and the sea and there was damn all I could do about it. After another gybe and a frighteningly near miss by the boom, I took the decision to drop the mainsail and lash it hoping to reduce speed and get some stability, but it made little or no difference. I needed to change the jib for a smaller storm jib I'd had specially made, but I had to force myself to accept the necessity. Scrambling precariously out of the cockpit and onto the deck, I inched my way to the bow, gripping the rails like grim death as the harsh weather tried to prise me from the boat. Clinging to the bow railing, my feet slipping over the side, ice-cold water crashing into my already numb body, with *Sharky* snaking and slithering in trough and crest through a rapidly darkening sky, it took around twenty perilous minutes to switch the jib and stagger back to the helm. Gone was my exhilaration, though not my confidence. I was fearful, respectful of the conditions, apprehensive but not cowed. I'd spent too many years and too much money to want to cry off. I'd taken a decision to be there and I was still glad to be so. Soaked, tired, aching, scared, hungry, pissed off but still glad to be there. I reached in to the cabin for a cigarette and found Chris sitting on his bunk, head in hands and thoroughly depressed.

'I'm scared, Dave,' he sobbed. 'I'm scared I'm going to die.'

To reassure him would have been futile and patronising. I punched his shoulder, the way men do when there are no adequate words, and swayed back to the tiller. It was now midnight and I'd been at the helm for most of the time since half past seven that morning, existing on tepid tea and yet more biscuits. Never had I felt so deadbeat, drained physically and emotionally, and I just knew I needed rest before exhaustion induced a stupid and possibly final mistake. Having lashed the helm opposite to the storm jib, *Sharky* seemed content, and lay well in the water, keeping her head to the wind. Going below to the cabin, I checked everything was secure, then slid back the hatch for a final look round outside. They say timing is everything. At that precise moment a wave crest hurled itself on the boat and water roared into the cabin. Chris screamed in distress but it was merely another soaking. Lethargically, I mopped up what I could with some towels and just sat hunched up, tired beyond belief but past the point of sleeping. Gone was the pristine organisation of the boat at outset, replaced now by a damp, semi-fetid claustral ravaged by close-living. I was reminded again of the time I first saw *Sharky*, a cabin the size of two adjacent coffins. Adding to the discomfort was the peculiar whine and whistling of the wind in the rigging, an eerie, discordant singing. It didn't take much imagination to believe we were in the presence of lost souls bemoaning their fate and warning us about ours. Not given to superstition, I did however grow a little anxious when the resonance hit a particular pitch. I'd spotted this before. It meant the wind was gusting to gale force with matching sea conditions; things were going to get worse.

The boat lurched and swayed every which way, like a person losing control of the limbs, twitching and tossing to no definable rhythm. We were indeed a small cork on an unforgiving maelstrom. I tried to reassure Chris we would be all right, but my words felt hollow and false. Staying in my wet clothes I slipped under the soaked sleeping bag and leant against the cabin wall. I had no energy left. Switching off the light, I stared listlessly into the pitch-blackness and braced myself as best I could. I knew that Biscay had the reputation of being rough but I couldn't figure out why the winds were so ferocious at this time of year. I must have dropped off, waking sharply about two o'clock in the morning. I sensed something wrong, something about to happen. Tired, not fully awake, instinct overruling rational thought, I had a dreadful foreboding. Chris was awake as I painfully moved stiff joints.

'Chris,' I said, my voice thick with sleep. At that point the conversation ended and it felt like the world had as well. *Sharky* suddenly lifted, as though we were in a fast-moving elevator. I had no time to be prepared. A powerful unseen dynamic scooped up our tiny craft and hurled it skywards. Helpless in the moment I felt my stomach hit my feet, arms and legs flailing in total disorientation. Deafened and dreading what was to come, now was the time to be scared. Completely out of control and in total darkness we lifted, held momentarily, then sharply angled over to a huge roar. As the crashing reverberated through the very core of *Sharky*, I sensed to my horror that we were going to roll upside down. Time slowed. Slow motion and disbelief took over. With no time or ability to react we were in a situation of no control and very real, very frightening, life-threatening danger. Trapped in the confines of the tiny cabin we were flung at the whim of the sea. A diminutive, pitch-black, frail capsule mercilessly bombarded by a fearsome, deafening fury. Water squeezed through the main hatch cover, the kettle and pan flew from the cooker, gear fell about us, everything colliding with everything else and everything thrown from its storage. As *Sharky* shuddered and righted herself I desperately scrabbled to find my torch. Controlling an urge to panic, I flicked it, on glimpsing Chris babbling incoherently. My orientation slowly returned and I cautiously opened the hatch cover. In the blackness and thunderous noise, visibility was limited to the white crests of the breakers as they continuously thrashed around us. Half-fearing that we'd lost the mast altogether, I switched on the masthead light and was relieved to see it and the mast in the right place and in one piece. I could see no obvious damage, just a slight undoing of the mainsail. Trembling with the aftershock of what we'd experienced I clipped my harness on, crawled on deck and re-lashed it down. I daren't stand as my legs were like jelly, my numbed brain barely controlling my hands. The noise from wind and sea was horrendous, *Sharky* was still being thrown around and I felt thoroughly horrible and sick. I clambered back into the cabin, shut the hatch and surveyed the damage. Virtually everything lay in forlorn sodden heaps. Chris was in deep shock, visibly trembling from the cold and fear, the white of his eyes stark with terror. The boat had been viciously knocked down on the port side, water had flooded up from the bilges and Chris had thought he was going to drown. I remember that we said nothing; there was nothing *to* say. We just looked at each other, shivering with relief, but also in the expectation that what had happened once might happen again. The small, still functioning core of my mind rationalised that we'd been hit by a rogue wave but I couldn't know for certain. We put the clutter back as best we could and sat stone-faced, nervously waiting for first light. I couldn't forget the suddenness of the episode. Some years later I watched a film called *The Perfect Storm* and found myself re-living that night. In the comfortable Sensurround setting of an urban cinema, I found myself drenched in sweat, unable to sit still as I was transported back to my memories of that disquieting night. Several years on I can still wake in the night, cold with perspiration, a haunting reminder of how near to death I might have been, the phrase 'two adjacent coffins' so nearly a reality.

The sea had again given me a glimpse of raw, unfettered natural power and reminded me of my fragile insignificance; a harsh and salutary lesson. *Sharky* had brought us through without real harm but I was beginning to wonder whether I had bitten off more than I could chew. Was I really up to an Atlantic crossing? Would stubborn self-belief be a poor obituary?

CHAPTER SIX

Camarinas

With a tranquil sea, the mountaintops and the ethereal haze, there was a spooky surrealism to our surroundings as we rounded the final headland.

THE DARK NIGHT DRAGGED on forever. Alternately dozing and shivering, we slowly emerged from darkness, through dawn's first wan light and into the best that the new day could offer; a particular light I've always referred to as suicide grey. Low on visibility, high on erratic swell, strong on winds and down in spirit we decided to clean up the boat and have a late breakfast – eaten more by necessity than desire. At the noon fix, conditions remained rough but at least we were still heading south, albeit slowly. A couple of hours later the wind was still howling but I sensed it was a dying cry. The sun had opened out bringing some much-needed warmth to heart and body. Chris however was still feeling ill and had little appetite for anything. The previous night had shaken him badly and he seemed to be retreating into a self-pitying state of lethargy, gazing blankly into nothing, the silence broken only by occasional monosyllabic grunts in response to my attempts at conversation or questioning. Although not as dispirited as Chris, I was chastened by the experience and had no particular desire to engage in much dialogue. As the wind dropped to a light flutter I shook out more sail and stayed at the helm until the early hours when the wind just died to a whisper. If it was as knackered as I was I knew how it felt. Setting up *Sharky* for the night I wriggled under my still-wet sleeping bag and tried to relax. Everything had been lashed down again; I was past caring where we drifted just so long as it was into sleep.

Early on Wednesday morning I felt rested and much better as I thrust my head out of the hatch. The sun was up but it felt chilly in the slight breeze. I treated myself to a set of dry clothes from the small pile double-sealed in bin liners and went up on deck. Early morning is a good time at sea when calm conditions abound. The light is different from the rest of the day and there is a freshness that somehow sparkles from the water. I had the full 360 degrees to myself and I'd recovered my zest for sailing. Gone were the earlier nagging doubts, and I was satisfied with how I'd come through the ordeal. Thinking back over my first brew of the day, I had certainly been terrified – who wouldn't have been? – but I hadn't panicked. Perhaps I'd been too exhausted to rationalise my level of fear and there had been little time for a planned reaction, but overall I was content. My life and sailing instincts had kicked in and, all in all, I reckoned I'd done the right things at the right times. That's why early sunny mornings are a special time of the day; it's the best time to convince yourself that all problems have been sorted, that you can cope with anything and that life begins anew. I'd got the visible world to myself and I'd eaten a substantial breakfast. Yup, I was a born-again seafarer. It was slightly worrying, in a perverse sort of way, that I'd enjoyed the experience. The following day I wrote in my log 'Man, I love this shit!' I couldn't let Chris read this entry – not just because he simply wouldn't understand, but in an already distraught state he'd suffer the additional nightmare of having a skipper with delusions of madness and self-destruction.

I helmed through a fairly uneventful day with little wind. By ten o'clock that night it picked up slightly so I set up Maurice, briefly wondering what the real person would be doing at that time. In earlier years Maurice (the person) and I had enjoyed deep and passionate conversations about the mysteries of life – what it was and whether our lives were at the mercy of fate or controlled by self-determination. He felt life was a dream, a precursor to a new life. I felt we should just get on with it. He believed in reincarnation; I wasn't sure, the present life was providing enough worry and excitement. He thought I drank too much, I thought he smoked too much dope. He didn't want material possessions, I did. We were two different characters with a shared curiosity, unhindered by no philosophical training or qualifications. Just two ordinary blokes intrigued by the intricacies and destinies of life and speculating whether there was another one around the corner. Being in tune with nature facilitates that reflective attitude, I think. There is so much of interest, so much at which to wonder, so little known. In a totally non-morbid way I've always thought that the upside to dying was that at last, finally, you'd get the answers to all those fascinating questions. If there wasn't another life, well, I'd be in no position to worry about answers anyway. Of one thing I *was* sure: much as I liked Maurice he wouldn't have lasted five minutes on *Sharky* and he would have pissed me off within the same timescale. It was comforting to know that I wasn't discriminating against Chris personally; clearly most people would piss me off given the right circumstances!

As the sun faded, I relaxed on deck with a hot drink gently lapping the cup's rim in time to the waves. Content within myself, I sat until the early hours enjoying the serenity. Chris had been asleep on and off for most of the day and was just desperately counting down the hours before we put into land. I was now checking on him quite frequently, ensuring he was taking sufficient fluids.

Waking at 7.30 to a perfect day I put a reef into the mainsail as the wind had picked up slightly. It was probably not essential but I found myself adopting a more cautious approach after recent events and wasn't going to take any risks. I awoke Chris and forced him to eat breakfast with hot, sweet tea. Still tired and looking grey, he picked up when, after the noon fix, I informed him we were 300 miles from Lizard with only 81 to Finisterre. At a steady three knots on a southerly course we were only a matter of days away from safe harbour, though averaging thirty-nine miles a day was not exactly rushing. There was little of consequence about the progress that day. I enjoyed the sailing for what it was and in its own right, a simple sail using mind and sinew; a chance to let my thoughts freewheel without deep and serious contemplation. I whistled and hummed, busied myself and enjoyed the moment. Chris surfaced and retreated as his mood and resilience took him. Not in an unkind way – he just ceased to exist as a priority at that time. I didn't ignore him and was concerned for his well-being, but essentially as a passenger. He was no longer part of my journey or my quest. To all intents and purposes, I had 'gone solo' and this was no longer a source of irritation between us. The inevitable had been accepted. Our friendship had changed, but hadn't been lost, though a dividing line had been reached. He was returning to a land life with anticipation. I was seeking a harbour with reluctance. We had become changed people even in those few days since we had cast off from Falmouth. And in that acceptance of change I relished the day, the wind, the spray and the sheer joy, perhaps relief, of living. I felt at one with the ocean and again experienced that aching, tenuous elixir of freedom. At one point I just shouted out because I could no longer contain myself. Simply put, I had a lovely day.

Thursday 30th July. There was a change in the colour of the water. The sea was flat and a bit lifeless. Gone was the translucent sparkle of earlier days and, while not murky, I couldn't peer through the surface. We were still heading in the right direction at a steady pace and I was noticing a mood change within myself. I'd run out of cigarettes and desperately looked forward to finding a tobacconist, but this wasn't the real reason for feeling as I did. This part of my voyage was creeping inexorably to its end with each gust of wind. Soon I would have to return to the drudgery of reality, my ultimate ambition still unfulfilled. Still there but put on hold. I would look forward to the planning and logistics while I accumulated more time and money, but this was scant reward for the real high of being aboard a living, breathing boat with its uncertainties and challenges. I knew I was going to be frustrated by this experience and would be a difficult person to be with when home. I had touched my dream, held it within my grasp for the briefest of moments. I had loved these few days with a deep intensity that I hadn't felt on other sea excursions. Having drunk deep from the well of desire, I wanted more and I was confident that I had the ability to succeed. As we sailed ever closer to landfall I was filled with an inner melancholy.

Chris on the other hand was pretty close to exuberance. He was feeling better and managed to enjoy a good tea. We'd spent most of the day together on deck watching the swell gently hiss past *Sharky*, listening to Dire Straits, Chris de Burgh and Stevie Winwood on cheap speakers wired to our Walkmans and pointing out the many dolphins that came and went. For the first time for a long time, Chris and I enjoyed each other's company. We weren't extrovert, silly or carefree, we'd gone past that, but I think we'd repaired our mutual respect and friendship. There was no 'side' to our conversations. We'd sit for long spells without feeling the need to talk and then chat inconsequentially before lapsing into another comfortable spell of silence; lost in our own space but no longer living apart.

With Chris looking forward to seeing land, I finally acknowledged that my original plan of sailing to southern Portugal wasn't going to happen. I decided to aim for the headland of Cabo Villano and Camarinas, a village down the northwest Spanish coast, which seemed to be the nearest safe anchorage. We'd had a good day and we were both tired; the sort of relaxed, satisfactory tiredness that comes from fresh air and contentment. We'd managed to dry some of the gear and clothing off in the wind so it was a pleasing experience to slumber under slightly damp rather than soaked sleeping bags for a change. I awoke during the night to flapping sails as the wind had died away, tied up the mainsail and jib and returned to sleep. Still windless next morning there was little rush to get anything done so we slept in and had a leisurely breakfast. The sea was like a millpond, highly unusual in an area feared and famous for its rough waters, and we were stuck, bobbing gently, with little or no forward momentum. I was perfectly happy to have a lazy day and wait for the inevitable breeze that would shove us on our way again but I could see Chris was restless and wanting to be on the move again. We agreed to start the engine and give it a bit of a blow out. To my surprise it started without much difficulty. I'd expected problems given its far from mint condition and exposure to the constant soakings, so, once underway, we motored until lunchtime when we stopped for a quiet meal. It felt odd not to be under sail and I found the engine's chug to be irritating and somewhat obtrusive to start with.

After lunch a gentle breeze did pick up. Conserving fuel and secretly delighted to get back to sailing, I put up the mainsail and jib. The breeze was light and frequently fluctuated in direction, necessitating some hard sailing – but at least it was quiet. Gradually a number of fishing boats appeared and we spotted an increase in lobster-pot markers and even a few yachts to the south. Having travelled about five miles in the last three hours even I was beginning to get a bit frustrated with the lack of progress, a condition not helped by the lack of cigarettes. There was little choice though as I needed to save fuel in case we required the engine in the harbour. We passed the time preparing a large meal of chicken and rice (again!) and I settled down with a book I had become absorbed with, *Kim*, by Rudyard Kipling. For the first time in many days I climbed into my sleeping bag just wearing underpants. Having spent so much time constantly dressed in waterproofs and warm clothing there was simple pleasure in just letting air circulate around my skin once more. My bag was not fully dry and felt salty but I was not concerned. It still smelt musty but I didn't care; this was relative luxury.

I took a while to drop off to sleep as we were heading into another shipping lane, and I had no desire for further close encounters. I was up four or five times during the night just for a quick look about and I did keep the masthead light on as a precaution. In the early hours of Saturday I awoke to a breeze blowing through the hatch, so dressed quickly, went out on deck to put up sail and grab a few miles. The masthead light had gone out after having drained the last of the battery power. This meant that the log was no longer working. I didn't care too much as I reckoned I could estimate speed and distance reasonably well. Within a couple of hours a revived and cheerful Chris was up making tea and cooking breakfast as I continued to helm, the sparse wind giving us around one and a half knots. As the afternoon wore on, a slight haze formed on the horizon and then, from within the partial obscurity, we sighted land. It had been ten days since we'd last been on terra firma and I remember we cheered, probably as much from relief as anything, the fix giving us a distance of eighteen miles to go. We could either wait for the wind to pick up or take a chance on the outboard, which would get us there in about four hours. Once again I was content to wait for the wind but Chris was positive we had sufficient fuel; I suspect this was ten per cent judgement and ninety per cent wishful thinking. We discussed it for a few moments then I acceded. Chris fixed up the outboard and we motored off at around four knots.

By seven o'clock that evening we were seven miles off. The forested mountains behind Cabo Villano were beautiful in the warm evening light though at sea level the haze was pretty thick. With a tranquil sea, the mountaintops and the ethereal haze, there was a spooky surrealism to our surroundings as we rounded the final headland. It was as though we were entering a lost world, the only sound being the popping of the outboard, no longer an irritant but a quiet encouraging accompaniment to the stillness.

Chris was now anxiously tipping the petrol can on its side trying to wring out the last of the fuel. It was going to be a close run so I kept a steady course close to the coastline in case the engine did stop and we had to anchor out. The heady aroma of pine needles wafted out from the peninsula. Chris was jumping about with excitement, alternating with worried glances towards the outboard. It was difficult to keep calm in the circumstances with just another mile or so to go.

'Come on, engine, good boy, engine, keep going, just keep going,' coaxed Chris, twitching about unable to keep still. 'The harbour, Dave!' he suddenly shouted. 'The harbour! We've made it!' Perversely the outboard took that opportunity to sulk, splutter and cut out. A split second of hesitation then, moving faster than I would have thought possible, Chris leapt towards the outboard and frantically jerked the lift pump like a man possessed – which in a way I suppose he was. Unbelievably the engine hiccupped and coughed itself back to life and settled down again to a gentle purr. Chris blew it a kiss, declared his undying love for it and rummaged for the anchor, pulling it through the hatch in eager anticipation. We rounded the harbour

wall and I felt like a king returning from a famous victory. We sailed past a few moored yachts, English, German and French, their owners enjoying relaxed evening drinks. We waved and received an unexpected, spontaneous round of applause as we cut the engine and dropped anchor, and for a while I wondered why. Then it clicked. We'd sailed in flying the ensign, the yellow quarantine flag and the Spanish visitor flag, so they would have known we'd sailed in from the UK or France. It was just their way of acknowledging our efforts, so I waved again in appreciation. The chain tightened on the seabed and the stillness returned. Chris was exuberant; delight, relief and energy showing on his face as he enjoyed his return to life. I sat down with a genuine smile on my face but with mixed emotions churning inside. I was happy and sad; a lump came to my throat and I felt like crying. A part of me still wanted to be on the open sea, a part of me wanted a shower, some fags and a cold beer. A part of me didn't want to leave *Sharky*. A memory of something I'd read years before sprang unbidden to my mind – for everything you gain, something you lose. I'd gained new experiences, confidence and the sheer pleasure of ocean sailing. In gaining them I'd lost the moment of happening. Each experience and emotion was now forever in the past. The memory, and probably a fading memory at that, was all that was left. But that is the rich condition of human life. We cannot live on memories alone. We strive forwards to replace them with new challenges that sustain us, an endless cycle of past and progression. My melancholy feelings passed. The here and now was a cause for celebration. 'C'm' on, Chris,' I smiled. 'Time you bought me a beer.'

We both slept well that night and enjoyed a long Sunday lie-in. Awaking to a warm but overcast morning I brewed a fresh mug of coffee and sat alone in the cockpit as Chris continued his slumbers in the cabin. It felt strange to be so inactive. No sails to reef, no long periods of helming. The sea calmly rolled around the harbour with seemingly little inclination to do anything energetic. For the moment I enjoyed the solitude, giving me time to reflect on our achievements. I was immensely proud of what we'd done and the long physical and mental journey we'd undertaken. In the best sense of the word I was very self-satisfied. With limited funds, basic equipment and fairly restricted experience I'd undertaken a trip I'd always felt was within my capabilities. True, there had been some anxious, even heart-thumping moments; Chris and I had had our emotional crises and I was not as far south as I'd expected to be, but all in all I felt pretty smug. Part of me wanted to start planning the next phase but relaxation and laziness held sway, so I remained content and enjoyed the surroundings. Besides, I didn't want to plan much without talking things over with Chris, who was still asleep.

As if on cue he sprang through the cabin, restored and revived, his cherubic smile back on show. We breakfasted to the sight and sounds of local fisherman returning with their catches. As they hoisted them up the quayside, the unintelligible jibber-jabber of local dialect cut through the village sleepiness, the sounds of industry eventually drowning out the earlier tranquillity. We washed and shaved before climbing precariously into the dinghy to row ashore. Dinghy is perhaps something of a misnomer. It was more a collection of ancient rubber and canvas patches that required a certain dexterity to inflate and operate. It had been given to me by the boatyard after I'd first bought *Sharky*. At the time I was grateful; *they* were probably grateful to get rid of it. The only rigidity came from laborious attempts to inject more air in it through the valve than was coming out from numerous other holes. Prior to casting off, a highly technical procedure was necessary involving calculations and strict discipline. Firstly a lengthy debate was necessary to work out the distance from boat to shore. This was to determine whether there was sufficient time to make it before all the air was expelled. Secondly it was absolutely critical to ensure the foot pump travelled with us in order to repeat the exercise on the return journey. Thirdly the dinghy had to be pumped up as near to the side of the boat as possible ensuring that everything we were taking ashore was already in the boat. Finally a delicately choreographed sequence of launching the blasted thing and agreeing who would clamber in was first practised on deck. Once launched it was simply a case of rowing like the very devil, trusting that the patches would hold and that the distance wasn't too great. The process was then repeated for the return leg. This was frequently more hazardous, and often more hilarious, depending on how much alcohol had been consumed in the interim. On this occasion we pumped up the dinghy, followed the procedures and rowed like crazy, watching the tiny puddles slowly ingress into the well. Camarinas had big harbour walls with steel steps and it proved quite difficult to get out of the boat, but at least we provided the locals with a few moments of entertainment. As had been the case the night before, we'd still got our sea legs so the morning was spent walking around in a rolling lurch without the benefits of being drunk.

Camarinas was a typical laidback fishing village tour operators would have described as quaint. Small and picturesque with that peculiar Mediterranean approach to living, where the beauty of flowers and well-tended houses sat juxtaposed with strewn rubbish and surely dangerous overhead wiring. We eventually found the post office through a mix of gesticulation, mime and schoolboy patois, changed some money and made our phone calls home. In the scheme of things we hadn't been gone for long but England seemed centuries away. I was pleased to speak to my mum and desperate to chat to Elaine, but found it difficult to describe what we'd experienced. I wasn't about to tell them of the rough conditions or the arguments with Chris and a rushed phone call was not the ideal way to describe the beauty or the thrill of the sail. I wasn't sure I could adequately express how I felt or that they would understand, so I restricted myself to a few inane sentences and listened to their narration of local events. Phone calls made, Chris and I retired to a bar and just watched the world go by. It is one of the most pleasant ways I know to spend time. To sit in a foreign land and watch a different life happen around you is both a delight and an education. The core of any organised society is probably the same anywhere but played out in so many different ways. To watch people interact, to examine their facial and body language as they go about their business, is to have a front seat in the theatre of the world. Add the colour, smells, language and sights and literally whole new worlds are available for your inspection.

While relaxing we met up with a couple who had sailed in a few days before us. Mike and Anne were ultra-keen sailors and had spent several years building their catamaran, so we had plenty of stories and incidents to exchange. Chris and I were invited on board *Dorad* – Gaelic for Dolphin – and were stunned by the luxurious fittings and huge amounts of space. It felt very homely, a bit like *Sharky* felt to me but there any resemblance ended. *Dorad* had no dank areas, no wet sleeping bags and definitely no Jammy Dodger crumbs. We rowed back to *Sharky* filled with red wine and a passing envy. As I succumbed to sleep I realised that our cramped conditions had at least one advantage; the *Doradions* couldn't reach over and make a pot of tea while still in bed.

We spent a few days doing nothing except sit outside bars and wander aimlessly around the village. I was surprised at my ability to cope with this, as I like to be continually active, but it felt right, though at some point I knew I would need to move on. Chris and I were getting to the point where I was getting fed up with his long spells in bed, when I wanted to get up and do things, even if it was just to wander around and observe my surroundings. One evening on my own I'd spent an inordinate amount of time in a bar knocking back more beers than was good for me. I'd got to that silly, inanely grinning state where nothing made much sense but everything existed within a warm, befuddled glow. My stomach growled an intense hunger so I illogically decided to head back to the boat for something to eat. Illogical because the bar I was in provided a perfectly good selection of tapas. Free from all sensibilities and mumbling songs to myself I happily staggered back to the harbour edge where I'd left the now semi-deflated dinghy. It took an age to pump more air in it but gripping the dinghy and oars under one arm, talking to myself as drunks do, I carefully placed my feet on the steel ladder affixed to the harbour wall. All went well until halfway down, when a dizzy head ruined my exaggerated concentration. My feet slipped and I fell ten feet backwards into freezing water, with an ungainly splash. Surfacing and spluttering I was very proud of the fact that I had managed to retain hold of the dinghy and oars. 'Bugger this,' I thought, I'll swim back.' So ignoring the hysterical laughter emanating from above, I chucked the oars in the rapidly deflating dinghy, tucked it under my arm and with a perfect stiff upper lip attempted to swim back to *Sharky*, encumbered by heavy jeans, trainers and a thick sweater. As I swam, dozens and dozens of tiny phosphorescent squid darted away from me, leaving fiery trails through the sea. If it had got to the point where even the fish were fleeing in embarrassment perhaps now was the right time to move on.

'Chris,' I said on sobering up, 'I'm going to continue south and try for Portugal, probably two or three more days' sailing. As soon as the wind's right I'm off.'

I watched his face carefully for the reaction, not quite sure what he would say or what I wanted him to say. The last few days away from the boat had done us both good and had got rid of some of the latent tensions that had been building up. I deliberately hadn't asked him his intentions; I knew I was going; he had a decision to make.

'I'd like to stick with it,' he said cautiously, and I knew he was balancing his words carefully. 'But can we do it in day stages, you know, go into harbour each night?' I looked at the charts, giving me time to check the feasibility of this and allowing my thoughts to gather. I had expected him to say he was leaving but logically there was nowhere for him to go to. Camarinas was relatively isolated, nowhere near a major city and it made sense to sail down to Baiona near the Portuguese border and fly home from Vigo Airport. Mixed emotions thrust themselves upon me once more. Selfishly I wanted the last few days to myself with no repeats of any acrimony, but the last few days had been quite good and I thought we were back as mates again. If we could just handle a few more days, well, I had the rest of the Atlantic to look forward to on my own – and would probably be clamouring for company. It made sense.

'All right, you bugger,' I grinned, 'but you're buying the drinks.'

CHAPTER SEVEN

Home Again

As I enfolded her in my arms, tiredness evaporated and all thoughts of sailing fled my mind.

In the days before leaving Camarinas I again met up with Mike from the *Dorad*. He'd been in the Merchant Navy and to my delight agreed to tutor me in the advanced points of astronavigation. I'd been dabbling with this on the run over from Falmouth but I was not about to miss the chance of some expert help. I also re-stocked *Sharky* with what provisions we could find and afford but couldn't find batteries for the radio in order to tune into the weather forecasts. I was anxious to get away but the north to north-westerly winds were building up and becoming gusty, which I thought might get stronger once in the open sea. Finisterre has a reputation for malevolent winds and I saw no reason to take unnecessary risks. What was increasingly worrying was Chris's attitude once more. He seemed to be becoming more petulant and forever nagging on about getting to the airport and getting home. In my darker moments I seriously thought about chucking him off the boat and to hell with him. The irritation with each other festered like an open sore and we frequently just ignored each other through long periods of silence. I kept telling myself that I ought to be more tolerant but on a small boat with nowhere for privacy even small differences were magnified. Try living with another person with polarising interests in a minuscule living space and then check your tolerance levels!

For three days we didn't move off the boat as the wind lashed to gale force; three days of reading, mashing, studying charts, staring into space, watching Chris sleep and observing the other boats in the harbour being buffeted by chilly onshore winds. I put out two anchors, which helped keep *Sharky* as stable as possible, but kept an eye out for any slippage that might have driven us onto the quayside. I felt isolated without a radio and expected to have to leave without it functioning – even getting petrol had meant an inland journey of eight miles. These operational niggles gnawed away and with the enforced inactivity these times were not my finest hour. Phone calls home were not guaranteed, the antiquated phone system sometimes taking up to three hours to get a connection. The post office ran out of stamps so all in all it was a miserable time. It wasn't much to ask, just a decent drop in the wind to effect my escape and get me focused on sailing once more. If there is such a thing as the call of the sea, I was certainly all ears, just frantic for the chance to get back to it. At the back of my mind was the growing concern that time was running out. My five weeks were slipping away like sand in an hourglass.

By the third day of being tossed around in the same place I felt very low. The sluggish, slow days, the confines of the boat and the uncertainty of Chris's moods were beginning to get to me. The novelty of Camarinas had given way to a need to leave this now cold, depressing backwater. My original plans for South Portugal had been thwarted. I had no clear plans for getting home and no interim berth guaranteed for *Sharky*. I felt trapped and isolated, sensed a depression that was more than just self-pity and misery. While wanting comfort from others I also craved solitude. Chris's sole conversation piece was now restricted to getting a plane and how I would help him get home. Each time he mentioned it the crack into my tolerance widened. Eventually I exploded into blind rage.

'For fuck's sake, shut up!' I bellowed. 'If we go now we'll hit the sort of weather you got screwed up about before; if you want to leave then piss off now and walk home.' I flung my arms around in frustration. 'Just fuck off!' I found myself trembling with rage, raw emotion casting rational thought aside.

His face crumpled; shock, brief anger and distress registered, and I thought he would dissolve into tears. At that moment I realised just how much he needed me to sort him out, and just how much I didn't want to.

'Chris,' I said harshly, 'I'm not your babysitter, so grow up. When we go ashore I've got to try and make arrangements for the boat so you're on your own. Sort yourself out!'

A cavernous silence opened up. He slunk into his sleeping bag and rolled over away from me. My misery felt compounded, not from any guilt about my outburst, but from sheer irritation that I was hampered by someone who was still a friend, but had the deadweight of an anchor. Had he taken me at my word, and packed his bags and left, I'd have felt remorse, but not for long. Confusion draped over my feelings like a damp, heavy cloth and I couldn't understand myself or my reactions. Chris was a decent bloke but totally out of his environment. Try as I might, I couldn't forgive him for that. It was unfair but I felt as though my plans were being thwarted and weren't as perfect as I'd wanted them to be. That evening was spent in absolute silence save the emphasised sounds of the chomping and slurping of meals.

When we awoke next day our altercation was never mentioned and a gradual cessation of hostilities ensued. The wind, though still gusting, felt manageable and I took the decision to slip moorings and head down the Galician coast. I double reefed the main and hoisted the working jib, but even that didn't prevent us from heeling over as we left the harbour behind us. Before long I had a fully reefed mainsail and a small jib, and we were still flying. The sun was out though it was chilly in the wind so we resorted to our familiar pattern of brewing up and munching biscuits. We began to converse again, a little hesitantly as though each was afraid that any comment would spark us off, but I was busy sailing so my spirits were up, and Chris knew he'd be in another port that night. For very different reasons we reverted to cordiality.

It felt great to be back on the swells again. Watching the constantly changing forms and patterns of the sea took me back to my young life at Thornheyes. A favourite pastime was to sit in front of the lounge fire and stare intently at the flames. I would watch the sparks and cinders drift upwards on currents of heat and draught and wonder where they would go. I'd gaze deeply into constantly swirling shapes trying to spot recognisable images around which I would weave imaginative and magical stories of derring-do, fantastical monsters and brave heroes – the latter always the part I'd reserve for myself. Staring into fires always produced a hypnotic trance-like state where my mind would go into freefall, to the exclusion of anything or anyone around me. Totally lost in my innermost thoughts I could easily ignore calls and pleas to come to dinner or go to bed. The flames took me into a world far less mundane. As I grew up and got into sailing I rediscovered that daydreaming ability, using the waves as substitute flames. With one hand on the tiller, sitting comfortably on the windward side, my instincts would control the boat while my inner being retreated to wherever it chose to go. Watching the waves is similar to a meditative state where good times can be relived, problems chewed over, wishes fantasised or deep meanings pondered. The sea would fill my vision; its noise muted in my concentration as I dropped out of the immediate reality, my mind swirling with the shifting of each tiny drop of water. I was glad to be under sail once more.

We stayed within sight of land during the day, catching the distant scenery of serrated mountains and the nearer jagged rocks thrusting themselves into the sea, the earlier patches of occasional fog receding as the sun burnt them off. By four o'clock that afternoon the wind was dying and I had to put full sail up. Cabo de Finisterre drifted into view and I pointlessly asked Chris whether we should put into harbour for the night. His response was immediate. Starting up the engine, for the sea was now a millpond again, he steered a course directly for our new berth, which was full of local fishing boats. Not wanting to struggle with the dinghy again we eventually moored alongside a half-submerged trawler, across which we would have to scramble to get us to the steps. The village of Muros had none of the charm of Camarinas, reeking of rotting fish and garbage, and it didn't have any apparent ambience. This was working Spain, no time or convenience for visitors; a little intimidating if you let the thought creep through your mind, but essentially live and let live. We ate on deck, a pasta dinner washed down with a bottle of Rioja, under the gaze of several inhabitants who peered down at us from the walls. Walking around the harbour after our meal, Chris remarked that the open sea looked crystal clear as the evening light began to fade.

'I'm going for a bath,' I said. Chris looked askance. 'Stay here, you smelly sod,' I continued as I moved back to the boat, 'I'm going to get the towels and the Vosene.'

Within minutes we'd stripped off all our clothes and were standing on a big boulder. Chris let out a strangled cry as he dipped his toes into the freezing water. Hearing the chatter of voices behind us we turned to find a large crowd of locals had gathered, curiously wondering what on earth was going on. There was no going back. The British stiff upper lip was again called into service, so, taking a deep breath, we plunged into the rapidly darkening waters. This was the first full immersion in water for over three weeks and was well overdue. Splashing around and throwing the shampoo bottle to each other, we gave our first naked entertainment performance to the now considerably enlarged crowd. I didn't care; I was clean and it felt good. Before too long all remaining and recognisable body parts were numbingly glacial so, bearing in mind we were international crowd-pleasers, we returned to our rock to perform our tantalising end of show towel-down sequence. As the evening graded to full darkness our fickle audience slunk away. Re-clothed and refreshed we went in search of them. Earlier suspicion melted away. In this smelly and refuse-strewn wilderness we were now regional superstars. As we walked through the streets around the harbour we were politely offered friendly greetings in excruciatingly poor English and expressively clear sign language. Perhaps it was as well our Spanish was restricted to 'hola' and 'gracias', as ignorance inevitably brings an uncomprehending bliss. We graciously accepted the good-natured bonhomie and eventually retired to *Sharky* for a well-earned rest.

'I reckon we'll be the subject of local folklore from tonight,' I smugly mentioned to Chris.

'Shouldn't think so,' he rejoined. 'I think they were laughing at the size of your dick.'

I silently but graciously conceded his winning barb. Not because it was true of course, but out of old-fashioned courtesy. I was still many points ahead in the nasty remarks game.

Friday 7th August. In the early hours I awoke to find rain lashing through the open hatch, which I guessed was from a passing squall, but at about eight o'clock I was again awoken, this time by the sound of *Sharky* crashing into the old fishing boat we'd moored against. A big sea, accompanied by a rapidly intensifying wind was pushing huge waves past the poorly protected harbour. We both dressed quickly, untying the lines and using the outboard to get us to the far side of the breakwater. We were thoroughly soaked but at least the turbulent swells had lessened considerably. Leaving it a couple of hours to see what the weather would do, I decided to head out and down to Cabo Corrubedo, another twenty or so miles. By ten that morning we were off, conditions still blowy with rain, but there were breaks in the cloud and the sun was daring to show itself. Once beyond the harbour I set a reefed mainsail and working jib and we fairly flew down the coast. Our speed was partly due to the conditions but also to *Sharky*, who was sitting higher in the water owing to depleted stocks of food and water. For two or three hours this was good sailing, Maurice performing well up to expectation, *Sharky* coming alive and responsive to the ocean swell, Chris and I working effectively together. Wind, sea, sun, friendship; exhilaration at the sheer joy of being there; even the dinner was perfect, creamed potatoes, mince in gravy and a tin of peas. I wished life could always be like that. I wished I could be at sea forever.

A sense of perfection occasionally comes with a delusion of complacency. After our meal the wind began to drop and within twenty minutes we were becalmed. I wondered whether the mountainous coast created these alternating conditions, but we had no choice but to start up the engine again in order to make landfall before dark. We left the sails up flapping aimlessly – a huge mistake.

I'd gone below when the boat swiftly tipped right over. Looking through the open hatch I saw Chris frantically gripping the helm. A sudden, strong gust of wind from nowhere had filled the sails and we'd keeled over. I quickly released the mainsail and the jib, shouting at Chris to switch off the outboard. This done he clung on to the helm while I reefed the mainsail and swapped the working jib for the smaller one. Once righted, I went below again to check the charts and pilots for submerged rocks near the shoreline. I heard a huge slap followed by a pouring of water through the open hatch. Another gust of wind and a changeable swell were trying to spin the boat around. Chris, already soaked, was helming with great concentration, but we were beginning to drift too close to the coast. I reefed the mainsail again and put in a tack to move us offshore and provide some room. Gradually we recovered control, but only just. The gusts of wind were sudden and unpredictable and it was quite hairy until we rounded the peninsula, where the calmer waters prevailed. A final gust blew Chris's hat into the water, where it perched forlornly − the first time it had been off his head for over three weeks. We manoeuvred using our man-overboard drill, eventually and successfully completing our first ocean search-and-rescue mission. Chris and his hat were reunited and delighted.

Corrubedo was a re-run of Muros, though lacking a harbour. We meandered through a collection of small fishing boats, beached *Sharky* as best we could and hauled the anchor onto the sand. Yet again we were the subject of much discussion and another crowd formed to watch us as we brewed coffee. Chris nudged me in the ribs and pointed across to the small village square. A huge stage was being erected.

'Told you we'd become naked folklore legends,' I joked.

'Doubt it,' replied Chris, deadpan. 'We're not that big.'

Uncertain as to what he referred to, I concentrated furiously on my coffee.

It was fiesta time in Corrubedo. The sun set to the aroma of freshly barbecued fish and we were soon drawn to the festivities. There was a distinct buzz in the air and a huge cheer greeted the rock band strutting onstage. I doubt if there is a Spanish word for 'quiet'. If there is it must hardly be ever used. To the deafening music pouring out of huge amplifiers the colourfully dressed locals went loco, dancing frenziedly, faces red with adrenalin and alcohol. Chris and I had no pesetas left, so changing a twenty-pound note in a friendly bar we settled down with a drink to enjoy the proceedings. We could see *Sharky* securely moored a few yards away and a feeling of utter contentment washed over me. I looked across to Chris and saw my feelings mirrored in his face. Silently we raised our glasses in a joint toast to our accomplishment.

We left the fiesta late but as I drifted off to sleep it was still going strong in the early hours. Fiestas in Spain can last a week; stamina is obviously a Spanish word. Saturday morning saw us up early, the only people around enjoying the morning sun. *Sharky* had floated off the beach during the night, so after a breakfast of fresh bread and cheese I hauled the anchor up, hoisted the working jib and tacked effortlessly through the myriad small boats to reach open water and set a course for Baiona. A perfect north-easterly wind drove us serenely southwards to the accompaniment of stunning mountain scenery, warm sunshine and friendly dolphins. About midday we rounded the breakwater to find a marina full of jetties, so quickly mooring up we set off to find hot showers. Whether the Baiona Yacht Club really has the best showers in the world is incidental. At that moment they certainly were – hot, pulsating, invigorating, made ever sweeter as they were the first civilised showers for what seemed like forever. As the salt cake and grime dissolved from my body so the pent-up energies and frustrations seemed also to disappear. I stood under that hot shower for over thirty minutes, letting mind and body cleanse themselves of all that was negative. Immobile under the enlivening deluge, shoulders drooped, eyes closed, I just let go and enjoyed the simple pleasure of hot water on skin.

Baiona was different again from the last two villages, and fishing, though still an important industry, vied with tourism for dominance. The town was mostly dedicated to Spanish tourism and the place still retained the feel of an indigenous people rather than from overseas. The streets were clean, houses freshly painted and flowers, especially the purple bougainvillea, permeated every sense. Fish restaurants and bars were aplenty and we soon discovered we had entered another fiesta town. The crowds were numerous and lively, bars were thronging and there was a definite air of expectancy around every corner. We grabbed a couple of empty chairs outside a bar and ordered beers. The waiter explained that tonight there was to be a firework display, which should not be missed, and sure enough shortly afterwards the first skyward explosions began. For over an hour starbursts and rockets peppered the night sky with a dazzling array of colour, punctuated by the cracking of whizz-bangs and firecrackers. The Spanish celebrate in style and the infectious happy mood was soon endemic. We drank steadily but sensibly into the night, then topped the evening off with a long walk before retiring to our bunks. During the evening Chris and I had discussed our return plans and agreed to leave at different times and days. This was a purely practical arrangement. I needed time to sort out a long-term berth for *Sharky*, which I thought would take a couple of days. Chris would leave a day before me, travelling to Santander, where he would catch a ferry to Plymouth. His leave from work was rapidly running out so an imminent return was essential. We still weren't communicating that well and it was a strange few days. Sometimes we conversed as we had done in the early sailing years, when we'd go almost for a whole day without speaking more than a dozen words. I liked to get up early and wander around Baiona, Chris preferred to remain in his bunk and sleep, which irritated the life out of me. I found myself trying to work out whether we'd meet up again once we were back in England, and I really didn't know the answer. There was no doubt we were still friends but increasingly distant and incompatible ones. We were fine in small doses but any longer together and the intolerant niggles would begin to surface. I'm sure he thought me selfish and inconsiderate; I thought him lazy and dependent. Sailing for an extended journey had emphasised the worst in our characters, which had been subordinated on our previous daily jaunts. That we'd polarised in our perspectives on sailing had added to the difficulties. I knew with an absolute certainty that while sailing had at one time been a common bond, it was now a fragile and tenuous link. Remove that bond and we were at opposite ends of the spectrum. He enjoyed what I called superficial, bright-lights socialising. I'd moved on from that. I'd found a focus to my life and a desire to be independent. Take sailing out of the equation and it was inevitable that Chris and I would go our separate ways. From day one in Falmouth we'd taken different journeys.

Chris left the following day, eager to be away. We left each other with no recriminations, conscious that we'd shared good and bad times.

'See ya, Dave, hope you make it,' he said.

'Take care, mate,' I replied, and that was that. I returned to *Sharky* strangely troubled. I phoned home later that evening then went for a walk around the harbour before turning in. *Sharky* lay peacefully in her moorings and it felt good to be back with my friend. The echoes of Chris still seemed to hang in the cabin and a depression washed over me. Alone, but this time lonely as well.

I awoke with much to occupy my mind and time. I needed inexpensive, long-term safe berthing for my boat. With the Plymouth ferry booked courtesy of my mum, I needed to get *Sharky* sorted before taking the twenty-hour train ride from Vigo to Santander. Finding a berth space was not difficult – finding a cheap one was. I moved purposefully from one harbourmaster to the next, wishing for more fluency in Spanish. With monthly fees hovering around the £160 mark they were all way off my budget. In desperation I left the yacht berths and found a port official near to the fishing fleet. I explained my circumstances and asked, begged, permission to tie up for what was likely to be several months. The official said it was not possible. Putting as much desperation in my face as possible I pleaded. I had but little money, I had an unfinished dream to sail the Atlantic, I needed urgently to return home to see my family. I pointed to my grubby worn T-shirt, my threadbare jeans and my toes now ingloriously poking out from the degenerating ends of my trainers. The official's stance softened and the kindly man inside relented. Yes, it would be possible, but not with the fishing boats. However, for £30 a month I could anchor out behind them in the bay. With this much reduced monthly fee negotiated and a great weight off my mind I returned to *Sharky* to transfer her mooring, stow gear and pack my things. I leisurely took all day over this, only returning to the port official to gift him a bottle of wine. He grinned, accepted the gift but took no details of *Sharky*. As I had earlier suspected, this was a backhander arrangement, but on my intended return the following year I could at least slip anchor without the problems of paperwork.

The last evening on my boat was spent gazing over Baiona marina under a full moon. From the expensive yachts, the gentle clanking of chains and rustle of rigging wafted over the still air to my budget accommodation. I could hear the murmurings of conversation and the odd tinkle of glasses. I felt no jealousy or envy; I'd had the richer experience. I went to sleep trying to convince myself that Baiona was no longer a port of debarkation; it was my port of embarkation for the next leg of my voyage.

Glancing through the rear window of the taxi next morning, I took a final view of *Sharky*. She looked abandoned, I felt – as though I were betraying her. I observed that I was more upset at this parting than I had been when Chris had left. I wished her au revoir, hoped I'd firmly cabled the anchors and prayed they wouldn't drag. I resolved to be back no later than as soon as possible.

Settling into the train at Vigo and surrounded by vast amounts of baggage, I reflected on my transfiguration from seafarer to landlubber. As the train pulled away from the coastal oyster beds and plunged into the wine-growing regions, I focused on the countryside and the thought of being homeward bound. I'd left one love in Spain but was returning to another. One part of my adventure was over and now the immediate enforced reality of work beckoned. It was just another challenge to face until I met up with *Sharky* again.

The journey from Santander was uneventful. I knew I was at sea but it wasn't quite the same. Overheated, overcrowded, noisy and with the baleful smell of engine oil permeating every cranny, the ferry shook itself from the quayside and stumbled its way into open water. I got a shock on seeing Chris as I boarded. He'd not caught the earlier sailing as planned but had stayed over with some Americans he'd bumped into. I nodded a greeting, he nodded and waved back – but that was it. We never once saw each other again during the twenty-four-hour journey. I spent the time strolling around the decks and bars, eventually meeting up with a guy who had crewed down to Spain with a friend. One meeting led to another and soon a small crowd of us ended up in the piano bar until after midnight. I left them to try and hustle a sleeping space in an out-of-the-way corner, but was delighted to finish up spread out across three soft seats, which were comfortable enough, though in a cold and noisy location. Waking in the morning, I was approached by a small chap who asked if I'd slept all right. Thinking this was extremely polite I replied that I had.

'It's just that I'd left my seat last night to go to the toilet,' he explained, 'and I came back to find you stretched across it and fast asleep. I hadn't the heart to wake you, and besides, you were bigger than me!'

Offering profuse apologies, I hurriedly gathered my belongings and escaped back to the piano bar for a guilty breakfast. A couple of hours later and we docked at Plymouth, grey, rainy and a million miles from Baiona. There was some dark humour in recognising that I'd left as skipper in a small boat with one other person and come back as a passenger with several hundred in a large one. I felt a momentary pang of anxiety for *Sharky*, then reality kicked in. I needed to lug several bits of luggage across this historic city and find a train. My whole life was revolving around transport.

I still felt tired after the ferry crossing and the train back home to Macclesfield gave me a little time to unwind. I wanted to meet my family in good spirits and I'd doubtless be expected to relate all my tales. But I knew the telling wouldn't last long; Mum would just be pleased to see me safe and sound and I had all the time with Elaine should she want a more detailed account. As I got closer to home I thought of nearby Rudyard Lake, from where I had taken some of my first tentative steps into sailing proper. I remembered the lake within its cocoon of forested sides, dappled blue-grey water with small running wavelets, where the wind would course down its length. Little had I known then where my interest would take me and how passionate I would become about life on a boat; a life without socks. Closing my eyes I remembered that I'd left a pair of damp, smelly ones on the tiny chart table. Ah well, they'd have to fester for a few months yet till I saw *Sharky* again. I'd progressed from Rudyard Lake, to the English Channel and down through Biscay. Soon, hopefully, I'd go on to achieve my greatest ambition, solo across the Atlantic to the Caribbean.

The train pulled into Macclesfield. Chucking my bags onto the platform I saw my darling Elaine shyly standing by the entrance, uncertain how to react. I gave her a huge grin and lugged my bags with a newfound vigour. As I enfolded her in my arms, tiredness evaporated and all thoughts of sailing fled my mind.

I was home.

CHAPTER EIGHT

Sharky Disappears

The security guard looked me up and down curiously. I realised I must have looked a bizarre sight, wet hair plastered on my head and clothes covered in mud and grass.

IN A FEW SHORT years I'd had quite a few homes. Born in Sheffield, then in a matter of months moved to Buxton. Aged five, I moved again to the outskirts of Harpur Hill. My parents split up when I was seven, so, with my elder sister Christine, I moved in with my grandparents. A year or so later we moved into Thornheyes, a dilapidated farmhouse in a Peak Dale village, where my mum got together with Norman. Four years later, I was out in Ajman in an environment totally alien and as far removed from the rolling hills of Derbyshire as I could have imagined. These were eleven disruptive years, not helped by the trauma of my family breaking up around me, and persistent bullying and under-performing at school. Disruptive, confusing, bewildering; but not without love. Although I saw little of my father my new 'dad' took his responsibilities seriously and from him I learnt practical skills and how to fight and stick up for myself. It also meant I took on a level of responsibility way beyond my years. As a youngster I adapted to my situation as it happened, simply because I knew no other. In the relative wilderness and solitude on the misted moors of the Dark Peak, then later in the isolation of Thornheyes, I developed independence, a liking for my own company and above all else, a love of nature and wild places. I was not without friends, but I was as comfortable roaming the moors, fields and woodlands alone as getting into schoolboy scrapes with my partners in crime. It wasn't just the open spaces themselves that held me spellbound, it was the sensation of freedom. There was an indefinable joy at being unfettered, a space without rules and regimes. The countryside appeared as a vast auditorium where I could reign without reins, think quiet thoughts or shriek with the pleasure of being alive. On some days, when the mist was down and swirling thickly across the gritstone moor, it was a land lost in time and space; ghostly shapes, muffled sounds and a schoolboy's fearsome thrill of something unknown that might be lurking in the murk. On other, rarer days, when the moors and hills came alive with sunshine, wild flowers and birdsong, they were magical places. And then there was the wind – always the wind – a special element I loved to be in whatever the weather. The wind was my friend, running with me, scattering my hair and pinching my cheeks; playing with me as a leaf in its clasp. At times gentle on my face, at others ferociously slamming into me without thought or care. In the fields behind my home I was learning more important lessons than those imposed on me at school; I was attuning to a particular elation, more instinctive than articulate, that would grow into my love of outdoor adventure. I was a zillion miles from my later passion for sailing, but perhaps the unremitting winds that blew across Stanley Moor were an exhilarating portent for future blusters I would come to love and fear.

Immersing myself in the relaxed lifestyle of Ajman, I began to get invitations to join older lads and men on their sea fishing trips. Such trips were invariably held on Fridays, and they became a real highlight of each week. A group of six or seven of us, often including my dad, would assemble at the harbour around seven in the morning and load our day's supplies on board – food, water, alcohol and fishing tackle. The boats were Arab dhows, motorised as well as sail, and we would venture out into the Gulf, miles from land, searching for grouper or any kind of fish we could eat. I used a hand line at first then bought a rod. The variety of exotic fish was incredible. Most amazing were the squid, spurting black ink everywhere as they were landed, but greater caution was necessary with puffers. As they were pulled on deck they blew themselves up into little balls covered with vicious, barbed spikes; there was no messing around with these devils and we handled them with great care. The edible fish were stored in the icebox for taking back; others were caught for sport and returned to the ocean. I revelled in the atmosphere, of being accepted in the company of men and in the sheer excitement of being on a warm, blue ocean, catching glimpses of the submerged coral while half-blinded by the sparkling and dancing iridescence of sunlight. The warm air would breeze around the sails and once the engine was switched off the only sounds were the banter and laughter of friendship and the lapping of water. Within a few weeks I was allowed to take the wheel on a regular basis, feeling very grand and important. Fishing trips were the nearest to heaven I could imagine; long, lazy, carefree days just living for the moment. If there was an early defining moment when the sea and sailing entered my life as a passion, this was it.

The more I went out in the Gulf, the more I became interested in the vessels we were in. At first fishing was the focal point but I gradually became equally interested in the boats themselves, how they were built and how they were sailed. Watching boats being built was not new to me – I'd seen them since arriving in Ajman and had observed both Arab and Indian builders at their trade – but it was merely the passing and casual interest of a young boy alive to the many new wonders around him. Now I took a more detailed interest in these beach-based craftsmen and began to study their methods.

The Arab dhow is a boat from ancient times and can take many forms, though each with the distinctive features of a high-profile stern, a low sweeping line through mid-ships, then the gentle rise to a long, elongated prow. Traditionally built for sail only, the dhows at Ajman had fallen victim to the mechanised age and were equipped with diesel engines. Nevertheless the basic construct seemed not to have significantly changed. Dhows came in several sizes depending on their purpose, and could range from the five- to six-metre fishing boat through to trade carriers of fifteen metres or more. The boats originally built at Ajman were *Shu'ai*, established workhorses with the well-recognised lateen, the fore and aft rig displaying the two scimitar-shaped sails. I was to learn much later in life that this alignment had been used since the dawn of civilisation, as it reduced the amount of sail necessary for travelling faster close to the wind. To think the apparently more technological Western nations were still using cumbersome square-riggers well into the sixteenth century!

Down on the beach there were always five or six boats in various stages of construction. The part-shaped stem and stern planks were driven into the sand to form the length guide, then a wooden keel made from teak or similar hardwood was attached between them. Slowly the hull sides were built up using thick ribs and planks, conventionally being sewn together with coconut fibre, but now fixed with hammer and nails. There were never any paper plans, the boats were built by eye, with experience and centuries of passed-down skills, each boat individual in its identity and customised with carved wooden panels attached to the hull. With the reliance on diesel, longer masts weren't now necessary, so short stubby alternatives were fitted for smaller sails. It has always been a marvel to me that ill-educated people, so easily dismissed as ignorant peasants, can produce beautifully crafted works of art with recourse only to the simplest of tools. To see piles of beach lumber transmogrified into skilfully functional treasures was a miraculous daily event, acknowledged by the builders and their observers as nothing more than just another unit of production. The Ajman boat area was a constant hive of manual activity, and even today, if I close my eyes, I can recall the assorted aromas of sweet tea and freshly chipped wood mingling with the powerful resin scent of hard timber. Sawdust would hang in the salty air as the nearby sea crashed along the shore, the line of little galleons resembling a swarming ant house of sawing, planing, hammering and chiselling. Day by day the outlines would change as the wooden skeletons were slowly dressed in their hewn finery. Then came the day of the launch. The completed boat would look ungainly and restless, its prow facing the shoreline as if anxious to be away from its sandy confinement. With much noise and effort it would be dug out, towed, rolled down to the water's edge and into its true environment. Accompanied by cheering and applause, the boat would seem to be momentarily surprised, then, coming alive, would surge through the surf in its full release. A true sailor will tell you that boats have souls, and I like to think that they get them at the moment of launch. Sailing on the finished boats enhanced that understanding and appreciation. Any boatyard, however sophisticated or primitive, is a cradle of birth. Put any boat or a ship to water, particularly a sailing vessel, and it adopts a graceful persona of its own, and these boats were no exception. My natural curiosity and growing love for sailing soon found me many friends on the beach as I added the boat builders to my growing list of tea stops.

At the age of fifteen my idyll came to an end. I was to be returned to Peak Dale and Kents Bank School to take my GCSE exams. Mum was insistent but, reluctant as I was to leave, I knew it would only be for six months or so, then I could return to Ajman. Nevertheless, going back to England was still a bitter disappointment. On the morning of my departure, I awoke early and went down to the beach, walking as I had done for the past three years, barefoot, sandals in hand. The soft sand scrunched between my toes and I tried to imagine what it would be like to have my feet imprisoned again in the strictures of grey socks and black shoes. The rising sun flooded the beach with a morning glow, and I felt its warmth seep into my skin. I curled my toes deeper into the sand, feeling the heat of the surface giving way to the cool dampness beneath. I couldn't believe that in a few short hours all this would be replaced by an autumnal chill. It wasn't fair; I didn't need rotten exams, I wanted my friends, the sea and my Elysian life. Reluctantly, I took a last lingering look around the deserted beach and the sparkling surf, then slowly trudged back home, feeling another incomprehensible sense of loss. I waved goodbye to my friends and family at Dubai Airport and several hours later found myself in the wintry cold and rain of Britain. Returning to Thornheyes, I lived with my blood father and enrolled at the grandly named Buxton

College – in reality the fourth and fifth year of Kents Bank, but in a different location.

It took a while to adjust to the constrictions that seemed to beset my life. I had spent three years in splendid independence and was supremely confident. Returning to full days of education, with only six months before exams and surrounded by petty rules, regulations and authoritarian teachers, I found it difficult to fit in. The friends of earlier years now seemed pathetic and immature, with limited vision and experience. They in turn were envious of my lifestyle, and we discovered little by way of common interests. I quickly fell into a lethargy, resulting in much truanting from school, though I surprised myself by my ability in maths, for which my teachers felt I had a talent. I also enjoyed woodwork and other practical lessons, probably as a result of time spent messing around in my dad's workshop and fixing things. When skipping school, I would mooch around Buxton or at home feeling a growing sense of frustration at time wasted. I felt as though I had reverted from a respected and responsible young man to a schoolboy. I'd sit in warm cafés, windows running with condensation, or trudge the dismal streets trying to picture what I'd be doing if I were back in Ajman. I was missing my family, my fishing and sailing, the sunshine, in fact everything I had taken for granted. Was six months of purgatory really worth it for a few measly and pointless exams?

The gut-wrenching, awful bombshell stunned me a couple of weeks before my first exam. My dad phoned to say he and Mum were returning to the UK for good. He'd had enough. My world fell apart absolutely as dreams of an Arabian homecoming were now shattered beyond repair. I saw no prospects, no future and no aspiration. The news was a body-blow and I felt sick, my life kicked to bits. I thought back to the people I had not properly said goodbye to and realised I would probably never see them again. Great pangs of remorse, regret and bitterness welled up in me, and an emotion I hadn't felt for quite a while, fear. I experienced the anxiety of uncertainty about my future as I had done all those years before when my parents split up. This time I was older and better understood the emotion, but it was still unsettling. I now felt a stranger in what for me was still a foreign land. On the evening when I knew I wouldn't be returning I went out into the fields behind Thornheyes. I watched as the darkness crept slowly westward over the landscape, the sky's hues turning from blue to purple to velvet-black. As the birdsong fell away and the bleating of sheep became muted, I recalled similar feelings on that last day in Ajman. I felt my eyes moisten and roughly wiped them against the sleeve of my sweater. With my future uncertain I had lost an important part of my adolescent life. Memories of Ajman and my friends would now remain just that, memories, and I felt that familiar ache of loss course through me. My friends had strengthened my character, building experiences beyond the ken of most people of my age. I bade a mental farewell to them all. I was going to miss them terribly.

I was missing *Sharky*. A grown man pining in this fashion seems rather pitiable, but several months after my return from Baiona I was desperate to get back to sea and worried sick about my boat. Winter gales could have torn her from her moorings, the port official might easily have sold her off for a quick profit, a fisherman might have found her a nuisance and cut her loose, or the harbour authorities might have discovered the scam and impounded her. Perhaps *Sharky* had resented her abandonment and sailed off into the sunset with some macho Spanish pleasure craft! These and other similarly alarming scenarios occupied much of my waking hours and interfered with my work. Thinking about the next leg of my trip though was also keeping me energised and helped block the nagging worries about *Sharky*. I decided that I would take another month or so off work in the June of 1993 and attempt the sail from Baiona down to the Canaries, taking in Madeira en route. A month was about as much as I dared absent myself, but I wanted to experience some ocean sailing on my own before I put myself in the hands of the Atlantic gods and sailed to the Caribbean. Basically, I wanted to test myself mentally and physically, and finding a tiny island in the middle of a lot of water seemed to fit the bill. I ordered the charts, and when they arrived I spent hours in rapt fascination, ultimately deciding I would head for Tenerife via Madeira with a start date of 8th June.

It was exciting to have a target date again and good to get involved in detailed planning. So confident was I that I pre-booked the flight. I realised however that I couldn't wait another six months before I checked my boat out. Christmas over I made the New Year resolution that I would fly out to Portugal immediately, head for Spain and sort things out. I didn't really know what I was going to do when I got there – sail *Sharky* back to the UK, take her a little bit further south, sail her part way back to France, or just make sure she was moored safely. Since I'd booked a June flight none of my thinking was making sense. It was a confusing time and I lacked direction. I just wanted an escape.

In mid-January I boarded a half-empty plane to Oporto in Portugal, looking to catch a train to Vigo, then a bus back to Baiona. As the plane descended for landing we entered cloud thick with torrential rain and a most horrendous buffeting by strong winds. The plane shook, rolled and rattled, the pitch of the engines alternating between roaring and whining until, to my great relief, we bounced onto the runway in an undignified fashion.

Oporto was a cold, dismal terminal with just a scattering of people and officials. In this bleak building I eventually teamed up with a Welsh businessman who offered to share a taxi to his hotel, which was opulent four-star. Walking into its reception area, I realised I couldn't afford an overnight stay, so wandered out into the still torrential rain to seek more affordable lodgings. For two hours I wandered around, soaked to the skin, unable to find anything suitable. In desperation I entered a bar and after a couple of beers asked the landlord if he could recommend anywhere. A series of rapid phone calls ensued, none of which I could understand, but eventually he came back to me beaming. His friend had a room I could use and he, the landlord, would be pleased to offer me breakfast with his family the following morning. European generosity had prevailed once more, so it was with light heart that I knocked on a dark doorway that was opened by an elderly courteous gentleman with a perfectly trimmed beard and moustache – straight from the sherry adverts, I thought. The spotless room was perfect, the price ridiculously cheap and the television was showing *Rambo 3* in English. Stripping off my sodden clothes I hunkered down for a quiet night unable to believe my luck.

The money saved on the room enabled me to hire a morning taxi to take me with my luggage to the railway station, only to discover that the Vigo train didn't leave until three o'clock in the afternoon, arriving at eight o'clock that night. There was nothing for it but to wait at the station, listening to the rain steadily dropping through a murky fog. A cold January in a Portuguese platform bar is not a pleasant experience but I whiled away the hours dreaming up impossible get-rich schemes, fretting about the boat and generally reflecting on my life. Before leaving home I'd ordered thirty pounds-worth of red roses for Elaine and I tried to imagine her surprise on receiving them. Would she be delighted or think the gesture too extravagant? I didn't care; I loved her very much and this was my way of showing it. Finally I boarded the train, regretting again how much luggage I'd brought, and slumped into yet another seat for yet another journey. After so much listless sitting around all day, the taxi ride from Vigo to Baiona certainly brought my senses back to life. I must have chosen the taxi driver with the greatest death-wish in Spain. A large excitable man grabbed my luggage and unceremoniously threw it all in the boot, virtually pushed me into the car and jammed his foot down on the accelerator. I shot back into my seat as he threw his car around with all the ambition of a Formula One driver. Crossroads and traffic lights flew past in total abandon as he chattered animatedly in unintelligible patois, frequently taking both hands off the steering wheel to demonstrate a particular point, usually on tight bends for some reason. In good weather this would have been hair-raising, but the fine drizzle was still in evidence so I just gripped the seat in front, braced my knees against its back and prayed St Christopher wasn't having a night off. Ten miles later we skidded to a halt near Baiona harbour and I dripped from the car, a thin film of glistening sweat cooling my body. The luggage was dumped beside me and off shot the taxi driver, looking no doubt for another passenger to terrorise.

It was now about half past nine in the evening. Baiona was a silent, damp antithesis of its character the last time I'd been here –

a few streetlights littering the quiet darkness, with only an occasional open bar dotted here and there. I quickly peered around the harbour but in the darkness could see no sign of *Sharky*. I walked up and down for an hour or so anxiously searching to no avail, then realised that I was being stupid: she must be out there but it was too dark and wet for me to see properly. I needed to find a hotel otherwise I'd be sleeping on the beach; the search could wait until daylight. Finding cheap accommodation I had a quick shower but couldn't settle; I needed to reassure myself that *Sharky* was all right. I donned my one-piece Musto waterproofs and set out again, passing a very mystified receptionist. After several minutes and a few hastily puffed cigarettes I was getting nowhere. My boat was not where I had left it. Panic began to creep into my mind and it needed a few more smokes until I came up with a plan. I would borrow a small tender from the back of a fishing boat and row out into the sheltered bay. Casually looking around, I inched my way over the slimy rocks and into the craft, slipped the knots and quietly rowed out through the dormant fleet. Feeling faintly crazy, I rowed among and beyond the fishing fleet, softly muttering my boat's name all the time, a rising anxiety inching its way through my body. Where the hell was she? Eventually, satisfied that she was not with the fishing boats, I reasoned that the marina and yacht club were my next objectives. The Baiona club was very elite, built within the remains of a centuries-old castle and designed to keep money in and the riff-raff out. Retying the tender I effected a casual saunter across to the yacht club, to discover that the main gates were locked. By now all reason had been left behind. It was past midnight but time was immaterial. Looking quickly about, I crabbed up the rocky castle walls, heaved myself over the crenellated tops and dropped heavily to the ground, my waterproofs noisily scuffing with the effort. In the distance I could see a security guard walking his beat, the powerful beam of his torch spotlighting boats at random. Trying to crawl as best and as silently as I could, I slithered through the sodden grass and onto the muddy beach, wondering about the consequences of being caught and subsequently arrested. Dodging the security guard, I bobbed up and down among the masts when, in the distance, I glimpsed the familiar outline of

Sharky silhouetted against the marina lights. A powerful sense of relief overcame me and I just sat for a few moments collecting my thoughts. Relief still overrode rationality and without thinking I stood up and walked across to the guard, who, startled, shone his light in my face.

'Señor?' he questioned, stepping back to leave a substantial space between us.

Giving him no time to think and assuming attack was the best possible form of defence, I began my explanation in halting Spanish, assertive English and wild gesticulations. 'Could you take me out to my boat, please? I want to see if she's all right.'

The security guard looked me up and down curiously. I realised I must have looked a bizarre sight, wet hair plastered on my head and clothes covered in mud and grass.

'It's one o'clock in the morning, señor,' he replied patiently, 'surely it can wait until daylight?'

'Ah,' I said, 'but I've just arrived from England and couldn't find my boat, but now I have and I'd like to see if she's all right.'

I could tell from the guard's face that confusion had set in. Not only was he trying to cope with my poor Spanish and risible explanation but he was trying to determine why anyone would arrive all the way from England in the early hours, damp and dressed in a one-piece grassy waterproof outfit and muddy trainers. I noted that he hadn't yet queried how I'd managed to get through the marina's locked gates, so I rattled on about my boat being anchored out in the bay in a different place from where I'd left it, and could someone possibly take me out for a quick look?

A penny dropped and he beamed. 'Hah!' he guffawed. 'You are the big mad Englishman.' To my great surprise he whistled up the security boat and there followed a short discussion in which the only words I recognised were 'mad Englishman'. Apparently word had spread during the summer about the madman who had sailed from England in a tiny boat. The pilot invited me on board and we motored out to *Sharky* as if it was the most natural request he'd ever had. Perhaps it was; I made a mental note to play the madman card whenever future tricky situations might arise. The boat nestled up to *Sharky* and I leapt aboard. The locks to the hatch were still in place, so I just gave her a quick, external visual examination and everything looked fine. Ten minutes later I was taken back to the jetty, greatly relieved and suddenly very tired. The pilot told me that there had been a huge storm at the end of November and my anchor chain had snapped. *Sharky* was being blown out to sea but luckily a worker in the yacht club had seen it and went out to tow her back in. I sent a silent prayer of thanks to my unknown benefactor; how easy would it have been simply to have shrugged and turned away, the bad weather itself being a justifiable reason for doing so. Talking to the marina manager the next day, he confirmed that I wouldn't be charged salvage for the effort in bringing the boat back in; my trip from England and my plans for a full Atlantic crossing, though regarded as foolhardy, had been held in high respect. All in all I'd been incredibly lucky.

Next morning I was back on *Sharky*, having decided to check out of the hotel and live on board for about a week or so. The locks had seized solid in the salty conditions so using an old screwdriver I broke them open and went below. The cabin smelt of a dank, damp graveyard, the walls and bunks covered in grey-green mould. The socks I'd left on the chart table lay in a disgusting festering heap and there was a general air of putrefying decay. Was it only a few months before that this had been my idyllic home? Now the forlorn space silently echoed my feelings of guilt; I had a lot of work to do to restore *Sharky* to her former glory. The next few days were spent scrubbing, cleaning and making things shipshape, but the damp conditions didn't help. The weather remained cold, wet and windy though I managed one quick sail out in the bay. I felt pleased to be back at the helm but something was missing. I felt detached, remote, isolated and lonely. Baiona was out of season and resembled the wintry northern seaside towns back home, slowly seeing out its lingering grey hibernation. As the watery cold sun disappeared every afternoon Baiona became even drearier in its desolation and I added sadness to my list of feelings. Alone I made my way ashore each night to find an uneasy solace over a few beers before returning to my boat, the alcohol fuelling my increasing misery. A major problem was that I simply didn't know what to do. I considered sailing back to Falmouth and starting the whole adventure again from there but I couldn't even get *Sharky* out to sea. The conditions were not favourable and I'd lost some confidence in my sailing ability. To make matters worse, I discovered that the engine was knackered beyond repair and I still had no replacement anchor for the one lost in the storm. To attempt a return trip with huge Atlantic rollers crashing onto the rocks would be reckless in the extreme.

During the daytime, once I'd checked things out, I'd settle on my bunk and read books and doze with no real purpose or motivation to spur me into action. The damp weather was causing condensation to run throughout the cabin, soaking my clothes, so on the odd occasion when the rain stopped I'd venture out on deck to dry them out as best I could. Sitting out, I started chatting to a seagull perched on the masthead. I threw a piece of bread, which it caught before flying off. Before long the gull returned so I threw an apple core, which it swallowed whole, jerking its neck back and forth, forcing the morsel down its throat. Every day the damn thing returned, fixing me with beady eyes until I relented with more food. I seriously began to wonder if I was suffering from depression; the only living thing I'd befriended in Baiona was Señor Seagull, and I was beginning to look forward to its daily visit. The inclement weather made further sailing impractical, and I didn't really know what I wanted to do, such indecisiveness being uncharacteristic, unsettling. I was lonely but couldn't bring myself to return home, and phoning Elaine only compounded my desolation. I could find no explanation within myself and hated the aimless drifting in this 'couldn't be bothered' state of mine. I began to question whether I had the confidence to sail the Atlantic at all, which added to my anxiety and despondency. After a few despairing, lethargic days of continuously pouring rain, when all I seemed to do was brace myself against the rocking of the boat and drink endless cups of coffee, my self-pity eventually spurred me into action. I packed my bags and after an interminable wait caught a bus down to Oporto and managed to grab an earlier-than-planned flight home in the early hours of the morning. I'd explained to the marina manager that I'd be back in June and he kindly offered to keep an eye on the boat for a very reasonable mooring fee. I left

Sharky for the second time, and again with mixed feelings. Sitting on the plane, I felt dirty and unshaven, with a nagging headache. It had been an awful week and I'd never felt so low. I still wondered whether I should just have picked up *Sharky* and sailed home and to hell with it. Despite my disheartened state, deep down I knew I wanted my Atlantic journey back on track – I just wasn't sure I could hack it anymore.

CHAPTER NINE

Back to Sea

No one knew where I was, a tiny insignificant spec on the earth's crust, alone in the silent vastness of all creation.

BACK HOME MY CONTINENTAL depressions soon left me and I became absorbed once more in work and, whenever I could spare the time, planning for my next Atlantic leg. Running the shop remained a hard track to be on; open seven days a week from a quarter to six in the morning until ten at night, with only Sunday afternoons off. We even opened for a few hours on Christmas Day. All in all I reckoned we did the equivalent of three weeks' work every week – no wonder I looked forward to the liberty that sailing granted me. Somewhere within the constant demands of running a retail outlet, once described to me as the freedom to work twenty-five hours a day, eight days a week, I managed to pore over the charts that would get me to Madeira the following summer. As ever, I was restricted by a very tight budget and the amount of time I could afford to be away from the shop. I was conscious that I was putting additional strain on my mother, but bless her, she encouraged me to follow my dream in her own bluff way. It didn't stop her moaning about my time off but I think she was proud of what I'd accomplished the summer before, as I hadn't really gone into great detail about the problems and challenges I'd encountered. She was forever saying, 'How am I going to manage?' or, 'There's some of us 'as to stay and work hard' and so forth. I reasoned she was content for me to go off again despite the barbed comments, but would take any opportunity when conversing with customers to remark, 'Our David's off bloody sailing again this summer.'

The trip from Baiona was going to be my first real solo sail in the Atlantic and I was reasonably confident I could handle the experience after the previous year's Biscay encounters. I'd finally decided I couldn't afford to replace the outboard, trusting instead to my sailing skills. My confidence had been restored now that I was back home, partly because I knew *Sharky* was safe and in the hands of a top-notch marina. After my first detailed look at the North Atlantic charts, I knew I was committed to the June date and contacted the marina to arrange to have my boat lifted out of the water and washed off. I was back on track. I'd actually booked the flight out the year before, so being a tight sod I wasn't going to lose the cost of the ticket by chickening out.

What I hadn't reckoned on of course was Simon. Simon, whom I'd met initially as a customer, also ran a business in Buxton just a few minutes' walk away round the corner. He and his mum ran a jeweller's shop, selling a range of bought-in stock, but he also made much-admired crafted pieces, which were in great demand. We were of a similar age and it wasn't long before he became part of our Friday night out with the lads. Simon was a quietly spoken, thoughtful guy who fitted easily into our social scene. The perception of him as intelligent and well read was supported by a rapidly thinning head of hair, which gave him a slightly professorial appearance. Like me, he was very combative at chess and backgammon, and we rapidly became good friends. Talking to him one evening, the conversation turned to my exploits with *Sharky*, the Baiona sail and my plans for the whole Atlantic dream. Without a notion of what was to come, I waxed lyrical, relating the adventure in glowing terms, building up the tension, describing the feelings and adrenalin rush, the stunning scenery and painting a far too rosy description of life on a small boat. I was grateful for an uncommonly attentive audience and the well-thought-out questions I was being posed, but it may have been the excellent Irish whisky that dulled my ability to spot the gleam in his eyes.

'You're a lucky man, mate,' he said, draining his glass. 'Not many blokes take the chance to do what you're doing.' There was a short silence as he stared at his glass, turning the tumbler this way and that in his hand as the ice cubes swirled around the sides. A short silence, a wistful sigh, and then he struck. A short question made even more pointed as he delivered it in his quiet intellectual manner. 'Any chance I could come with you on the next bit?'

Mellowed as I was by the drink, something in my brain screamed out 'Not again!' There was an awkward silence, which Simon refused to fill while my mind went into overdrive. Previous glowing images of bravado were replaced by a succession of snapshots hurtling through my mind. Screaming and swearing at Chris, a cabin filled with vomit and seawater, a panic-stricken, tearful companion convinced he was going to die, a sailing mate who wouldn't or couldn't pull his weight. I also drained my glass, looked at Simon and purposefully shook my head.

'Sorry, mate,' I said. 'I've tried it and it just doesn't work. It's taken a while for Chris and me to sort ourselves out and I don't want to risk another friendship.'

Simon shrugged and said he understood and respected my decision. 'Shame though,' he replied, 'I've knocked about a bit in a dinghy but I'd love a few days in the Atlantic to see what real sailing's like.'

The weeks progressed and I continued working flat-out, the thought of the June sail making me impatient. As winter worked its rigours, I stumbled into a freezing cold shop each dark morning, clutching the damp newspapers thrown into the doorway, becoming ever more desperate to get away to that once-tasted freedom. I'd find myself absent-mindedly stacking shelves, poring over the sailing magazines and wishing myself into their pages. At the end of long exhausting days filled with single mums and their prams filled with screaming kids, dirty old men sneaking top-shelf magazines between newspapers, under-age kids trying to buy cigarettes and booze, shoplifters of all ages, handling staff problems, wholesalers who wouldn't budge on the slightest of margins, and bank managers who treated you with contempt – at the end of each day, dog-tired, I'd think back to those heady Biscay days when life had been more extreme, more simple, simply more fulfilling than life at home, where I was permanently exhausted, knowing that in just a few hours I'd get up again and repeat the unending cycle of making a living. I wasn't ungrateful, it was a good living, and I had the independence of running a business, but I knew I couldn't do it forever. In my late twenties I was becoming irrationally anxious that life was passing me by, stuck in a dreary northern suburb where mindless gossip, television and survival were the main topics of conversation and of life. I wanted to be back on the sea. I wanted to be with *Sharky*, revelling in a passion for life, screaming at the top of my voice again as the wind filled her sails and the spray stung my face. June simply couldn't come fast enough.

On my rare evenings off, I'd share these thoughts with Simon. As an armchair dreamer he could relate to my desire to escape into a *Boy's Own* world. I went round to his flat one night clutching a couple of takeaway curries, some cigarettes and the obligatory Irish firewater. We'd both learnt to play guitar so it was a delightful night in, jamming our favourite songs and driving oxygen from the room with spiced and smoke-laden fumes. The whisky wove its magic and I slumped comfortably on the floor, my back against the settee.

'Come on, June,' I half said to myself.

'Had any more thoughts about that?' The sound of his softly spoken voice drifted across the room, borne aloft on two perfectly formed smoke rings.

'Huh?' I replied, lost in the ambience.

'Your trip,' came the languid response. 'Just wondered whether you'd made up your mind about me tagging along.'

A warning bell rang distantly in my mind, but it didn't seem too loud. Nevertheless I sat up, wafting the fug around in an attempt at clarity, trying to recollect a distant conversation and what exactly it was that I had said. 'Tagging along?' I questioned, stalling for time.

'It'd be great,' slurred Simon. 'Just a couple of mates on a great ocean journey. It'd be great.'

The bell rang a little clearer, and I sensed a trap opening up but I wasn't sure I was that bothered. Simon hadn't the same skittish mind as Chris. True he'd had little sailing experience, but I could teach him. After all I'd been virtually solo on the days when Chris had not been at his best. And we wouldn't be in such unpredictable waters as those in Biscay. We shared similar interests and he was an engaging, likeable guy.

'Heh!' I cried, picking up my instrument and launching tunelessly into Clapton's *Tears in Heaven*. 'We could take the guitars and jam on the ocean waves!'

Simon responded with Rod Stewart's *Sailing* and thus the deal was done.

Back at work next day I had time to reflect soberly on the rashness of the previous night's exchange. What on earth had got into me? I didn't want a companion, even one as good as Simon. I wanted a solo adventure, a chance to pit my wits to see if I truly had it in me to attempt a complete Atlantic journey. I began to consider ways of reneging without losing face or a friend, but as with Chris, Simon had seemed genuinely delighted at the arrangement. Even before I'd left his flat that night, he'd begun to plan how he would take a month off from his business. It took a couple of days for me to formulate a possible way out, and the more I thought about it the more I became certain it was a convincing option; one which would accommodate both our wishes. I approached him and explained the plan. I would sail solo down to Madeira, a distance of 740 nautical miles, then meet him out there. With a lighter boat and a desire to sail flat-out, this might take me around ten to fourteen days or so. Simon could then accompany me on the remaining leg to Tenerife, where we would enjoy a short holiday. He was immediately enthusiastic and I felt we'd agreed on an excellent compromise.

Finally the day of departure arrived. I'd spent the previous month ensuring the shop was fully stocked and my mum happy with the arrangements. We had a mix of full- and part-time staff, plus Norman and my sister, who were helping out, so I was content that Mum was not going to be left with too much on her plate. I bade my second set of farewells, a lingering kiss and cuddle with Elaine and a perfunctory, though genuinely warm 'Take care, son' from Mum. Simon drove me to Manchester Airport for the start of a journey I was not looking forward to, as it involved endless changes weighed down with enough gear that would have made Hannibal wince. I couldn't trust Baiona to have the supplies I'd need so I had little option than to take it all out myself. A few days before the flight, I stood in my bedroom surrounded with mountains of equipment and wondered whether it really was all going to fit in. A dozen or so tins of food, clothes, waterproofs, charts and pilot books, batteries, navigation equipment, radio, sextant and, unbelievably, an anchor with sixty feet of chain. I should have been worried sick, but I wasn't. I was deliriously happy at the prospect of adventure and laughed out loud when Elaine looked at the anchor and chain and gasped, 'You're going on a plane with that!' I got a very similar response from the girl at the check-in desk. I staggered up, passport clenched between my teeth, clutching a large suitcase and box, two large holdalls and a cabin bag. I heaved it all onto the weighing conveyor, and the girl said, 'It weighs ninety-five kilos.' I thought she was impressed with the fact that I could lift that amount, until she added, 'You're only allowed twenty-four.' Across came the supervisor, and I decided to chance my luck. Taking him aside I explained what the luggage was for, while surreptitiously slipping a few quid into his hand.

'No problem, sir,' he said with a wink, 'have a good trip.'

I was amazed I'd got away with it but delighted at saving the excess baggage fee. It was another example of what it was possible to get away with by adopting a fresh-faced, innocent brazenness – a trait I'd been practising for as long as I could remember!

The nightmare journey lurched ever closer to Baiona; from Manchester to Barcelona, change of plane to Madrid before catching a shuttle flight to Vigo, and finally a bus to Baiona. Each stop necessitated the unloading and reloading of all my possessions, the weight subconsciously increasing every time I grabbed a handle. Eventually at half-past ten in the evening I dropped my luggage for the last time outside the yacht club entrance. Gone were the winter gales and driving rain. Baiona was back to her fairy-lit best, recumbent in the warm dusk with clusters of people leisurely meandering through the streets and bars. As I'd hoped, *Sharky* had been taken out of the water and stood on the cradle by a jetty. Pretty exhausted by now I loaded the gear, shut the hatch and fell into a deep and dreamless sleep. It felt as though I had hardly been away. Next morning I awoke to a sunlit dawn, knowing I was in for a busy few days. There was much to be done; in particular I had a thick mass of seaweed and barnacles to scrape off the bottom of the hull. The weed grows at such an amazing rate that within a year or so the drag would have been sufficient to stop *Sharky* sailing at all. It was hard work for twelve hours but eventually the hull was clear to receive a couple of coats of red anti-fouling paint, freely donated by the boatyard lads who took a keen interest in my trip while helping with odd jobs and encouraging my Spanish pronunciation. The next task was to stock up with fresh fruit and vegetables from the local supermarket. So impressed with the amount I was buying, the owner insisted on personally driving me back to *Sharky* and helping me unload, all the time showing a genuine interest in my exploits. This sincere curiosity and willingness to help is something I've encountered wherever I've travelled, and it seems particularly prevalent in non-English speaking countries. In many places people haven't acquired the reserved nature evident among the British, and once you realise that they are displaying interest, not poking into your affairs with bare-faced interference, life becomes much more interesting and amenable. I discovered this particularly in Arabia and among Asians who show none of the inhibitions we have in these isles.

Within three days of my arrival *Sharky* was shipshape and gunwaled up with provisions, so I had her craned into the water where she sat rather low, though not as over-laden as in Falmouth the previous year. By now it was early afternoon and I went to pay the various charges and make a couple of calls home. With most of the hard preparatory work done, I was surprised to find myself feeling quite anxious and apprehensive. A touch of self-doubt washed over me and I fussed around trying to put off the actual decision to take to sea. I really didn't like this emotion and I worried whether I had forgotten the skills I would soon need to use. The prevarication was forced aside by the arrival of the lads from the boatyard, who came to wave me goodbye. The die was cast. With a last look around and a salute to my friends, I hoisted the jib, slipped the lines and tightened the sheet carefully to tack through the moored yachts, heading for the bay. The weather was a mix of sun and cloud with occasional rain forecast. A strong force five to six was blowing, so I hoisted the mainsail and tacked up and down the bay for an hour or so, taking in and shaking out reefs, getting my sea legs back and generally checking for leaks, loose keel bolts and the like. Growing in confidence but still wary, I left the shelter of the bay and headed out into the Atlantic. Once beyond the bay, the wind gusted and the sea responded in its swell. Swathes of spray coated the deck and *Sharky* knuckled down to the task, glad to be back to the job for which she was made and eager to show me her prowess. The wind increased and *Sharky* began to heel over too much so I put another reef in the mainsail and changed to the smaller storm jib. I felt a curious mix of pleasure, fear, relief and fleeting loneliness. Not a desperate ache for company, more a wistful jumble of indefinable happiness and sadness. Memories of the first leg flooded back and I realised just how badly I had missed the sailing. I had been granted the privilege of being in this wonderful and humbling environment once more and had chosen to experience it alone. As dusk fell I stared out into the dimming horizon, random recollections of my life flowed unbidden and haphazardly; experiences that in many ways had led me to this point and to this ambition. From somewhere words from T E Lawrence's book *The Seven Pillars of Wisdom* sprang to mind:

> All men dream: but not equally. Those who dream by night in the dusty recesses of their minds wake in the day to find that it was vanity; but the dreamers of the day are dangerous men, for they may act their dreams with open eyes, to make it possible. This I did.

I set *Sharky* up for the night, checked the self-steering gear and retired to my bunk, the author's words still in my mind. I'd been a dreamer all my life, was still a dreamer and perhaps now I was beginning to make my dreams become those of the day. Very little in life seems extraordinary at the time of happening. It is only later, on reflection, that we can stand back and declare ourselves proud of our achievements. Learning to sail had no other initial defining goal than that of enjoyment; sailing across the Atlantic had crept up on me in stages and almost by stealth, but I felt now it was becoming not a daydream, but a dream of the day. Drifting off to sleep, I knew with a quiet confidence that I had achieved things I could be proud of and that I was capable of achieving more. Thoughts of work and even of home slipped away under the hypnotic rocking of the swell. Confidence much restored, I slept the sleep of a man satisfied with life.

The confidence remained longer than the sleep. Within a couple of hours I was awake again, still not fully familiar with the boat's movement, so I brewed some tea and lay listening to the tinny sounds of music playing through the Walkman's minute speaker. The sea was a bit choppy and it became a long, rough night with several strong gusts making the boat pitch and roll quite violently. I had to get up and fully reef the mainsail as *Sharky* bounced around like an uncontrollable child. I was glad when the sun at last showed itself through an overcast sky, and by noon I'd travelled eighty-three miles, with which I was well pleased, celebrating with another hot tea and several of the ubiquitous Jammy Dodgers. I wrote in my log 'The best day's run in *Sharky* to date.' The next twenty-four hours slipped by in much the same fashion, cloudy, gusting winds and waves crashing over the deck, Madeira steadily closing in about 400 miles to the west of us. Already some of my clothes were back to their familiar damp condition and I would dearly have loved a warm wash and shave, but the weather controls everything and such luxuries were not yet on the list.

For seven days I endured rough, unrelenting weather that offered no relief from pitching, yawing, rolling in heavy seas and cold, driving spray. The one consolation was it was a good wind and we were eating into the miles. My confidence ebbed and flowed in equal measure and I forced myself to spend a few hours on deck, in between times staying in the cabin gripping on to any surface that kept me more or less upright, with frequent anxious glances through the hatch

1 Sharky outside my flat and shop where I worked on her in preparation for the sea.

2 (above) The strengthening work carried out on the windows to ensure Sharky was as safe as possible for the Bay of Biscay crossing.

3 (right) Chris on the helm on our first Channel crossing.

4 (above) The last view of Falmouth, England as we head off into the Channel

5 (left) Cooker.

6 (right) Maurice the self-steering gear working well as the evening draws to a close.

7 (above) Sometimes the sea would just kick up some small irregular waves. Any closer to the boat and this one would have given me a soaking.

8 and 9 (above & right) Cooped up in the cabin and very wet outside with waves breaking and washing over the decks.

10 and 11 Sea picking up in Bay of Biscay.
Confused waves giving Chris and me the sail of our lives.

12 (above) Sharky tied up to a buoy in the Spanish yacht club that rescued her. You can see her in the centre of the photo with the blue hull.

13 (left) Sharky in Northern Spain all painted up and ready to be lowered into the water.

14 (below) Good conditions but wet decks made being outside uncomfortable.

15 *Accepting a generous tow from a fisherman in return for my emergency bottle of scotch. I had been drifting just off the coast of Madeira for most of the day and was relieved to be heading for the safety of the harbour after ten days at sea.*

16 *Simon enjoying the great conditions on the way to the Canaries.*

17 (left) Full sails set on a perfect sailing day.

18 (below) Sharky and I posing for some inquisitive tourists in Tenerife.

19 Sorting out the contents of Sharky in preparation for the Atlantic crossing. I sometimes wonder how it all fitted in!

20 Sharky about to become engulfed by the Tami lift that would lower her into the water. Always a very tense time!

cover, gulping in fresh air before sliding it shut again. Despite the constant erratic movement of the sea, there is still an underlying rhythm to a boat and that motion gets locked into the brain. It becomes part of the whole essence of sailing, as natural as breathing, always there but never acknowledged, until it changes. And so it was on the second stormy night. I was wedged in the cabin, reading by torchlight when I suddenly felt a deviance from that rhythm. My heart skipped a beat and a flash of fear shot through my body, which instinctively stiffened. After a split second, seemingly lasting for ages, my brain kicked in and I realised what was going to happen. *Sharky* had left the crest of a wave and I just knew we were going to be catapulted into the next trough. We hung out of the water, helpless in the moment, the roar of the sea against the hull disappearing, then, with the impact of hitting a brick wall at speed, we slammed down into the trough with an almighty crash. I remained frozen on the spot, fear drying my mouth. I looked fearfully around for signs of a splitting hull and the inrush of seawater, but *Sharky* had somehow survived the impact and the natural rhythm returned. I went back to my book but it took a long while to get the concentration back. My eyes sightlessly read the words as all other senses were tuned to the sea – listening, feeling, willing the rhythm to remain. On another occasion, the self-steering rope snapped in the maelstrom, leaving the gear turning uselessly and at the mercy of the conditions. There was nothing for it but to hang on to the stern like grim death, while my numb hands attempted a repair, rather like tying a rope while hanging on to a bucking, sodden roller coaster. Time spent on deck was gruelling. Wet, cold and windy, the spray came in bucketfuls, with waves sloshing continuously down and across the boat. The misery was worse when I couldn't vent the ordeal on anyone. I had chosen to sail alone but there were times when I wished Chris were there, just to see another human face, even a pasty, fear-stricken one. After a couple of days, even though conditions remained unpleasant, a stiffer resolve forced much of the melancholy away and my deeper levels of determination helped to defeat any notion of wretched self-pity. I had chosen to make this particular bed, I would now happily, if somewhat soggily, lie in it.

There is one particular inescapable act at sea, however, that remains forever wretched, a regular requirement that might euphemistically and politely be described as a necessary bodily function. Using the heads, going for a number two, having a dump, using the toilet or, in the vernacular, going for a crap, is just about the worst thing to do when at sea, and unless you are seriously well disciplined or wish to die an unpleasant death, it is not something that can be put off for any length of time. Those of a sensitive disposition may well choose to ignore the next paragraph. Those with a curious disposition will read on and discover why you should forever bless the inventor of the flushing toilet.

Thomas Crapper and his later disciples appear never to have seen the necessity of troubling themselves with nautical waste disposal. Boat designers equally never gave it much thought, probably thinking that, as they were earning vast fortunes from their profession, they were more likely to sail on larger boats where a more civilised modus operandi was incorporated. Real sailors therefore must grit their teeth, if not their bowels, on long voyages, safe in the knowledge that constipation is not a finite state. At some stage something has to give. Taking a crap at sea takes two forms – the civilised crap and the rushed crap. The former is done in calm seas with no rain and every opportunity should be seized to take advantage of such conditions. A bucket is filled with around four to six inches of seawater and placed on deck or in the cockpit and sat on while the bodily function is performed. The level of water is critical. Too much and any resulting splashing tends to be a tad messy, too little and it can be quite difficult to part the faeces from the bucket. Once the mission is completed the bucket is tied to a rope and it and said contents are tipped over the side, the bucket subsequently being washed out on its return. The rushed crap, usually taken in rough seas and cold, driving rain or spray (in other words most of the time) is altogether more dangerous but arguably more interesting. Timing is everything and the decision to 'go' must be delayed until the absolute last minute. The procedure is to strip naked in the cabin, difficult enough being pitched about, then clip on the harness. Clothes only get in the way and will become soaking wet in the weather anyway. A mad dash is then required to anywhere on the boat where it is possible to hang on to a rail or any fixed object and quickly void the bowels. Even in the worst of conditions there is a sublime and somewhat ridiculous point where a sigh escapes involuntarily from the lips and a brief smile appears before the freezing reality kicks back in. Once the motion is completed, the bucket (with rope) is flung over the side and a gallon of briny sea is then deployed to wash the ordure away. Defecation complete, phase two is then brought into play. Toilet paper has no place on board a small boat for fairly obvious reasons, it not being the most robust of materials. A clever device, known as a 'squiddy', is thus deployed, which consists of a flannel tied to five feet of thin line towed behind the boat. When required the 'squiddy' is pulled in, used appropriately, then slung back into the water – the ultimate in self-cleansing.

Picture the scene therefore, which would not go amiss as a filmed comic caper. In the middle of the night, from the bowels of a small boat being violently thrown around in the worst of weather, comes an unshaven, wild-eyed individual, naked save for a fluorescent nylon harness. Staggering through the elements he grips the nearest boat rail, simultaneously being lashed by heavy rain and swamped by crashing waves. He squats in an undignified fashion, the grimace on his face gradually giving way to a fleeting smile as he proceeds to find the 'squiddy' line, which is invariably in a different location from where he has so recently rushed. Clinging on with one hand he wipes his bum, the grimace returning to his face as the salt-encrusted flannel comes into contact with his nether regions. Then, flinging the 'squiddy' back, he drags, still single-handedly, a bucket of water from the depths and attempts to find his excreta in the black night in order to wash it away. Then and only then will he clamber back to the cabin and relative security. Thus is the rushed crap performed. Three final, vital points need to be emphasised. It is pretty important to ensure the rope is securely tied to the bucket to ensure its retrieval, unless you have a penchant for several spares. Secondly, if throwing the faeces overboard from the bucket, it's a good idea to check the direction of the wind. Finally, after several weeks of trailing behind the boat, the 'squiddy' can become home to an assortment of little sea creatures and crustaceans guaranteed to wipe the smile off just about anything!

Back to the journey. On the eighth day out from Baiona the weather improved insofar as the rain cleared, but the wind also died, leaving me barely making any headway at all. As night fell so did the remains of the wind. On deck for a smoke, I looked around in the low sea mist, at the sails flapping slightly and a completely flat sea. I took in the sails and just relaxed on deck watching the stars come out. It was an eerie but not uncomfortable feeling and before long I drifted off to sleep, waking after several hours as the night chill wreathed my body. I awoke to an enchanted sight, a clear, black night filled with thousands and thousands of stars. For an instant I went back to my childhood days in the desert of Ajman, then realised where I was. There was no noise, an absolute deafening silence, not even the water lapping against the hull. The ghostly mist still hung over the glass-like sea and I felt suspended in time and space. A jolt of fear shot through me and I shivered. I was completely and utterly on my own. No one knew where I was, a tiny insignificant speck on the earth's crust, alone in the silent vastness of all creation. It felt weird, as though I was somehow intruding into the realms of God, who or whatever that might be. My fearful mind gradually relaxed and that moment became the most peaceful I have ever known. I entered a profound state of overwhelming joy and serenity that I couldn't comprehend. I felt the existence of a life force that transcended mere flesh and blood, more than just electrical and chemical stimuli. I don't claim to have had a religious experience in the established sense, but I felt an affinity with something powerful that I couldn't understand. I lay back on the deck, my brain not big enough to take in the wonders around me, and let my thoughts go into freefall. Despite the chill, I floated back into another deep and secure sleep.

By morning, the wind had picked up slightly but progress was slow. At seven o'clock that evening I at last spotted Porto Santo Island in the distance on my port side. The island lies to the northeast of Madeira, and I was hopeful I would be approaching Funchal harbour some time the following day. As Porto Santo loomed ever larger on

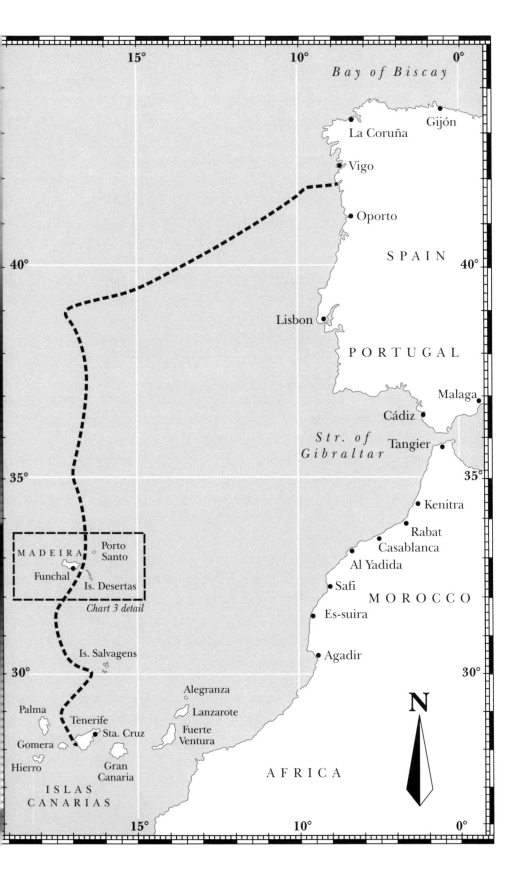

Bay of Biscay

15° 10° 0°

Gijón
La Coruña

Vigo

Oporto

SPAIN 40°

40°

Lisbon

PORTUGAL

Malaga

Cádiz

Str. of
Gibraltar Tangier

35° 35°

Kenitra

Rabat
Casablanca

Al Yadida

MADEIRA Porto
Santo

Funchal Safi MOROCCO

Is. Desertas

Chart 3 detail Es-suira

Is. Salvagens Agadir

N

30° 30°

Alegranza

Palma Lanzarote

Tenerife Fuerte
Gomera Sta. Cruz Ventura

Hierro Gran
Canaria AFRICA

ISLAS
CANARIAS

15° 10° 0°

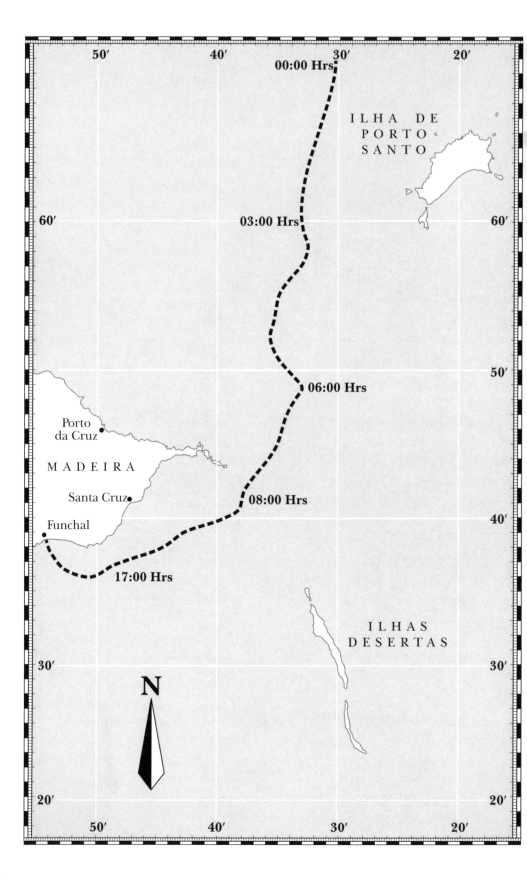

the horizon the wind suddenly increased dramatically and I sensed I was in for a long night. I fully reefed the mainsail and shortly after hit a vicious squall with heavy stinging rain driving into my face. The squall lasted several hours, the wind surging and gusting without warning. I helmed through the night keeping myself alert and awake with numerous cups of coffee from the flask I'd thankfully prepared before the conditions deteriorated. Despite the weather, I thought it might be a good idea to take a photograph of the night swells, so managing to hang on to the helm and somehow keeping my camera dry, I attempted a shot low along the deck to the bow. A blinding flash erupted in my right eye and I realised I'd pointed the camera the wrong way round. With vision consisting of two ultra-bright red spots and the beginnings of a headache, I unceremoniously ditched the camera and attempted to helm *Sharky* as best I could.

By five in the morning I was a couple of miles off Badajeira Rock, the most eastern part of Madeira, and could hear the breaking waves and surf crashing on the rocks. Two hours later I rounded the point and entered the calm millpond conditions in the lee of the island. Tired and still with a throbbing headache, I dropped the sails and went to sleep for a few hours. By ten o'clock the warm sunshine woke me for breakfast, as I waited impatiently for a breeze to take me into Funchal, now only eight miles away. There was a sudden bump at the front of the boat. Rushing forwards, I spotted a dazed turtle erratically swimming away, the daft thing had run into *Sharky*.

The breeze I had waited for duly arrived mid-afternoon, so, upping sail, I plodded slowly towards Funchal, at no more than two knots. By seven o'clock the wind died once more and I made preparations for another night on board. Taking down the sail, I heard astern the approaching 'phut-phut' of a fishing boat and had the glimmer of a bright idea. Rummaging in the cabin, I found my bottle of unopened emergency Scotch, so grabbing a length of rope I rushed back on deck, held them aloft and gesticulated to the fisherman. Without hesitation he got the message and within half an hour I was tying up in the harbour. The fisherman was delighted with his gift. I was delighted at the prospect of a decent bed, shower, a cold beer and meeting up with Simon. A quick phone call home to let my family know I was safe also confirmed where he was staying on the island. I made my way to the hotel and found him relaxing in the lounge. It was good to end the first part of this leg with a friend, and he was keenly interested in my journey.

That night was spent in non-stop chatter as I recounted my tales. Although the sail had only been ten days in length, I felt I had made a number of voyages. I'd re-found my confidence in sailing and confirmed my determination to cross the Atlantic. I knew I had the ability to sail solo for a lengthy period and could cope with the conditions I had encountered. I had sufficient strength of character and determination to keep me going in hazardous and trying circumstances. What pleased me more than anything though was an affirmation of a core appreciation that had been with me since very early in my life. Whether on land or at sea, but especially at sea, I could still admire and wonder at the beauty of the natural world. I had thought many times about the reasons why I wanted to sail the Atlantic, what my true motives were, what I hoped to gain from the experience. The last few days and especially that one magical night had convinced me I was doing it for the right reasons. I wasn't doing it for glory or self-aggrandisement. I wasn't doing it for other people. True, I wanted to attempt it as a serious personal challenge, but overriding all was a very simple, ridiculously simple, reason. I loved the environment of the sea, its changing hues and moods, to the point where I just wanted to be part of it.

CHAPTER TEN

Going Bananas

Now fully awake, I was astounded at what I found. I almost pinched myself to see if I was hallucinating, but the scene was live enough.

MADEIRA IN JUNE WAS a beautiful green island, bedecked with flowers and bursting with life. From the harbour and marina looking inland the capital Funchal spread wide across the natural amphitheatre of wooded hills and scrabbled up towards the dizzy rim beyond. Towering above the residential limits, the mountaintops of the island's occasionally snow-capped hinterland peeked through. The Picos das Torres and its lofty sisters stood guard at 1,800 metres or so, and I found them an intriguing backcloth to the large, busy harbour at their feet. Boats of all sizes were littered across the water, most several times larger than *Sharky* who, as ever, failed to be intimidated by her neighbours. My boat had proved her worth far more than these floating hotels and looked every inch a seasoned traveller. From the shoreline promenades, luxurious gardens, trees and small cafés stretched along Funchal's waterfront, and above the traffic noise of the busy and impressively named Avenida do Mar e Comunidades carriageway, you heard the mournful siren of the regular ferry to Porto Santo some seventy-five kilometres away.

Simon had already been on the island for five days or so and had done his tourist exploration bit, so he was content to laze away the days by his hotel pool. I was pretty knackered after my sail but, having been cooped up in a confined space, revelled in the chance to explore this fascinating island. I started with Funchal and rapidly discovered that its initial beauty was more than skin-deep. From the Avenida, wide roads and narrow streets furrowed straight up the hills and into the mountains beyond, regularly criss-crossed by tiny lanes crammed with an impossible number of cars, lorries and motorbikes. As I strolled ever upwards, I was drawn to the heady scent of perfumed exotic flowers suffusing the usual urban sprawl. Running down the centre of the largest roads were carved deep gullies to funnel the winter rains and melt-water. Stretching over these cavernous channels, fine wire mesh trapped thick masses of bougainvillea that, seen from afar, resembled huge purple snakes winding their way through the streets. The capital was awash with tropical flowers I'd never seen before, minuscule gardens jammed ridiculously into tiny spaces, imposing churchyards with immaculate flowerbeds seemed to assert themselves at every corner, while, higher up still, the tropical lushness of the Jardim Botanico cast its floral eye over the town far below.

I resolved to experience the thrill of the levada walks, of which there were several, leading from different parts of Funchal. Working my way up to the football stadium, I discovered the end of a small concrete channel, half-filled with softly flowing water, no wider than eighteen inches or so with a walking surface about a foot wide on either side. This was the levada, a centuries-old water channel that meandered down through the contours to bring water from the hills to irrigate the lower fields. Clearly a sense of balance was required on the narrow ledge, so I set off, a little hesitatingly at first, while my mind and eye adapted to the narrowness of the footway. The channel traversed the hillside, working its way through banana plantations, with people's gardens giving me an unusual view down to the sea. I was climbing upwards and after an hour or so the agricultural vistas abruptly stopped. Turning a corner, I was now in true mountain country, with vast drops from steep rugged cliffs intersected by spectacular waterfalls. The silence was overwhelming and I took time to absorb the scenic splendour before continuing my journey. At frequent points the levada simply clung to sheer cliff walls, seemingly defying gravity itself, and it took nerve to walk along the thin platform for several yards while trying to ignore the several-hundred-foot drop to the valley below. Eventually I found the source of the channel where it took water from the hills, and sat for a long time staring at the mountains and reflecting on the twists and turns that had brought me to this spot. Rested and with an inner contentment, I returned along the same route with a firm timetable in mind, two days of preparing *Sharky*, and for that matter preparing Simon, then we would set sail for Tenerife.

Simon was a bit of a curry fanatic and considered himself an authority on the subject. While I busied myself with the mundane tasks of replenishing supplies, fresh food and water, Simon scoured the street markets for curry powder and the aromatic spices that he assured me would enable him to cook the best meal I had ever had. That evening as we were generally tidying up we had what was by now the regular call from Freddie. 'Coming over for some gammon then?' Freddie was our newfound neighbour on his boat *Sunset Touch*, a graceful thirty-six-footer with a gleaming wooden deck. Freddie was one of those archetypal larger-than-life blokes who seem to inhabit every port anywhere in the world. Mid-forties and looking every inch a rugged streetwise bruiser, Freddie had sold his London nightclub in search of a simpler life at sea, but after several years or so was running out of money and running into boredom. Speaking with a slurred lisp acquired from having his jaw broken a few times, he enjoyed teasing and winding people up, so he and Simon hit it off straightaway, each trying to outdo the other with tall stories and practical jokes. He was a very competitive character and loved to indulge in his favourite game of backgammon, something we thought we were quite good at as well. For a few evenings now, we had been invited over to his boat for games, good company and what seemed like an inexhaustible amount of beer and sweet Madeiran wine. After the rigours of the sail from Baiona these near perfect evenings of hospitality, companionship and bonhomie, set against the backdrop of an island bathed in the setting sun, were accumulating more treasured memories that I knew would stay with me forever. In the dazed pleasure of alcoholic conviviality I occasionally and guiltily thought of Elaine and family in that detached but well-intentioned way that men do when far from home. I was missing them of course, but, heck, I was glad I wasn't missing these evenings either. Way past midnight we would carefully effect the exaggerated stagger back to *Sharky*, knowing that dry mouths and sore heads would be our morning fate, but caring little for the ill-feeling to come. Life was good again but Tenerife beckoned and I knew we would soon have to leave this bit of paradise behind. The last evening before our departure saw us yet again on the *Sunset Touch* as Freddie plied us with more beers. I'd noticed that Simon was beginning to show signs of anxiety as the time for sailing approached, and I think that Freddie sensed this as well.

'Simon,' he said in his inimitable cockney twang, 'I've sailed this boat for a few years now and I've been across the Atlantic four times, let me give you some advice just in case you have a bit of bother.'

Simon edged forward in his seat while affecting an 'I'm cool' manner.

'Simon,' continued Freddie, 'if you get to the point where the boat starts sinking, get some black trousers on quick and flap about like a seal. Don't shout and scream because there's no one about to hear you, just bark like a seal.'

Simon for once fell for the line and asked in all seriousness why he should do that.

''Cos sharks eat seals and it's a quicker way to die than hanging about waiting to drown!' guffawed Freddie, throwing his arms wide in self-congratulatory triumph.

The joke set the pattern for a last great night and it was with much reluctance and affection that we said our final goodbyes. As we made our way back to *Sharky* all we could hear in the darkness was the sound of Freddie barking like a seal amid peals of laughter.

With furry tongues much in evidence the next morning, we popped into Funchal for large quantities of black coffee and a chance to wake up the sober side of our brains. It took until lunchtime to decide we would go and, as luck would have it, I found another yacht departing for Tenerife at about the same time. The owner readily agreed to tow us out for a few miles off the coast, so Freddie, now up and about, undid our mooring lines and passed them over as we pulled away. I turned and waved at the people on the nearby boats with mixed feelings. It felt as though I was leaving an exotic film set, knowing I would never see these friends again. A brief pang of genuine regret gave way to the excitement of new adventure. I gave the thumbs-up to the receding figure of Freddie and turned forward to sort out the sails.

Within thirty minutes I could see a gentle breeze was starting to ripple the water and decided we could now get underway. A shout of thanks to the yacht-owner and he slipped my towline and pulled rapidly away. I hoisted the mainsail and working jib as we crawled south at barely two knots, initially on a heading for the uninhabited island of Selvages. I quite fancied a night ashore on a deserted, if not desert island, but rumours of giant spiders confirmed our decision to continue. For a couple of hours we drifted with the wind until, clear of the island's influence, it increased to around fifteen knots. I set Maurice up, put a reef in the mainsail and settled down for the first night. We chatted away inconsequentially as I let Simon adjust to his new cramped (and moving) surroundings, noting that his earlier anxieties were being overcome with the novelty and excitement of it all. As darkness fell I suggested we took three-hour watches in turn, with Simon taking the first until midnight. Buoyed up on adrenalin, he readily agreed, so I retired to my bunk and fell soundly asleep. All too soon I was wakened and reluctantly took my turn, clipping on my harness still half-asleep. The wind had picked up slightly and we were skipping along steadily. Simon enthusiastically described how he'd seen two ships and worked out their direction by their lights, but I showed little interest. As he went below I said I'd wake him at three, all the time yawning and wishing I was still in my bag. As I hunched into my helming position, *Sharky* began to take some spray and quite soon the decks were wet. Despite the discomfort I quickly slipped into a deep sleep, and the next thing I knew I was being roughly shaken awake by Simon at 4.30 in the morning.

'Just nodded off, mate,' I muttered, but I could tell he didn't believe me.

'Bollocks,' he replied, 'you were fast off.' I doubt he had a good night's sleep for the rest of the trip, eternally wondering whether his confidence in my seamanship had been ill-judged.

The next day was just perfect – sunny, a slow north-easterly wind and an amiable day spent gazing and lazing, interspersed with chats, meals and endless drinks of tea. Simon was adapting really well, had had no sea-sickness, and other than concerns about my ability to keep watch was feeling very relaxed. I decided to put him to the ultimate test. Could he cook an excellent curry as he had promised? Within a few minutes, the smell of chopped sautéed onions and garlic wafted through the open hatch, followed by a rich amalgamation of spices, which tantalised my taste buds mercilessly. At long last, Simon emerged from the cabin, a white towel turbaned round his head, jabbering in mock Indian dialect and carrying my largest cooking pot laden with a fantastic tuna vindaloo. We ate our fill, then some more, still leaving enough curry for another meal. Replete in body and mind, we returned to the chore of sunbathing and congenial banter. Sun, sea and sky were coloured to perfection. It was one of those days when it was pure joy to be at sea.

That evening, as the sun dipped low to starboard I had the deck to myself. Simon had gone below to escape the earlier heat and was dozing in his bunk. I was in a reverie, thinking a lot about nothing much, just reflecting on the day past, my eyes half-shut in contemplation, and to shield them from the now dimming glare off the sea. Suddenly I was conscious of a slight slowing down and a series of muffled bumps coming from the bow. Now fully awake I was astounded at what I found. I almost pinched myself to see if I was hallucinating, but the scene was live enough.

'Simon,' I called down. 'Fancy a snack?'

Wondering whether I'd totally flipped he scrambled up on deck and burst out laughing at the bizarre sight. For several dozen yards we were completely surrounded by empty box crates and thousands of floating bananas. We'd sailed into a nautical plantation presumably ditched by a passing freighter. The scene was so unexpected that we could do nothing but gaze at the green and yellow vista with incredulity. Eventually, pragmatic as ever, Simon grabbed the boathook and began to haul the jetsam aboard, tentatively sampling the fruit. Between us we hauled in several bunches, keeping the ripe ones but discarding the majority, which had gone soft and were beginning to split. For several minutes we ploughed through this Pythonesque seascape, bewildered and amused, then, as suddenly as they had appeared, the yellow carpet slid past our stern and we were back in clear water as if nothing had happened. So entranced were we by this odd occurrence we completely forgot to take any photos, but any time I eat a banana nowadays I still expect to taste that enduring flavour of saltwater.

The sailing over the next few days was nigh-on perfect, and while I still held a preference for solo journeys, Simon's companionship was good and he respected the times I needed solitude. He'd also completely relaxed into the voyage and proved himself quite competent at the helm, though as I did point out to him, it was easy to be a fair-weather sailor. Once he'd resisted the temptation to lean over the side of the boat in brisk winds, as his dinghy experience had required, he quickly got the hang of *Sharky*. Much to my secret delight he always referred to her by name, a small but not unnoticed habit that got my full approval. The one dark cloud that hung over this part of the trip was a sense that I wasn't feeling one hundred per cent. As we had been leaving Funchal the hatch had jammed and without thinking I'd slammed it with my open palm to free it. In so doing I caught a sharp brass catch, which drove into my hand like a red-hot needle. Although the pain was momentarily intense and Simon had suggested stitches there was no way I was going to delay the departure, having been offered a free tow. I dipped my hand in the sea until the pain reduced to a dull throb, then wrapped my hand in a bandage and swallowed a couple of painkillers. At sea I first wondered whether it was some sort of infection that was making me a bit unwell, but going for a pee one night the pain of passing water was so excruciating that I nearly passed out. Clearly there was a bigger problem than a throbbing hand, and I was sure I had passed a small lump along with my urine. Fortunately the weather was holding fair but my anxiety increased as I felt myself becoming progressively weaker as each day went by.

The weather continued to stay fine with long sunny days, the wind maintaining a steady force two with occasional dips, when *Sharky* was all but becalmed, a situation that did not sit easily with Simon, as he relished the exhilaration of speed and spray. We frequently spotted dolphins and whales cutting through the watery vastness, excitedly pointing them out as they were sighted. This was the sort of sailing that any seafarer would give his right hand for and the drab routine of shop life remained banished from my mind. It was a life I wished could go on forever, a true freedom to roam without constraint or barriers. The sea was my world and I was content for it to be my master. The words of John Masefield's 'Sea Fever' seemed appropriate and I wondered whether he had felt the same passion when penning those immortal words, 'And all I ask is a tall ship and a star to steer her by'. I hadn't got a tall ship but I knew what he meant. My restless spirit had found its home again, not an acre of land or a building, but space. Far horizons and a seascape I had no wish or ability to conquer, but space without limitations, save those I placed on myself. I was master, not of my surroundings, but of my destiny, and I ached with the pleasure of that thought. I tried to encapsulate my feelings in one word but I hadn't the extensive vocabulary to find one fancy enough. In the end I settled for 'good'. Simple, ubiquitous, uncomplicated. With a fair wind in my sails, a faint spray playing over my face, the hiss of water against the hull and nothing else in sight, I just felt good about life, about myself, and my ability to direct my future. I must have had a right dopey look on my face because Simon called over to me.

'You all right, mate?'

I replied softly, 'Yeah, just lost.'

A look of alarm crossed his face. 'You mean you don't know where we are?'

I grinned back. 'Don't worry, just lost in my thoughts.'

Four days out of Madeira and we spotted the island of Palma, the most westerly of the Canaries. Perhaps sensing a berth, *Sharky* picked up her skirts and we fair skipped towards Tenerife at four knots. Before long the cloud-topped bulk of Mount Teide swept up on the horizon, giving Simon a further excuse to take photos.

The wind increased throughout the afternoon and by dusk I had thoughts about putting a reef in the sail. My pilot books had made mention of a phenomenon called the acceleration zones, so I reefed the mainsail and changed down to a storm jib. These zones are areas of sea affected by winds being squeezed between mountainous landmasses, in this case the Canaries. The wind funnels between the islands and the resultant compression brings gusts to the usually quiet leeward side. I was glad I had made adjustments to the sails as the air blasted over us at about six o'clock that evening. Simon took on a worried look and instinctively leant his body over the high side to counter the heeling. A sharp word from me to 'get yer arse back in' had the desired effect as I disconnected Maurice and took command of the helm, until, confidence restored, Simon took over and we zinged along into the lee of Punta Teno and Tenerife. Out of the zones the wind died completely as we entered a flat calm – a strange and almost instantaneous transition. Our destination of Los Gigantes, down the west coast, was still several frustrating miles away, and we spent a long night just bobbing around with little headway made.

By dawn and the promise of another hot, cloudless day we were still around eight miles away, so we dropped the sails, made breakfast and accepted that with no other boats in sight from which to beg a tow, we might as well become temporary tourists and admire the spectacular mountains and cliff scenery endemic to the northwest coast. By noon we were still becalmed, so Simon took to making a set of oars from the boathook and some scraps of wood from an old hatch board. Frustration makes fools of us all and we passed the afternoon sweatily rowing to achieve about half a knot per hour. About half-past eight that evening, desperate for landfall, a shower and a cool beer, I at last spotted a fishing boat motoring in. I hailed it over and we were rewarded by a friendly tow to Los Gigantes. My feeling of illness and weakness still hadn't gone away and I reckoned I ought to see a doctor, but the pressing priority was a hotel, a shower and some beers. That evening in a quiet bar we bumped into the two fishermen who had towed us in and, much to their delight, we stood their drinks all night.

By morning I was distinctly poorly and Simon insisted we find a doctor. Having a pee was still excruciating and I passed another small lump. My back was painful and I had stomach pains as well. By early afternoon we'd found a medical centre and I was given a thorough examination, which confirmed I had a kidney infection and had been passing small stones or parts of a larger one. Three injections followed by a prescription for heaven knows what and I spent the evening feeling much better but rattling with pills of all sorts, colours and sizes. I was delighted and relieved that the worst was over and full of praise for the Canarian medical service.

Restored to reasonable health, I had three priorities: sort *Sharky* out after her crossing, find a place to lay her up for the winter, and enjoy a short break on Tenerife before flying back home and the reality of earning a living. Simon and I gutted the boat's contents, cleaned, polished, made good and returned everything to its rightful place. When sailing in a small boat there is no time for housekeeping niceties, and it only takes a few days, a few hours even, before the cabin resembles a rubbish dump. It wasn't simply about being careless or uncaring about items. We often attempted to tidy up when the demands of sailing lessened, but often there is no time or will to be boat proud. Conditions on *Sharky* were comparable to a student flat. All students aren't necessarily untidy, they just leave or locate items in places different to the accepted norm. The floor becomes a wardrobe, the sink a shelf for pots and plates. Life on a small boat is similar. Items get put in convenient, not necessarily correct places, damp clothing is either worn or slung in a corner. Neither Simon nor I was congenitally untidy, it was just that conditions dictated custom and necessity dictated niches. Satisfied with our housework we hired a car and toured the island's coast and hinterland, visiting isolated villages and walking some of the mountain trails.

The national park of Teide was a fascinating region of deep ravines, pine forest and black and ochre-red lava, wind-sculpted into remarkable statuesque shapes. It resembled a stark moonscape, and I heard that the NASA space mission had tested out their moon buggies in the area. Teide was frequently encircled by a band of clouds just below its peak, through which we had to drive to reach the summit. Once through the cloud cover we would enter a desert world sweltering under a cloudless sky, eerily quiet, apart from the cries and shrieks of over-excited tourists. Back on the coast Los Gigantes was now in its death throes as a small, quaint fishing village. At the base of huge 500-metre vertical cliffs, and despite a fairly unattractive shingle beach, the once tiny community was being urbanised with all the rapacity that timeshares, holiday companies and local developers could muster. Cheap tack shops, 'genuine' English bars and gross hotels that wouldn't have looked out of place in Blackpool now scrimmaged for holidaymakers' money in a frenzy of neon and trashy frontage. Fishing boats were ousted by increasing numbers of pleasure craft, and I found it quite sad that the Tenerife authorities hadn't learnt the lessons of the appalling Playa de las Americas several miles further south. Nevertheless there were still a few isolated havens to discover once the beaten track was left behind.

It was now imperative to find a winter berth for *Sharky* before our flight home. We drove down the western coast, isolated and austere, before the blighted las Americas hove into view. Eventually we settled on San Juan, a proper fishing village about ten miles south of Los Gigantes and in halting Spanish I negotiated a deal to lift *Sharky* from the water for her winter sojourn. Away from the tourist traps the locals were inquisitive and friendly, no more so than a huge six-foot-four, 300-pound monster, complete with Mexican-style moustache and sombrero. Ramon was the crane driver.

He said, 'Bring her here in two days. You understand? Two days.'

I got the feeling that perhaps we should do exactly as he said. There was still little wind and I daren't take the chance of trusting to the weather to get up a blow, so I arranged to borrow an outboard for a few hours and we motored sedately into San Juan, where we were met by the friendly locals. Ramon was ready with his crane and before long *Sharky* was being lifted ungainly out of the water and into dry dock. Simon and I took some time to wash and scrub her hull and superstructure, then checking everything was in order we left *Sharky* to her slumbers. I patted her hull affectionately as I left.

'It's the big one for you and me next time we meet,' I whispered, shivers of anticipation and fear playing down my back. We'd timed our lay-up to allow us another couple of days to laze around, play backgammon and discover more of Tenerife's natural wonders. As the countdown to the return flight ticked away, I reflected on a month's superb experience. True, the weather had helped enormously and I was glad that the sailing relationship with Simon had endured without friction. He hadn't been tested like Chris but he'd pulled his weight and had achieved his ambition to undertake an ocean sail without the need to prove himself further. It was an interesting distinction between us. He was content to have had the opportunity and now he would move back to his life and his business. I wanted to go back to pick up the relationship with my girl but I didn't relish continuing to run the shop with any degree of enthusiasm. The year's delay for the second leg hadn't dented my eagerness to complete the final stage. I knew I was happiest when at sea but another long bout of frustration was looming, as once again I needed to save more money and keep the business going. My mood at the airport was one of anticipation at going home tinged with the inevitable sadness of leaving my boat behind yet again. This time around however wasn't as traumatic as in Baiona, and I didn't experience the deep sadness of the year before. This time the distant ambition of sailing west was not quite as far away. My ultimate dream was getting closer to becoming reality with every passing day. The chance to live my dream was tantalisingly still on course.

CHAPTER ELEVEN

Freedom at Last

*I kept returning to Kahlil Gibran and thought that for me freedom
was indeed that fusion of reason and passion intertwined with focused
hard work. There was no universal definition-each of us
must define it for ourselves.*

BACK HOME THE BUSINESS seemed to have been thriving
without me and, despite my growing doubts as to whether running
a shop was what I wanted to do with my life, I nevertheless threw
my energies into making it a going concern. It didn't help that I'd
returned in summer when I would really have preferred to be out
on my boat. Every time I went up and down the stairs to my flat, I
involuntarily glanced out of the landing window, expecting to see
Sharky's mast leading down to her deck. I couldn't help it, just a
habit that never left me. Occasionally I'd stop and look out, mainly
when it turned rainy or drizzly, and cast my thoughts back to San
Juan, wondering if my boat was missing me as much as I her. Meeting
up with Simon each week gave us both an opportunity to re-live
our adventures, and it helped keep my dream alive. I wanted to get
on with the next leg as quickly as I could, but work was pressing
and I was desperately short of cash, to the point where I really couldn't
forecast when I'd next be able to confirm a long break away. As

summer faded into autumn, itself eroding into the winter chill, I kept my spirits up, helped enormously by memories of the sail to Tenerife. This time I felt no deep depression at being away from *Sharky*, just a healthy wistfulness tempered by the thought that one day, one day I would be back in Tenerife, on my own and ready to cast off. And on that day I'd look back to now and know that all the effort, the waiting and the cost would have been worth it.

January is a strange month. Not just cold and dark but held in the strangled grip of superstition. A time for new beginnings, the subtle and not so subtle urgings to start afresh, reinvigorate the thoughts of pastures new, stir from the doldrums of post-Christmas and start once more. It's a month of resolutions stemming from old Pagan rituals that modern man seems reluctant or unable to leave behind. I don't think I actually sat up on New Year's Day and thought 'I need a life-changing decision' but time for reflection on my sailing trips had filtered my mind towards the prospect of selling the business and doing something else. Interestingly, I didn't feel fazed by these thoughts. I trusted my judgement that I'd be able to cope with the impact of any change and that I'd instinctively know when the right opportunity arose. I can't claim to have been supremely confident or arrogant enough to think everything would go well. It was just another quiet little thought tickling through my mind, a sensing of change rather than a dramatic resolution. Was it media and social clamour to think afresh, the result of introspective musings at sea or just a general restlessness attributed to age and the work I was doing? I don't think I was too bothered about analysis, I'd manage the situation if and when it arose.

In truth though, I was working what seemed like twenty-four/seven. Not only was I managing and running the shop but I'd taken to acting as a wholesaler for other similar shops in the area, trying as ever to squeeze a little more profit from my working hours. I'd also been involved in a couple of sideline businesses trying to develop a paint-balling market. The result? Constantly knackered, constantly over-extended and always anxious about money, to the point where my leisure was non-existent. I began to notice I was allowing my frustrations to show, becoming irritable, grumpy, tense and rebellious.

I used to catch the odd moment or two from *Coronation Street* and think, 'I'll be like that one day, just a moaning, grumbling old Alf Roberts wallowing in misery.' *Sharky* seemed further away than ever before and I started to fret that all the time and money I'd spent on her and learning to sail had just been frittered away together with my receding opportunities for an epic voyage. I felt like a caged and shackled wild animal, my horizons unattainable through the bars that confined my frenetic existence. One late evening, after I'd finally seen the last customer from the shop, I phoned Mum for a quick chat. I was just going through the figures and staff rotas when she suddenly interrupted me, tiredness erupting through her voice.

'David, I really don't know how long I can keep going like this,' she said.

Without any thought I replied, 'Okay, Mum, how about you retire and I'll try to sell the shop?'

From that casual aside I spotted my opportunity to move on, with no real plan, just a foolish notion that I'd sell the shop and get a regular job with enough holiday time to get back to sailing. Perhaps I'd found a way to loosen the shackles.

It took all of spring and summer to sell the shop, endless let-downs, countless promises broken, but finally in August 1994 I signed the sale agreement, handed over the keys and walked away. I didn't feel elated or unfettered, just numb. The big sigh of relief I was expecting failed to materialise. Instead it was replaced by an anxiety that actually I had no idea what I was going to do. I had no plans and no income. I'd grabbed at the last offer to sell because I didn't want to lose out yet again. I remember walking away from the solicitor's office and suddenly realising that I was a changed man. For the past eight years I'd lived and worked among friends, customers, trading partners, sales reps, suppliers and deliverymen. They'd been the fixtures and fittings integrated into my life, but now they had gone, or rather I had gone. I hadn't just got rid of a shop and the flat that had been my home, I'd walked away from a life I'd thought would be there forever. The people I'd surrounded myself with were now just fading ghosts with no part in my future. No longer was I Dave the shopkeeper, I was just Dave, unemployed, homeless, financially bereft and increasingly apprehensive, locked outside of what I'd regarded as my cage and wondering whether the big wide world was actually just another rather larger one.

Two months of disquiet and regret followed as I lost myself in a haze of uncharacteristic vagueness, drifting aimlessly in a current of ambiguity and insecurity, while the finances continued to tighten. Finally I found a job, based in Chesterfield, but working in York. I took it because of my experience with the shop. I was now Dave the Retail Trainer, working with young people to improve their chances in the business world. Solid nine-to-five work. No lifting, shifting or being the boss. I started my new life with recharged batteries, keen to learn with fewer responsibilities on my shoulders, hoping I could now find the time to resurrect my ambition.

> Your reason and your passion are the rudders and the sails of your seafaring mind. If either your sail or your rudder be broken you can but toss and drift or else be held at standstill in mid-seas. For reason, ruling alone, is a force confining, and passion, unattended, is a flame that burns to its own destination. Therefore let your soul exalt your reason to the height of passion…and let it direct your passion with reason.

These words were written in 1883 by Kahlil Gibran, the Lebanese poet who'd died in the early twentieth century. They'd been given to me by Maurice a few years earlier when I'd been at another set of crossroads in my life. I was several weeks into my trainer job and by strange coincidence I'd found the scrap of paper tucked away in a book I'd been reading. Their profundity hit me like a punch in the stomach and I felt a real shiver of discovery. The trainer job was, well, okay, but it was routine, non-challenging stuff. The earlier enthusiasm was waning and always in my head was the fact that it was getting on for eighteen months since I'd last sailed, had last seen *Sharky*, endless months without the uncertain thrill of a wild sea and salt in the wind. I read the text again and something welled up in my heart and mind. I felt like a dormant volcano, thrusting against huge forces, desperate to break through the weakest chink and release the massive forces that I'd held in check for so long. Reason and passion: for so long I'd held them at arms' length, distanced and separated from each other for very valid reasons, but now I had no real need to continue in this way. Now I had no real responsibilities other than to myself. Perhaps now I could dare to dream, dare to take that one final step towards my ultimate freedom. Dare to give up everything for the chance to sail across the Atlantic at last. Reading Gibran's words was like being launched down a slipway. With growing confidence I realised that now was the right time for me to break with convention and to hell with the consequences. While short of cash I reckoned I had enough to fly to Tenerife, get my harbour fees paid and have just a few hundred pounds left for supplies and possible repairs. Once in the Caribbean I would have no money, no income and no job to return to. Elaine was working and I was sure she'd bail me out if necessary. I'd miss her like hell but I knew that this was now my time. All my instincts screamed, 'Just go! Don't think about it anymore, take the calculated risk, just go!' So I did. I handed in my notice a few weeks before Christmas and feverishly set about studying charts, buying supplies and gear. Although it meant sailing from Tenerife rather later than most people had advised I wanted a decent Christmas at home with my family. I just wanted a good relaxed Christmas, the first for eight years without having to open up a damn shop!

The end of January saw me staggering into Newcastle Airport laden with luggage of every shape, size and hue. Maurice had again done the decent thing and accompanied me to the airport. His reward the first time he'd helped out was self-steering gear named after him. This time I gave him my car. Again I'd got far too much luggage, so playing the cheeky-chappie routine I attempted the charm offensive at the check-in desk. Smiles, pleadings, despondent looks and offers of cash-in-hand achieved nothing but a severe and definite negative. The excess baggage fee of £90 was more than the cost of my ticket and I spent the whole flight down to the Canaries fuming at the unfairness of it all, convinced that the check-in woman had vented her spite by allocating me a cramped seat next to the aircraft toilet.

It didn't help that the flight went via Faro, thereby adding several hours to the journey, nor was I pleased to be surrounded by manic, deliriously happy tourists who I would happily have despatched from the cabin in mid-air. To add insult to near-injury the landing at Faro was aborted at the last minute. Just into touchdown the pilot threw on full power and we shot off into the blue again at stomach-wrenching speed. At least it stopped the bloody tourists from their screeching inane chatter.

Leaving my fellow-passengers to the mercy of tour reps and sunburn I grabbed a taxi to San Juan and at last began to relax. It felt unreal. I hadn't seen *Sharky* for ages and as we approached the fishing port my apprehension increased. I wondered if I was truly mad. I hadn't sailed in all that time and was now contemplating sailing off for a journey that would take around forty days and cover about 3,000 miles, assuming of course I'd have good conditions and that *Sharky* would still be where I'd left her. The taxi drove into the harbour area and I hurriedly grabbed my possessions, all the while scanning the hard-standing yard where I'd last left her. To my great relief she was still there, a little faded and a bit grubby but indisputably still my boat. It was a strange meeting. I couldn't quite get the emotions in check. Had it really been such a long while since I'd left her? Seeing her this time also felt different. I knew I was on the verge of a significant challenge. I'd given up a business, a job and income just to achieve a frail ambition, but they didn't matter. They were as insignificant as yesterday. In the warm sunshine of San Juan I reunited myself with *Sharky* in mind and body. A feeling of utter freedom and release overwhelmed me as I dumped my gear into the still clean and dry cabin. I sat relaxed on the bunk remembering all the incidents and accidents that had filled this tiny space since I'd bought her. And now it was my kingdom again, population of one, just as I'd always wanted it. I was alone, not lonely, free of cares and wanting the feeling to last forever.

Having made my peace with *Sharky*, I went across the harbour with an overnight bag to find a cheap place for a good night's sleep. I found the ideal accommodation a stone's throw away, a simple clean room where I showered then went out in search of something to eat. The last time I'd been here I'd found a small South American bar in the next village along the coast, run by a guy called Domingo. I recalled it as a small, grubby bar but welcoming with excellent cheap food, a place in which tourists could feel intimidated, fearing rejection at their intrusion into a place for the locals. I was hungry, didn't regard myself as a tourist, so thought it might be an ideal place to rekindle the mysteries of the Spanish language. Nothing had changed. I wandered in as if I'd been there the day before. It was still grubby, still welcoming and still cheap. The first thing Domingo said, as indeed he always seemed to say to everyone was, 'Tienes hambre [are you hungry]?' I nodded, my mouth salivating at what was to come. There was no menu at Domingo's. You said you wanted to eat so he'd start cooking, never asking what you wanted. Plates of food kept arriving and pretty soon I was surrounded by deep-fried beef and cheese pancakes, banana pie, fried cheese, grilled fish and a whole host of delicacies that I couldn't recognise but which tasted delicious. This was real Spain, a thousand taste buds from the sanitised 'chips with everything' that passed as tourist fodder. My Spanish was halting as I tried to converse with the bar crowd but I was rewarded by genuine interest and hospitality.

As a boy growing up in Ajman I'd acquired the confidence and the curiosity to wander off the trodden path and discover real life away from that presented to transient visitors: I was now reaping the benefits of that upbringing, something in my bearing and manner cutting through the barriers and allowing me to merge into local culture without fear or hesitation. It was an attitude I was forever rediscovering in myself, confidence bred confidence. It was something in my inner core that enabled me to cope with people and situations, the same confidence that bore the self-belief that I could sail to the Caribbean. That thought brought me up with a start. Replete with a staggeringly good meal washed down with a bottle of house wine, home-made liquors and strong black coffee, I said my goodbyes and wandered contentedly back to my room. I had work to start on *Sharky* the next day and I needed to write some lists.

San Juan nestled on the western coastline of Tenerife, against a backdrop of gently rising mountains, inexorably leading the eye to the two-and-a-half-thousand-metre Teide mountain range. A small, well kept fishing village with a long concrete breakwater protected on the ocean side by stacks of huge rocks. The long wall provided safe moorings for the fishing boats and the handful of small yachts bobbing in the calm waters. Palm trees fronded the neat promenade; altogether a delightful setting to commence the necessary preparations for my journey. I reckoned it would take me a couple of weeks or so to sort out supplies, check my gear and ensure *Sharky* was up to the trip of her life. I was keen to get to sea but regarded the preparatory phase as part of the experience. At last I was not hidebound by the need to return to England. As far as I was concerned I had all the time in the world and I was going to squeeze every last portion of enjoyment out of it. The young kid in me wanted to rush everything through in a frenzy of excitement, the wiser head wanted to savour every precious minute. I set about unpacking my gear, books and the food I'd brought, stowed them away then began to calculate the amount of water I needed to take. This was crucial. I judged that twenty of my five-litre containers would fit under the cockpit and double as ballast. A further twenty-four two-litre bottles could be stashed around the boat where convenient, while a twenty-five-litre container of tap water would serve for washing and shaving.

The next job was to overhaul the two-burner cooker, strip it down, check hoses and connections and reassemble it. That done I realised I had two small empty gas bottles, which needed to be refilled at the gas factory at the north of the island – another task to be added to my list. I sweated in the hot cabin confines until dusk dictated a return to my room for a shower and a relaxing read. Refreshed, I was drawn to Domingo's again for more excellent food and company. I shared the bar with Alan, an English guy who'd made enough money to live a comfortable life painting and sculpting. He was an intelligent, well-travelled chap and I envied his attitude and approach to life, the more so after several bottles of robust red wine. A mellow if rather unstable walk back in the moonlight further highlighted my contentment and I slumped on the bed the most relaxed I had been for several months.

Each day saw further ticks at the top of my list and additional items added to the bottom, but I worked hard and was rewarded for my efforts. *Sharky* was retouched and given a new coat of anti-fouling paint, her rudder was de-greased and re-fitted, and a rotting bulkhead was patched up with fibreglass and resin. I was interrupted occasionally by interested tourists strolling through the yard, intrigued to know what I was doing and where I was going, one group asking if they might take my photo as they'd heard about the Englishman who had sailed from the UK. Clearly San Juan was in need of a very minor celebrity! A couple of guys even asked me if I wanted to sell *Sharky*, and got a very short, albeit polite response. The long sunshine days were some of the most enjoyable I have known, industrious, concentrated, purposeful work interspersed with coffee breaks and the chance to daydream of the journey that was nearing with every passing moment. I thought a lot about freedom, what it meant, how to capture it, how to define it. I kept returning to Kahlil Gibran and thought that for me freedom was indeed that fusion of reason and passion intertwined with focused hard work. There was no universal definition – each of us must define it for ourselves.

A few days into my preparations I met up with an English couple, Viv and Liz, who were giving their forty-foot boat a major overhaul following a sailing accident that had damaged their rudder. They'd been there about six months earning money by Viv playing guitar in the many bars dotted along the coast. Not only were they a delightful couple, they also had a van at their disposal and readily offered to help fetch the things I needed, including my major supplies from the supermarket. Yet again, as so often has happened to me, I was struck by the kindness and generosity of strangers. It reinforced the notion that there is a basic goodness in all humanity, which rarely makes headlines. For once I gave Domingo's a miss and sat with Liz as we listened to Viv play his gig in a local bar.

As the work on *Sharky* moved on apace, I began to experience dreams of huge breaking waves and churning seas, and, waking in the night feeling increasingly nervous about what I was attempting to do. The small, dark hours of the morning pressed upon my fears and tested my self-belief. The time for realising my journey was fast approaching and I'd still not sailed *Sharky* to assess my own seaworthiness. By breakfast time those fears had subsided and I'd regained much of my confidence but began to dread waking in the night, unable to settle, knowing that I was now on the edge of the precipice of my commitment. Within a couple of days, the enveloping comfort of San Juan would be behind me as I faced the biggest challenge of my life. Confidence ebbed and flowed as the tide but I knew I was going anyway, stubbornness and determination remained steadfast as other feelings waxed and waned. I wrote in my diary, 'I have decided to go on Thursday 9th February. I'm frightened and excited, the adrenalin is pumping now. Ready or not I'm going on the biggest adventure I've ever wanted to have. Here's to Antigua!'

Just days to cast off and I was fixing a new cleat when a hand tapped my shoulder. Turning, I was startled to see Simon, rucksack in one hand, backgammon board in the other, grinning like a child who'd played a huge practical joke.

'Simon,' I gasped, 'where the hell did you come from?'

'Got a three-day return flight,' he smiled. 'Couldn't let you loose without saying goodbye in person. Besides,' he added darkly, 'I might not see you alive again.'

That last remark warranted a thump on his arm, which he duly received, then it was off to the bar to celebrate his arrival. I was really chuffed that Simon had taken the time to fly over, a generous act I genuinely appreciated. After a bite to eat, he rolled up his sleeves and set to work on *Sharky*, which meant that by the middle of the next day I had completed all the work that needed doing. Simon then hired a car and we shot off to refill the gas bottles, followed by a rewarding drive round the island. His short visit was soon over and we said our goodbyes.

'You're a lucky bugger, but take care,' he said. 'Come back safely, I still need someone I can thrash at backgammon.'

True to his word, Viv drove me to the supermarket on the morning before my departure, where I crammed food and water into two huge trolleys. Back on the boat I stowed the water, then packed the food in bags, tying them securely wherever I could. I spent a busy day keeping myself active, not wanting to think too deeply about what I was about to do. The stomach butterflies were fluttering and I recognised the familiar mix of anxiety and anticipation beginning to overcome me. I didn't rest until evening, when I headed off for a farewell drink with Viv and Liz. They were as excited for me as I was thankful to them for all their practical and positive support. Viv promised to help with lowering the boat the next day, so I made it an early night and went back to my room. I slept fitfully, unable to relax, lists and 'what if' scenarios fighting for mind space. Here were my endless concerns, nagging doubts that questioned my sanity and competence, coupled all the while with a background eagerness to get back to sea – an eagerness that battened down these pessimistic thoughts. As a cloudy light yawned into daybreak, I got up and stared out of the window at the ocean. The day I was sure was never going to come had arrived. In a few hours I would be on my way, on my own and heading west to another continent. Success or failure was now down to me, my sole responsibility just as I liked it and had always wanted it to be. The new day banished any deep doubts, leaving just a healthy trepidation, which I hoped would go once I set sail. I wandered down to the grocery shop by the harbour and picked up a couple of cases of fresh fruit, which I stowed in what little space was left in the cabin. *Sharky* was still on her keels on the hard-standing, and she looked restless as if she knew she'd been out of the water too long. I searched out Ramon, the huge Mexican who operated the Tami lift, and asked when he could lower her into the water.

'Three o'clock this afternoon, señor, and good luck,' he replied, shaking my hand. My plan was to ask Clive, a guy I'd met, to tow me with *Sharky* out to an anchorage point, then return me to the shore where I'd make my final phone calls home. I had then to row back to *Sharky* in the dinghy, complete my checks and get away. Strolling into what had become my favourite bar for a last drink with the old men of the village, I chanced upon William, a wizened, one-armed local whom I'd got to know quite well. William and the other elders seemed to spend all day sitting in the bar reflecting on their lives and watching the world go by. Every day I'd been in San Juan their presence in the harbour bar had a timeless permanence amid the bustle around them. They were comfortably locked in a time warp of their own choosing, where contentment and languid movement were the only priorities. William seemed genuinely saddened when I told him I was leaving. He shook my hand slowly then, gripping it fiercely, he looked deep into my eyes with such intensity that I was taken aback.

'Don't be foolish with your life,' he said, with such power that I wondered whether he could see my future. 'Don't be foolish with your life,' he repeated strongly, refusing to loosen my grip until I nodded my understanding.

I swallowed my drink, said my goodbyes and returned to *Sharky*, struck by the force of William's words. Was he giving me a warning?

All went well as Clive, Viv, Liz and I nervously watched *Sharky* settle into the two bright orange slings that gently lowered her into the water. The ugly duckling had turned into my beautiful swan again as she rode the sea, bobbing as if eager to be off. Once the boat was secure on the anchorage I went back to the harbour in Clive's speedboat in an increasingly heavy swell. I walked over to a public phone. It was a strange feeling, standing in the booth not really knowing what to say. The enormity of what I was starting hadn't really kicked in so I mumbled a few pleasantries, told everyone not to worry and put the receiver down, feeling oddly detached from reality. Now I was anxious to be away. Tired from the lack of sleep, the long wait to lower *Sharky* and the drain on my emotions, I wanted to draw a line under the last fortnight and settle down to the challenge of sailing. I pumped up my rapidly deteriorating dinghy and rowed out to the anchorage, struggling against a gathering northerly wind. A few moments later, I saw Viv and Liz rowing furiously towards me. Holding the two vessels together, they solemnly presented me with a wooden parrot before bursting into laughter.

'Better to talk to the parrot than yourself, Dave,' chortled Liz.

'Good luck, mate,' added Viv, 'send us a postcard from Antigua.'

Again touched by their kindness I watched them fight their way back to the calm of the harbour. I would miss their company greatly but made a mental note to ensure they got their postcard.

The wind was now very strong and I wondered about delaying my departure until it had died a little, but felt it might move to a north-easterly, which would have kept me in the lee of the island. I noticed squalls approaching, so slipped on my waterproofs then put up the mainsail with two reefs and the smaller of my working jibs. I note with quiet satisfaction that I had slipped into the routines again quite smoothly, which boosted my confidence greatly given the less than ideal conditions.

'This is it,' I said to myself. 'C'm' on, *Sharky*, let's go for a sail.' Taking a deep breath, I upped anchor and sailed out of the bay just as dusk was falling. I turned at the sound of a foghorn to see Viv and Liz waving madly from the end of the harbour wall, the last people I might see in a very long time. Now I could start the journey of a lifetime.

CHAPTER TWELVE

In a Blaze of Glory

I genuinely thought I was going to die as I clung on desperately waiting to see if she would right herself.

The wind was now gusting severely and it started to spit with rain. Even with all the weight in *Sharky*, she was sailing well, ploughing doggedly through the waves on a heading of 240 degrees and seemingly pleased to be back where she belonged. It wasn't long before I had to reef the mainsail fully and change down to the storm jib. The further I left Tenerife behind the more I began to feel the swell of the Atlantic, powerful surges that left me in no doubt as to who was in charge out here. The thrill of being in a small boat is that you are literally so close to and at one with the sea. The swells have a raw energy that is tangible and forceful, a truly living environment that is omnipresent and omnipotent. The green-grey surface wells up, twists and turns then dissipates in another direction. There is no cessation of movement, just a vast amount of fluid restlessness that obeys only the laws of nature. It is both fearful and fascinating to watch and always a timely reminder to be respectful of the sea.

As the winds increased in strength so did the waves, and a momentary thought flashed through my mind that perhaps I should have delayed my departure until the weather had improved. However, without an engine I had to take advantage of the good northerly wind in order to clear the islands. Sailing is often about seizing the moment, not waiting for something better that might come along. Too late anyway, the time had passed for fanciful thinking, and I expected to be in for a combative night. I dropped the storm jib, making a bit of a hash of it through lack of practice, crawled back to the helm and decided I would run more easily with a fully reefed mainsail. In the maelstrom that was my whole universe

I left myself in the self-steer hands of Maurice and went below to make a cup of coffee. Wedged into the cabin to offset the bucking of the waves, I flicked on the radio and tuned into the local English-speaking radio station, which made a useful change from the one I'd been regularly listening to in a tenacious attempt to improve my Spanish. I picked up a news item reporting that driving conditions on Tenerife's main motorway were becoming hazardous due to the increasing strong winds. Braced into my cabin with the cooker gimbals manfully struggling to keep my kettle upright, I gave a wry smile: they should try being out here! Drinking and spilling my coffee in equal measure, I staggered out on deck and quickly harnessed up. We were now into a real blow, the mast and rigging were whistling under the strain and *Sharky* was yawing terribly. Squally rain, salt spray and foam drove into my face like sharp pinpricks, and my eyes soon became red-raw with the stinging attacks. In the encroaching darkness all I could see was the bright glow from the masthead light, the fading glimmer of Los Cristianos and the indistinguishable fudge between sea and sky. I reckoned this was definitely going to be a long, uncomfortable and extremely wet night.

I thought back to the warm bars and good friends I'd left behind only a few hours ago, and wondered why I just couldn't have settled for an easy life instead of all this hair-raising stuff. But I wasn't complaining. I'd spent a long time waiting for this moment and still regarded myself as privileged to be where I was, master of my destiny, here by choice and, despite the appalling conditions, grittily determined to see it through. I let out a huge, crazy whoop of resolve as yet another wave crashed over the deck. There was no one in my circle of non-sailing friends who would have understood the sheer enjoyable madness of pitting myself against the elements like this, no one who could see beyond the superficial recklessness and foolhardiness no doubt seen as stupidity. It would take another adventurer to understand the deeper soul-call that had brought me to this spot, a call that combined my love of nature and the outdoor life and the challenge to my skills and determination. I saw myself as just an ordinary man, I was an ex-bloody shopkeeper for heaven's sake, but I had taken a conscious and selfish decision to set myself a personal challenge. Part of that challenge was to confront the obstacles and overcome them. Either that or I was certifiably insane as many people thought.

The fact that I was happy to be where I was did not mean I wasn't scared. The blow had turned into a full gale interspersed with occasional and violent gusts. As *Sharky* and I were slung around in the turbulent spin cycle, I had good cause to wonder whether I would see the next daybreak. Adrenalin mixed with real fear kept me alert as I tried to control the boat as best I could. I raised the storm jib again, receiving another underwater dousing as the bow dipped into the troughs flinging ice-cold water over me and through my foul-weather clothing. I dropped the mainsail and altered course slightly. With the wind coming from the north I headed southwest on a reach, taking the seas on the starboard quarter to make conditions as bearable as they could be in the circumstances. *Sharky* seemed to handle easier on the new heading but I thought it would be preferable to helm myself rather than trust to Maurice – if nothing else it would keep me busy and better able to feel the way my boat was responding.

I deliberately shut out all negative thoughts of impending peril but I was beginning to regret not having a life raft or transmitting radio. My only form of salvation if *Sharky* did flounder or break up was my next-to-useless, rapidly perishing hole-filled dinghy. On dry land I hadn't wanted the extra expense, but given the current position I wished now I'd borrowed the money and to hell with it. In the blackness of the night and the whistling of the rigging I could have sworn I heard the mocking seal bark of Freddie from Madeira.

Was that just the wind or the echoes of his black humour? 'Put your black trousers on and flap like a seal, it's a quicker way to die.'

There was no let-up in the wind, sea or squalls, and my earlier elation began to diminish. As the night progressed and I moved further into the acceleration zones, the wind gusted viciously, creating huge breakers that chased down the boat. I was now very nervous indeed, reacting more instinctively than rationally as the noise levels saturated my ears, banishing all thoughts from my mind. *Sharky* was surrounded by the boiling white-green glow of a phosphorous sea ominously waiting to claim us. Never had I felt so alone, the vastness of the empty sea chillingly apparent. Noise levels would suddenly drop and my stomach would churn from the knowledge of what was to come, a relative quiet then an almighty gathering roar as the wind powered down again swamping the decks with swathes of ice-cold waves threatening to engulf the boat. The one overriding thing I was dreading eventually happened. A huge gust of wind knocked *Sharky* broadside sending her flat, mast and boom slamming into the sea. I genuinely thought I was going to die as I clung on desperately waiting to see if she would right herself. She did, like the old warrior she was. Slowly she shook herself from the water as a dog shakes droplets from its body, and lurched somewhat ungainly to resume her journey. Once upright again I scanned the boat for damage and discovered that the gooseneck joint between boom and mast had broken and that the rudder had twisted out of true by about thirty degrees. Minutes later a rogue wave bore down on *Sharky* and I was nearly washed off the boat, panic rising as I scrambled for a firm footing, legs flailing desperately for any solid surface.

Throughout that long night the weather refused to let up. I helmed with no other respite for food or drink. I was desperate for a pee but daren't lose control of the boat for even a few minutes. In the end I just peed in my waterproofs, my groin being momentarily the only warm part of my body. Several times more *Sharky* was knocked flat to the water and each time, like a battered boxer, she sluggishly and heroically refused to accept defeat, returning to right herself and grimly slugging on. I was cold, tired, famished, miserable and soaked, and William's words came back to me. Was I being foolish with my life? Could I endure this for another forty days or so? Had I reached the dividing line between going on or giving up? It was my call. What value did I place on my life compared to the desire to achieve my ambition?

An apology for daylight embarrassingly filtered through, posing as dawn. Still the unremitting weather refused to let go, gusty winds driving me on. The plan, the ideal, was to have gone south for a couple of hundred miles before edging out in a more south-westerly direction, until I picked up the trade winds that would then carry me westward, somewhere about latitude seventeen or eighteen degrees north. I could have opted to try for more southing but given the current conditions and the damage to *Sharky* I decided it was preferable to match the boat with the sea's motion than constantly fight against it, a southwest heading not looking too bad for now. I was unable to take a noon fix as it was too rough, the only difference from the night before being that I could see what was around me, though it was still a gloomy murk. I desperately needed sleep and something to eat, but first I had to repair the gooseneck joint as best I could. Armed with thin wire and a roll of gaffer tape I clung to the mast and with wet, numb hands eventually formed a crude repair, which I hoped would last until a weather break allowed me to attend to it properly. There was little I could do with the rudder trim so I set Maurice up again and went below for what would have to pass for rest.

Try as I might I couldn't relax, couldn't sleep. Conditions were far too rough and my stomach was playing me up, either through irregular eating or just plain old anxiety getting to my nerves. Twenty-foot waves were throwing us about willy-nilly, noisily crashing over the boat, which shuddered under each impact. I felt my resolve beginning to wane, just couldn't see how I could last out if the weather didn't break soon. As the gloom of the day relinquished itself to night I eventually managed to keep down some biscuits and a little water. While I needed food I didn't want to go on deck for a crap, so stuck to the minimum intake, hoping that was the right decision. In the end sheer fatigue wore me out. I huddled my sodden sleeping bag around me, jammed myself in as secure a position I could find and just crashed out. I remember thinking back to the first time Chris had got really depressed in similar conditions and how I, in effect, had dismissed him as wimpish. If he could have seen me at that low point I think he would have levelled the same accusation with some justification. I drifted off to sleep hoping against hope that the gale would blow itself out before I woke.

I spent a fitful night racked with hunger pangs and general anxiety, in my damp clothes and with the motion of the boat. About four in the morning, after thirty-odd hours of gales, the weather eased and a bright moon flooded into the cabin. The swells were still mountainous and the temperature decidedly chilly. I blamed myself for taking the decision to leave Tenerife when I did, a mixture of deep annoyance and retrospective frustration. I should have waited for better weather, should have had a practice sail, shouldn't have been over-zealous to get away. It was made worse because I knew there was no one else to blame, which compounded my anger. Short of self-harm or chucking myself over the side, I had to sort the situation out for myself, with commonsense and self-pity vying for mastery over my thoughts. Eventually I calmed down and mentally tossed the self-pity aside. Throughout the night and the next morning I made fairly slow progress, and was still heading more west instead of the south-south-westerly I needed to get into the steady trade winds. A frustrating, though often delightful aspect of sailing is the constant search for the maritime Holy Grail, otherwise known as the perfect heading. All competent sailors know where they want to be and how to get there. Unfortunately the sea and weather are never party to this calculation and blithely go their own way, on the basis they've been around a lot longer. Sailing therefore assumes a one-sided competition between the aspiration of man and the indifferent stubbornness of the elements. Hope springs eternal in a seafarer's breast, but never in a straight line. People sail because they like the challenge of finding and keeping a perfect heading – nature just lets them get on with enjoying their delusions.

For a couple of days *Sharky* and I got much needed respite to recover and recuperate. The wind and sea both eased considerably, down to an absolute calm for a few hours. At least the calmer conditions gave me the chance to look at the emergency repairs I'd done to the gooseneck and carry out a stronger job. I was now enjoying the sailing again, revelling in the solitude, turning my head constantly to view the whole empty horizon. On the fifth day I was 230 miles southwest of Tenerife as I took the noon fix. Big rolling swells appeared from nowhere, and, with the accompanying cooler winds, the temperature seemed to drop a few degrees. With the swells came a small flock of storm petrels, their fluttering, bat-like flight, short wings and square tails easily identified as they skimmed the waves and disappeared from view. A breeze picked up, gusting frequently as I kept a watchful eye on the gooseneck repair. I fully reefed the mainsail and ran up the storm jib as the swells continued to build and slap against the side of the boat. I thought I ought to grab something to eat while I had the chance, but still had little appetite, which concerned me.

Forcing myself to grab some biscuits, I returned to deck to find Maurice increasingly unable to cope with maintaining a steady course. With the rudder still out of true, I was pushing the tiller hard across but not getting the maximum turn I needed. By midnight the breeze had turned into another real blow, with the sea heaping up white foam and *Sharky*, not under full control from the rudder, slewing about as the sea ran into her. Worse, the rudder seemed to be getting stiffer and stiffer, indicating a more serious problem. While I still had some control I didn't want a situation where something would completely break. Now was a time for mature reflection and decisive action. There were several key facts that I couldn't ignore. I had a damaged boat, I had been going more west than south too soon after Tenerife, and the weather and sea were still not conducive to the course I needed. Sometimes it's more important to do nothing than take action that might make matters worse. Given I had no engine I was to a large extent at the mercy of the wind and tides, which were entirely unpredictable. It was possible the weather could change. It was possible I might make a wrong decision. In the absence of any clear alternative I decided to give it a few hours to see if things altered, and if they didn't I'd gybe and head south. If necessary I'd run with my new heading and see what happened. It didn't feel like decisive action but I managed to convince myself it was. In the back of my mind was the inkling, nothing more, that perhaps the Cape Verde Islands, several hundred miles further down the African coast, might make an enforced landfall if absolutely necessary. In the morning, with no change in the weather, and another full gale lashing around me, I went aft to sort Maurice as best as I could, and decided that no matter what, I just had to get further south before too long. I threw in the gybe then retreated to the cabin to escape the full force of the gale. I remained cooped up in the cabin all day and night trying to keep warm, occasionally dashing out to check on the steering and boom. Constantly tossed around in the large swells, sleep was impossible, the muscles in my legs aching and cramped from straining to keep myself steady. In the gale's fury the sea condition gave *Sharky* a constant buffeting, with the distinct possibility of being blown anywhere at all.

Much as I love the wind at sea, and certainly prefer it to a listless dead calm, there are times when it can become unbearable. As a new dawn broke I again suffered a drop in spirits. Looking and feeling rough, weak through lack of substantial and sustaining food, I reached a point where I seriously thought about giving up. I'd been wet, cold, hungry and miserable plenty of times before, so those factors in themselves were only minor as to how I felt, but my mental attitude was under strain. My expectations and anticipation for this final leg had been higher than I had perhaps realised. My emotional high had been at an all-time peak, and I'd been at fever-pitch to wring every last ounce of enjoyment from the journey. The terrible gale when leaving Tenerife had been challenging, but I'd fought it despite moments of despair. I'd spent a lot of the time since then stowed away in the cabin riding out the weather, but I'd done that plenty of times before, so what on earth was different this time that so filled me with doubts? The wind was no longer a comforting element and it seemed to drain my energy. I remembered films I'd seen of Arctic and Antarctic explorers struggling through and holed up against the constant driving wind, with its eerie and persistent moaning. I felt cowed beneath that selfsame sound, which had now been around intermittently for some days. I realised the other major distinction this time was a different sense of space. My mind had distinguished a subtle disparity between the earlier legs and this one. Previous legs had been shorter and I'd ended up more or less where I had intended. This time I was expecting a voyage of over forty days and a few thousand miles, when I'd literally be on my own in the middle of a vast ocean. Coupled with changes of direction and a damaged boat, my mind had planted seeds of doubt that perhaps this time I'd over-stretched myself. Add the fatigue, sleep deprivation, et cetera, et cetera, and the gulf between high expectation and enforced reality was being widened.

It didn't help that it was February 14th, St Valentine's Day. Hunched in misery, I opened my cards from Elaine and burst into tears. Far from being enveloped in a bubble of love, I just felt more alone than ever before. I missed her, I felt remorse for all the times I thought I could have treated her better, I wanted to tell her that I loved her more than anyone, I wanted to kiss her and squeeze her tight. I sobbed my heart out in a wallow of regret, homesickness and guilt. And all the while, *Sharky* ploughed through the gale-heavy seas, and the wind moaned its haunting wail. I sensed through the tears that I had reached a low point I'd never experienced before, and it scared me. The whole empty day dragged on as I slunk in the cabin, venturing out only for a pee or a quick breath of fresh air, a whole empty day caring little for anything. I half-heartedly started a book, then slung it away in an explosion of impotence. Endless cups of coffee became cold in my hands as I stared red-eyed and unseeing at the angry sea. Bruised and battered in mind and body, I turned in early that night, knowing I'd wasted a precious day of my life, and deeply questioning my desire and capacity to see the voyage through. The dark humour of a friend of mine sprang to mind. He'd been asked to provide a mission statement for his company and tongue-in-cheek had suggested 'Success is never a possibility, failure is always an option'. It seemed to sum up my day exactly. Perhaps I should just get out of this stinking boat and jack the whole bloody journey in.

I awoke after another fitful night as *Sharky* continued to be pounded by heavy seas and gale-force winds, and I wondered if all this was some form of punishment for something evil I'd done in a previous life. I wrote in my log: 'One week since I've left Tenerife and eighty fucking per cent has been cold, miserable and wet. Please stop being windy.' Another day spent in the damp and smelly cabin that had become both my cell and refuge from the atrocious conditions. For a full week, bar a couple of calm days, I'd been at the centre of a sodding, sodden and noisy roller-coaster, enduring increasing worries about how *Sharky* was soaking up all this punishment. The gooseneck repair was still holding, the rudder still giving problems. The wind remained strong with severe gusting.

Angrily shaking off my misery, I knew I needed to stop wallowing around. The only rational thing to do was grab a coffee, grab some charts, and do something positive. I realised I was in an area for which I had no small-scale charts, the best reference being a pilot book for the Eastern Atlantic. The Cape Verde Islands were an achievable option, a safe harbour about seven days' sailing away, which did give me a possible bolthole. There were advantages. The islands could give me the opportunity to repair *Sharky* and continue my voyage, and secondly I realised that if I continued sailing south I could still sail due west from Cape Verde and make for Barbados instead of Antigua. It was not what I really wanted to do, but if pushed my ambition was still within my grasp. I grasped the nettle, commonsense overriding emotional desires. The situation I was in demanded only one solution. I had to make a diversion to the Cape Verdes.

It is remarkable how quickly the human spirit can revive. The smallest glimmer of hope releases the lock gates of despair and renewed vigour floods back through the veins. I gave the chart table a triumphal thump with one hand, raising the other in an exultant fist. The will to carry on, the spirit to overcome the weather and the desire to attain my goal resurfaced phoenix-like: eight inexorable days from Tenerife I stuck my head out of the cabin to spot a bright moon and partially clearing skies. The second gale was blowing itself out after long relentless days, though conditions were still very fresh. Perhaps this was an omen and a cause for some celebration. With increasing confidence and buoyed-up enthusiasm, I celebrated my good fortune with a much-needed crap.

I'd confirmed my decision to try for the Cape Verdes, a course which I felt was unfortunate in some ways but clearly the right thing to do. Elaine, family and friends crept into my thoughts occasionally, but I wasn't missing them in a disconsolate way. They were about me in a warm, snug fashion, comfortably in the background but not intruding. I had the best of all worlds, doing what I wanted to do, knowing I was still in the bubble of a loving family. I was also a little bit smug. From the small-scale pilot chart I'd hand-drawn a larger-scale chart for the Cape Verde area, though I was still plotting my course on the former. From this chart, covering the whole of the North Atlantic, I picked out the island of Sal, only two millimetres wide, an insignificant pinprick, which put my overall journey into perspective. A few stabs with the dividers and Sal was eventually obliterated, which, with grim humour, I realised might also be my fate. I took the longitude and latitude and transferred the coordinates to the large-scale chart, sketching in the island's shape by hand. I needed to get this landfall accurate, as without an engine I was committing myself to this course of action. Get it wrong and there was no way I would be able to beat my way northwards again in this wind. This was pioneering sailing stuff in the style of Magellan and Drake, hands-on practical navigating, which gave me much cause for satisfaction. The only irritant was an increasingly creaky mast, which gained a relentless rhythm that bored into my brain. Try as I might to shut it out the blasted squeak-squeak took on a prominence I thought might drive me mad. I started singing some of my favourite songs out loud, but to no avail – the bloody high-pitched creak tore through mercilessly. From such trivial matters do sailors go insane. Completing the chart, I realised the decision to go for Cape Verde had been the right one. Although running repairs to the rudder had reduced the deficit to about ten degrees out of true, I was beginning to ship water in the rudder housing, which necessitated a bailing-out every day. I'd also noticed cracks appearing in the bulkhead above the mast, which was still creaking badly, audibly crying out for a new gooseneck. I needed a break, and *Sharky* needed respite before *she* broke. Ditching Antigua as my original destination, I was left with only Hobson's choice.

One day merged into another with no lull – gusting breezes and hammering seas. My norm consisted of fitful dozes for five minutes at a time, snatched food and drinks, rushed trips to bail out the rudder housing, quick checks on the storm jib – my only sail up – and the odd moody contemplation of why and for what purpose I was in this situation. The earlier deep depression had not returned, and, while everything in my small and immediate world was wretched and uncomfortable, I was beginning to rise from my desolation. I can't pretend to have been enjoying the experience, but it was becoming slightly more bearable. Importantly, I was coping again, and, most importantly, I was beginning to cope positively.

I think the decision to try for the Cape Verde Islands gave me back some sort of purpose. There'd been a point a few days earlier where I'd been vacillating about what to do, and my indecisiveness had been oozing like a running sore. Now I concentrated on my homemade chart and set out to aim for Palmeira on the island of Sal. While the physical tribulations of being on *Sharky* were still an important health factor, I knew that if I could get my head around my situation then I'd be all right. The utter desolation on Valentine's Day had been a sort of wake-up call. I knew that I was capable of extreme emotional ranges and that I'd had to dig really deep to force myself to keep going, and from what I'd read by other seafarers these emotional peaks and troughs were not unusual. Long sea journeys taxed mind and body to the limits, but also rewarded people with a sense of being that was worth the price. Sailing the wild oceans demanded much and promised rich personal bounty for those who tested themselves.

A few days earlier I'd seen my self-pity and melancholy as weaknesses, now I saw them as a necessary though dislikeable part of my condition. If I could fight them but also accept they were inevitable composites of my character I would be in a stronger position to overcome them and carry on. I also realised that this inner contemplation, this ruthless and often uncomfortable self-analysis, was one of solo sailing's rewards. There was time for reflection, time to question the million issues about life itself. No answers were guaranteed, but subtle changes to self were inevitable.

The sea was probably the best personal counsellor I could ever have asked for.

Now on a steady heading of 190 degrees, progress appeared pretty slow, with just a storm jib, though in fact I was making good ground, the strong breeze occasionally swamping the boat with big seas. I rekindled my interest in books and buried myself in *Atlantis of the Sands* by Ranulph Fiennes, his fascinating account of the search for the lost city of Ubar. It was strange to immerse myself in a book concerned with desert, heat and quiet when I was in conditions at completely the other end of the spectrum – perhaps the subject matter helped keep me warm!

Well into my second week out of Tenerife and I was finding it increasingly difficult to remember what warm sunshine felt and looked like. The winds remained brutal for most of the time and the cold and damp were playing havoc with my back. I'd taken to using a hot water bottle to lean against, which relieved the aching somewhat, but I'd now resigned myself to a state of permanent damp and cramp. When necessary I attempted the occasional hot shave – a challenge in itself to hold razor and stubble together against the wishes of the heaving Atlantic. If I'd cut my throat by accident and been found they'd probably think I'd committed suicide, when all I'd really wanted was to get rid of my thickening stubble. I laughed at the irony and cheered myself up. *Sharky*, however, needed more than a good shave. Without complaint she'd got her head down, got stuck into the ocean swells and just carried on regardless, though I was still bailing out the rudder housing on a daily basis. I kept a concerned weather eye on the creaks and cracks, but reckoned if she could hold out for a bit longer I could make good the damage. I was repairing my own emotional damage and coming to terms with the interminable weather. I spent a lot of time thinking about my life, my experiences and what the future would have in store for me. At the back of my mind was a feeling of commitment and a desire to settle down, trying to establish some regularity in my life, odd thoughts for someone who wanted the freedom of the seas. I spent many hours trying to figure out whether those desires stemmed from a reaction to the conditions I was in or whether I was just getting to that age where some permanence was required. It was good to feel positive about a future though, and to know that the detail would sort itself out soon enough. For now the priorities were a lot more prosaic – needing to keep dry, needing to keep on course, and needing another crap in a force six.

At the noon fix on Saturday I'd sailed 70 miles in twenty-four hours, under just a storm jib, and judged I'd another 260 miles to go before I hit Sal, probably on Wednesday morning. After the first day's gale, the short period of relative calm, followed by another lengthy gale, the weather now held steady and the daily bump, thump, bang, the grind of the rock-and-roll motion, remained the backdrop to my existence. I'd noticed though that the water was getting warmer. Washing dirty plates consisted of holding them in the sea to get rid of stubborn bits of food, and there was a distinct if slight increase in temperature. About bloody time, I thought: I'd also noticed that the wind was not gusting as much, even though it remained steadfastly strong. I'd spent so long in these conditions that wind speeds of around thirty knots were now the norm, as was, fortunately, the occasional abnormal wave, which rattled down to swamp the boat. That very evening I was to experience a major wave, throwing me down the side of the boat, bruising my arms and legs quite badly, a sort of nautical reminder that there was still no room for complacency. I awoke on Sunday with a sense of foreboding. I'd been having strange and often disturbing dreams for several nights and, while I couldn't remember what the last one was about, I woke disturbed by it, bringing on a feeling of hopelessness and listlessness. Still on an emotional switchback, I sensed a lack of enthusiasm for continuing this sail, and thought that when I reached Cape Verde I might just pack it all in and go back home. I kept this mood for most of the day and barely noticed that the clouds were beginning to clear and the spray was easing despite the big seas. After several hours of inattentive sailing I eventually discerned that the rudder, Maurice and a slight wind shift had been turning the boat onto a more westerly course. I hastily corrected the error as the brief interlude from a grim sky dissolved, and was replaced once more by low clouds and precipitation. Would this journey ever end?

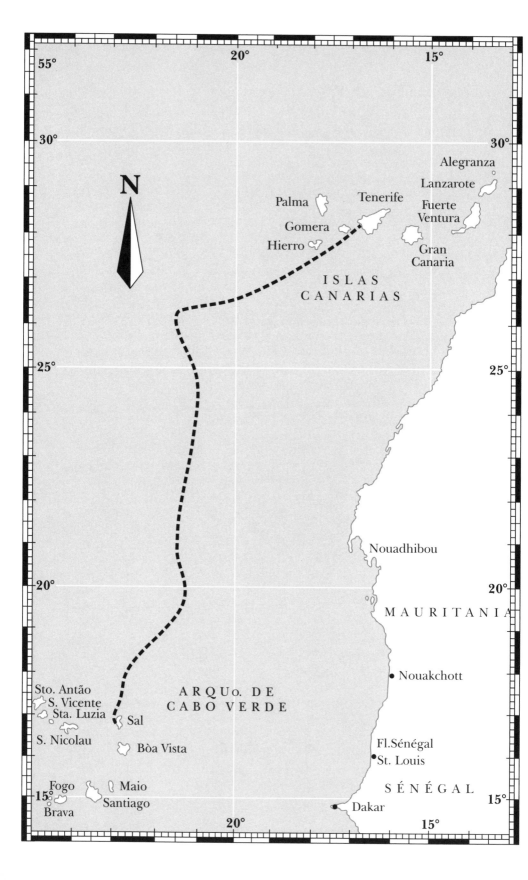

Time dragged by on Monday, though the weather improved slightly in that the sun briefly appeared and I managed my first strip wash for quite a while. Large waves continued to swamp the boat and I now had to bail the rudder housing out at least three times a day. I put up a partially reefed main, together with the storm jib, and we fairly flew through the water. I was very keen, almost frantic, to make landfall as soon as I could, and reckoned that a bit of extra sail would add to the already impressive sixty miles or more I was making each day with only the storm jib. On Tuesday morning I altered the heading to due south, reckoning on an estimated time of arrival in seventeen or eighteen hours' time. For nearly a fortnight I'd been more a passenger than a sailor. I felt manipulated by the sea and the weather, tossed around like a plaything, with little other to do than read, drink, smoke, sleep and put up with my own company. I was quite pleased at how well, in retrospect, I coped in sustained, appalling weather, but now I'd had enough. I wanted the security of dry and stable land, a decent non-moving bed, a lot of warmth and human company. I tried not to think about the next important decision I needed to take, to jack it all in or continue my way. I still had a vast distance to travel, and in some ways I was no nearer the Caribbean than when I'd left Tenerife, and I wasn't sure I was in the right frame of mind to make a rational choice. One thing at a time, I thought. Firstly just get off this sodden boat and try to rejoin the human race. I might not know what I wanted to do but at least there were no immediate pressures to influence my choice. As the Cape Verde Islands drew ever nearer I wanted no part in long-term decisions. Right then I'd have sold my soul for a warm, luxuriant bath.

I went to sleep early and woke at eleven that night, my hair a mass of sweat beads after another dark nightmare. I tried to recall what terrors I had imagined but the images faded quickly, leaving me with nothing more than weird, spooky feelings that made my skin clammy. *Sharky* was spinning again in the seas and I had no option but to get on deck and steer by hand if I stood any chance of keeping on course. The wind was still strong and breezy, a virtual calm by comparison to the earlier gales, and despite thick cloud a half-moon flickered briefly and occasionally into view. I felt comforted by the sight, the only external contact I'd had with anything for a long, long time. As dawn broke, the island of Sal appeared in the distance and I let out an audible sigh of relief – no cheers this time, just gratitude that I'd stayed on course. The wind gusted infrequently and spits of rain fell as I made for the village of Palmeira, with no other thought than to lay up, sleep forever then find a phone. About half-past ten in the morning I sailed into the harbour through the maze of small fishing boats and a couple of local yachts. Once beyond the jutting harbour-wall-cum-breakwater, the northerly wind prevented me from sailing directly to a mooring, so I spent a good half-hour frustratingly zigzagging across the harbour expanse, advancing only slowly. I noticed a number of locals on the wall curiously studying my efforts, and I'd have given a lot at that moment for the luxury of an outboard. Slowly, exasperatingly, I made my way towards the slipway, eventually anchoring among the small fishing vessels. Tying up, I glanced around at my surroundings. Palmeira was not an impressive sight, a collection of Third World huts and an air of faded weariness, but at least it offered temporary shelter. I contemplated rowing ashore to find somewhere to sleep, but suddenly lost all my energy and will to do anything. I felt unwell, shaking and trembling, not really coming to terms with ending up where I had. Part of me just wanted to burst into tears, but I was too exhausted even for that. I wrapped myself into my sleeping bag and fell into a dreamless sleep.

CHAPTER THIRTEEN

Second Thoughts in Cape Verde

I needed to get to the island's airport and check out the possibility of getting home and abandoning the whole affair.

I SLEPT THROUGHOUT THE morning and much of that afternoon: an exhausted deep sleep without waking and without any reference to where I was. Accumulative fatigue had closed down any extraneous intrusions and I was oblivious to all sounds and movement. Eventually I awoke, slowly, first trying to recall where I was, then staying in my bunk, listening to the world outside and gradually attuning to my circumstances. If all had gone better during the previous days I should by now have been well into the central Atlantic waters, but fate had decreed otherwise so I now needed to explore my new environment and decide what to do. Still weak and not feeling at my best, I grabbed a quick coffee and went up on deck to see what was what.

I'd made land on the Ilha Do Sal in a small port called Baia Da Palmeira close to the larger town of Espargos. There are ten volcanic islands in the Cape Verde cluster and Sal was one of the smaller ones lying to the northeast about 300 miles from the coast of Senegal. A former Portuguese colony, the Cape Verde Islands were slowly emerging as an independent nation, but with poor national resources and prone to drought. They were to all intent and purposes very much a Third World country, relying heavily on imports while trying to scratch a living from basic foods and rural industry. Sal is Portuguese for salt, the island getting its name from the large lagoons where salt was extracted from the sea by evaporation. As I peered across the harbour a dusty haze permeated the lunar landscape, dotted with shacks and oozing desolation. The initial signs were not good but experience of other countries and of living abroad had taught me not to make snap judgements. It was time to find out whether Sal had a soul. My first task though was to dry out my gear after the ravages of fourteen days of sailing turmoil. Essentially if it moved it was wet, if it was part of the boat it was wet. T-shirts, trousers, underwear, trainers, sleeping bag, boxes, everything I owned festooned *Sharky* so that she resembled a gipsy caravan. Clothing flapped colourfully in the breeze like a line of little Tibetan prayer flags. The rigging sported my underwear and T-shirts, the boom became a drape for my sleeping bag, and trousers and shorts hung from the grab rails. I had a photo of Maurice (the person, not the self-steering gear) in my cabin and I reckoned he would have approved of the haphazard garlanding, which would have reminded him of his Asiatic travels.

With *Sharky* now affronted and ignominiously bedecked, I dragged my decrepit dinghy from its stowage and began to inflate it madly with the hand pump. If anything, there seemed to be even more small holes than before, and it felt as though I was giving a wheezing, breathless old man a few desperate gasps of air. Following the oft-practised routine I slung a few items in the well, chucked in the oar, then paddled furiously the thirty-odd yards to the shore, all the while the dinghy steadily taking in water, old-man dinghy not quite deciding whether death by drowning or asphyxiation was the preferred option.

My landing was watched with much amusement by a small horde of excitable, ragged and barefoot children chattering and jabbering in a patois I found out later was called Crioulo – a Creole derivation mixing Portuguese and African languages. The kids crowded round as I heaved the sloshing dinghy from the sea. My hesitant smiles and waves were rewarded with big grins filled with glistening white teeth. It was a humbling experience being surrounded by children of all ages, some shy, some bold, all of whom wanting to shake my hand and become my friend. It's frustrating when the language barrier prevents a real exchange of friendship, but a delightful opportunity nevertheless to transcend that obstacle with nothing more than genuine smiles, some pulled funny faces and the raw pleasure of being accepted. In under ten minutes since landing I was rejected as a stranger and welcomed as part of a community, an astonishing transformation brought about by innocent lives and a real sense of welcome. Any reserve I had about Palmeira melted away. In the dry dust clouds of the village I had struck gold.

The children wouldn't let me go. Noisily crowding around and constantly shaking my hand, I wondered if they thought I was some sort of celebrity. Unable to converse with them, I reasoned that finding a bar was probably as good a start as anywhere to get my bearings, as much as a well-deserved drink. Dragging the dinghy over the boulders and above the tide line, feeling like the Pied Piper, I began to wander towards the collection of nearby shacks. Rapidly closing in on me loomed an animated local with a booming voice who shooed the children away while extending his arm for my first adult handshake.

'Hello!' he shouted in English. 'My name is George. I have made it my duty to help all travelling yachts. I can help you find anything you need. My name is George Housha and I live in the small green house over there.' Hardly drawing breath, he pointed vaguely behind him and ploughed on. 'Ask anyone in the village for George and they will show you my house. What is your name and where have you come from? Where are you going?'

Slightly taken aback by the barrage of information and questions, I dutifully replied and shook his hand again. George, who worked at the airport, had made himself the unofficial village ambassador, whether through civic responsibility or just a smart move to increase his local standing I could never quite decide, but nonetheless a good ambassador he was, courteous, helpful and a fount of all local knowledge. It seemed everyone likely to be of use or value to me was either a cousin or an in-law or a very good friend. I had only to mention his name and doors would be opened. He pointed to a marginally less tattered building and explained that it was the customs building. 'You have no problems, Mr Dave,' he said. 'Customs people are friends of mine.'

Another good friend of George was Antonio, a mountain of a man reminiscent of a nightclub bouncer. With eleven brothers and sisters and the owner of a thirty-metre fishing boat, he was clearly a dominant character and a man of local standing, who employed many of the fishermen. Of swarthy complexion, with huge hands and a bear-like grip, he looked a hard man and not one to cross, his sharp piercing eyes boring into me as we were introduced. His English was limited but passable and I told him of my journey from England and my ambition to sail to the Caribbean in *Sharky*. He looked at my boat and nodded, a gesture of genuine respect from one seafarer to another that pleased me greatly. He turned out to be a kind, honourable man, a shrewd, rough giant who lived from the sea, who was prepared to acknowledge my journey and who understood what it meant to me. I instinctively sensed he regarded me as an equal and would offer any help he could. And help he did. Each day he would solemnly hand over a couple of lobsters from an earlier catch, shrugging off thanks with a desultory wave of his gigantic paw, and I knew better than to offend him with payment.

George led me to one of Antonio's brothers' bar, where he encouraged me to speak my first words in Creole, 'El ciris cervesa', and a bottled beer duly arrived. I took it and sat outside on the dusty street and began to take in my first real view of the village and the surrounding landscape. It felt strange again sitting in the back of beyond as old memories flitted in and out of my head. Despite the remote beauty of the heat-haze rocky hinterland, and the empty beaches, at first glance there was little to commend Palmeira, a shanty, derelict village with breezeblock hovels, water standpipes and doom-laden posters warning against cholera. A small, well-stocked shop sold vegetables, flour, tins and fruit, just enough to satisfy basic needs. Kerbstones lined unmade dirt roads, and people sat around in groups or singly, simply passing time. A disused fish cannery rusted away at the harbour edge, its reddening sheet metal coated with dust, giving it an eerie glow in the evening sun. If a place could have made a living from dust it should have been Palmeira. Dust was in the air, on buildings, on everything, it added to the lethargy of an apparently pointless existence, but still there was a sense of community. People got on with their lives and there was laughter and ease with their lot. Shaken out of my reverie by George, I was invited back into the bar to face a huge bowl of chopped-up offal in a spicy gravy, accompanied by freshly baked bread. Around the communal bowl lay twelve forks, all of which soon gained an owner directly related to Antonio. His brother Domingo became translator for the evening and there was genuine interest in my travels. An offer of payment for the meal and for drinks was curtly but not disparagingly refused. I was their honoured guest, invited to share their meal and hospitality. Eventually I returned to *Sharky* after a solemn shaking of everyone's hand and my profuse thanks. I felt humbled by their interest and invitation, reminded once more of man's inherent good nature and courtesy towards others. I had been accepted as an equal because of my respect for them and for the sea. I thought again about the meaning of richness and poorness, which had nothing to do with material possessions and everything to do with humanity. These were poor, simple fishermen. They knew no other life, yet they had unhesitatingly invited a stranger into the intimacy of their home. With such people as this there was still hope for the human race.

I also thought of home and the need to let Elaine and my family know I was safe. Yet again I reminded myself that, just a few hundred miles away and barely a fortnight before, I'd left people in air-conditioned offices, shops and hotels living in a westernised, so-called civilised society, with everything and anything they needed. Now here I was on the same planet but in a totally different environment, dust, abject poverty and a barren existence. What a comparison between rich and poor, yet I pondered who had the greater riches? Still battered and bruised from the journey, I began to nod off, realising I hadn't had my quota of sleep, was still feeling a little bit queasy. My exploration of Sal could wait another day, a day I needed to get to the island's airport and check out the possibility of getting home and abandoning the whole affair. I wandered back to *Sharky* still very uncertain about what I wanted to do and my capability to keep going. Yes, I'd enthused many days ago about using Cape Verde as an alternate jumping-off point for the Caribbean, but I still had real misgivings about the state of *Sharky* and my own ability and willingness to continue. It hit me just how much the sail from Tenerife had taken away my resolve and confidence and I couldn't determine whether it was the wretched tiredness that was making me think this way or if, deep down, I knew I really didn't have it in me to complete the journey. I'd hit all-time lows in the endless gales and buffeting and my spirits had ebbed more than flowed. I simply couldn't sort my intentions out so I resorted to the best possible action in the circumstances. I ambled back to *Sharky* and went to sleep.

The world improved overnight and got even better after a decent cup of coffee and a cigarette. The morning was already warm, *Sharky* riding a calm sea under a blue sky laced with white clouds. As I attempted to take stock of what I wanted to do there was little noise from the village, just background chatter and workaday sounds. I sat for a long time just watching the sea, trying not to address the decision I had to make. I'd been in this position plenty of times before on this long journey starting from Falmouth. Plenty of occasions when my head had screamed 'give up' and my heart had nearly followed; plenty of moments when I felt I'd taken on too much too soon with too little experience; plenty of opportunities to miss my loved ones. Alone with my thoughts, indecision washed over me. I had little money, a damaged boat, no job or prospects, and a growing fear that I'd been in perilous sailing situations where luck had perhaps played a significant hand. What had William said back in Tenerife? 'Don't be foolish with your life.' I don't know how long I sat on *Sharky*, my thoughts focusing and blurring as I tried to make sense of my life, my ambition and my future. I thought back to all the times when sailing had consumed me with an acute passion, when the sheer joy of unfettered freedom at sea had claimed my soul with an intensity I hadn't believed was possible. Then again I wasn't deciding whether to give up sailing for good. At the end of the day the basic decision was simply whether to pack up now, go back home and think about completing my ambition some time in the future or decide that enough was enough and stick to coastal sailing or carry on from Sal. In that moment I knew I had made my decision. This was not about sailing skills, fear, confidence, cash, prospects or anything remotely logical. The decision was made on something much less tangible, involved no logic and had no genesis in the mind. I took the decision, or rather reaffirmed it, on the basis that I had made it in the first place three years earlier. I was going on to sail across the Atlantic simply because in my heart it was what I wanted to do. I knew that if I left Sal now I would never return to continue. I understood William's words in a different light. To be foolish with my life would have been to give up my ambition and forever regret not accomplishing it. To carry on was my great test of skill and character. I shook my head to clear my thoughts. What on earth had I been thinking about? Of course I was carrying on!

With a lighter heart, I set out to find a phone and report home only to discover that the nearest one was in Espargos, a larger town just a few miles away. George readily agreed to accompany me so we begged a lift in a ramshackle old truck, the three of us chattering away in halting English and my equally halting but newly acquired Creole and basic Portuguese. Espargos at least had tarmac roads and some public transport, but it was obviously a place with little money. The shops, stuffed with a jumble of low-quality items, were barely the size of small rooms. I bought some batteries knowing they were rubbish and wouldn't last long. Two incongruous newish hotels stuck out like alien structures, forlornly awaiting the influx of tourists who had yet to discover the island. I couldn't help thinking of the huge culture change waiting round the corner for these simple, friendly people. Tourism would bring much needed income, jobs and prosperity, but in exchange take away their innocence and way of life. It would be nice to think that an environmental balance might be achieved, but somehow I doubted it and felt saddened. In twenty years' time the Cape Verde Islands were fated to be just another holiday destination looking like all the rest. Espargos was a dusty oasis in a barren landscape desperate to be modern and westernised, without fully understanding the impact. Stay as you are, I wanted to scream, but then I saw the dog.

I'd wandered away from George to use the phone and have a look around when I chanced upon a side street, where there was a small dog, rather like a whippet. It lay panting on the roadside unable to move on account of a badly smashed and twisted back leg, splinters of the bone jutting through the broken, swollen skin. It looked as though it had lain there for a while, and with no attention from anyone was just waiting to die. Sad, brown eyes locked into mine in resignation and I imagined the pain it was feeling. Anger and helplessness washed over me and I felt ashamed as I walked away. There were people on the street who had passed by without a glance, and without compassion, their own survival seemingly blocking out care for one of God's creatures. Perhaps the negative impact of tourism was worth the price if it meant this callousness could eventually be eradicated. Right then I hated Cape Verde.

Saddened by the experience I found a phone in one of the hotels and made contact with Elaine. It started as a difficult, stilted conversation as I explained in general terms where I was and why. I started to apologise for putting her through the anxiety of my being away, and moved on to say I was missing her, and then, to my astonishment as well as hers, completely out of the blue I asked her to marry me! There was a short silence as a million thoughts rushed through my head, one of them being that this was probably the most unromantic proposal I could ever have dreamt up.

'Do you really mean it?' came her hesitant response.

'Yes,' I blurted out, 'I love you.'

'Then I will,' she said, and that was that, totally unplanned, unpredicted and low-key. We chatted inconsequentially for a few more minutes then said our goodbyes. I dropped the phone in its cradle in a bit of a daze. That twenty-minute call had cost me £60 and my bachelorhood. Today's trip was turning out to be an expensive jaunt, and I had yet to call my mum, which cost another £30, a further sum I could ill afford. I spared her the sailing details that I knew would just add worry and tried to be as light and upbeat as I could, though she was more concerned with the matrimonial news anyway. I put the phone down again glad to have heard their voices but knowing the physical distance between us would only bring on despondency later, plus, I couldn't get the image of that damned dog out of my mind. It had been a strange day all in all and I needed something to jolt me out of my confused state. I needed to find George, buy him a drink and tell him my good news. George was knee-deep in friends and insisted on introducing them all to me, including two doctors, the only ones on the island. I jokingly asked them who was looking after the hospital, which brought hoots of laughter but no response – clearly it was important to stay in good health in Espargos. At least everyone was delighted I was making an honest woman out of Elaine, and none more than I. I was getting to like Cape Verde again.

Feeling somewhat restored after another good night's sleep, I went to work with a vengeance on *Sharky*. Although I was getting to like Palmeira and its people and would happily have stayed a while longer, I was casting an anxious eye on the time. Most sailors aim to be in the Caribbean for Christmas and it was now late February. The trade winds tend to strengthen as they blow themselves out before the onset of the hurricane season, and with over 2,000 miles yet to cover I didn't want to hang around any longer than necessary. I needed to make good repairs to the rudder housing, gooseneck, keel bolts and cracks around the mast bulkhead. With no facilities to speak of, I slipped over the side so that I could work on the bent rudder and its housing. The water was about twenty feet deep, a filthy, swirling mess in which unidentified and extremely dubious and unhygienic matter floated round the hull. Undertaking external repairs in this depth was going to be bad enough without wondering what sort of detritus I might swallow if I inadvertently opened my mouth. Donning a facemask and gulping in as much air as I could, I slid underwater and gave the whole structure a good inspection, hull, keels, rudder and skeg. It all seemed okay though it looked as though it was the tiller rather than the rudder that had strained out of alignment. This I fixed in traditional fashion, a couple of whacks with a hammer, a lot of brute force and a dictionary of profanities.

Tightening the bolts seemed to bring it back into true, but I added another strengthening fixing for good measure. To check the keel bolts meant I had to clear the cabin of gear and wriggle down to the bilges. It all seemed fine and I guessed that with *Sharky* on hard-standing so long in Tenerife the wood might have shrunk, allowing water to seep through. The worst job by far was tackling the leaks in the rudder housing, which had required all the bailing out in the gales. Difficult to access via the back hatch under the self-steering mechanism, I mixed and applied the gooey fibreglass, a horrible, sticky, sweaty job done more by feel than sight, but helped along with regular bouts of intense swearing. Finally all the repairs were done. I had spent much of the day neck-deep in fetid water and I fantasised over a long hot shower. The reality was a less than satisfying strip wash in bottled water.

Towelling off, I realised that for the inhabitants of Palmeira life was completely devoid of even the most basic amenities. In a few months I could go back to a westernised lifestyle with as many hot showers as I could want. For these villagers water came from an unhygienic standpipe or a visiting bowser truck that pumped water up to big storage drums on the roofs of some of the shacks. Drainage was non-existent, sewage being carried out and dumped in the sea. Many villagers merely squatted down and defecated by the harbour rocks, relying on the incoming tide to wash their waste away. Pigs, goats and hens wandered at will, leaving excrement anywhere and everywhere. On several occasions I witnessed women washing animal intestines in the street in preparation for an offal meal, something of a delicacy in a place where fish was the staple diet. Dust, dirt, decay, desolation. Any photograph would reveal that image of Palmeira, but actually being there exposed a vibrancy that somehow transcended the impoverishment, and I continued to be embraced and welcomed by these people. Perhaps it was because I also dressed in a desultory fashion, faded and torn T-shirt and shorts, bare feet, unkempt hair. I didn't see myself as a tourist and tried to blend in as much as possible, so perhaps acceptance was easier to acquire. Other than the horrendous squalid conditions, my abiding memories of the people of Sal are all to do with community and generosity of spirit.

On my fourth day in Palmeira, with repairs finally completed, I knew I wanted to leave the following day. After yet another lobster breakfast courtesy of Antonio, I resolved to take my camera ashore and get some snaps of the place. It was as though word had got about. The children in particular were fascinated by, and desperate to be in, the shots. I would line up a picture of some buildings or a general view, would be about to press the shutter when a smiling, grinning face would appear in the lens. I was still the subject of much handshaking, so taking photographs was quite a lengthy affair. In the end I became embarrassed to take pictures of villagers, feeling I was intruding into their underprivileged lives, but there would always be half a dozen children hanging around the harbour insisting on having theirs taken.

Antonio arranged to exchange my last few pounds so I could restock with supplies, much of my fresh fruit and vegetables having gone mouldy through a combination of damp conditions on *Sharky* and the heat of the island. The 'fresh' food in the shop looked even worse than the stuff I had slung so I settled for tins of fish and corned beef, bottled water and packets of pasta and rice. Back on the boat, after the obligatory reverse paparazzi run, I decided I'd go for a final evening stroll before cooking dinner, up to the small Christian church – in reality no bigger than an average lounge – at the edge of the slipway. I'd been there a couple of times and found it to be a quiet, solitary, contemplative spot to refresh and recharge my mind. I had been on Sal for only a few short days yet so much had happened. I'd experienced the warmth of a close community, the harshness of poverty, the aching wrist of friendship and the aftershock of engagement. I reflected how different things would have been if the weather conditions from Tenerife had been more tolerant. Clouds really do have silver linings, I mused.

A shadow fell across my body. It was Manuel, another of my many acquaintances. He was an interesting, intelligent chap who also worked at the airport. We chatted for a while about life on the islands, about liberation and independence, then I mentioned how genuinely sorry I would be to leave Sal the next day. Immediately he insisted I return with him to his house for a drink and a meal. I gravely accepted his invitation and we duly went to his house for a meal of mixed fish with plates of vegetables brought in by his wife and son. I sensed Manuel was embarrassed by the poverty of his village, wanting to know how I felt living with such poor people. I sipped my red wine, put down my glass and looked him straight in the eyes. From my heart I gave my honest and non-contrived response.

'Manuel,' I replied. 'I have been thinking about this a lot on my boat, about the generosity I have received here and in other poor places I have visited and lived in. Many poor people have a richness in their hearts and they give willingly without expectation of return. Many rich people are self-centred, poor in heart and expect a return. The people in Palmeira may be poor but they are rich in their hearts. I can tell you honestly this is one of the best places I have ever been to.'

He looked at me sombrely for a while. 'You are right,' he said. 'Thank you. I think you are right.'

By eleven o'clock next morning I had washed, shaved and put on fresh clothes. My old trainers were barely holding together but I had no others and anyway they'd become part of me. How perverse, I thought, that I had chosen to live in these old shoes when a few yards away there were people who had little choice – they had no footwear or socks. I paid my fees to one of the happiest customs officials I'd ever met, who wished me 'bon voyage' and proffered the inevitable hand for shaking. I had a feeling today was going to be pretty well national handshake day. My intention was to set off at two o'clock that afternoon, to take advantage of the natural light, and later, when darkness fell, the lights from the other islands I'd be sailing through. First I needed to grab a lift into Espargos and let Mum know that I was setting off, then I needed to say goodbye to all my village friends. Phoning home was perfunctory. I had virtually no money left so quickly told Mum not to worry and that it could be forty or so days before I got back in touch. That was it. I left the phone booth smearing away tears and telling myself fiercely to get a grip. For Christ's sake just get a grip!

I wandered back in Palmeira saying and waving goodbye to everyone I'd got to know, endless smiles, endless handshakes and my heart getting heavier by the step. I wanted to go, anxious to get back to sea, but there was also a reluctance to leave these happy people. I got back to the harbour to find Manuel searching for me. His wife had prepared a special lunch for me that he insisted I attend.

'It is your last meal,' he said, with no trace or intent of irony.

I accepted his invitation but insisted that I must leave by two o'clock that afternoon.

'Of course,' he replied. 'But first you must have a good meal to give you strength for your journey, my wife has prepared such a meal for you.'

I was delighted to see that George was also present. I'd grown very fond of him in just a few days and I'd appreciated his warmth of sprit and friendship. We entered Manuel's house to find a huge bowl of bean soup, in which floated a severed tuna head complete with eyes and a number of pig's trotters, complete with hairy skin and fat. Already anxious about leaving, I knew my stomach was not going to cope with this so I ate sparingly, sticking to the beans, while George and Manuel tucked in enthusiastically, teeth ripping into everything with gusto. Trotters and tuna apart, it was an enjoyable time in the company of friends, and although it was tempting to offer continual toasts to friendship I restricted myself to one small glass of red wine. Eventually, two hours after my intended departure I bade them goodbye and returned to *Sharky*. If she'd had arms I think they would have been folded in exasperation, fingers tapping in vexation and all the while thinking, 'Men!' Down at the harbour Antonio wandered across with Domingo and shook my hand vigorously. His gaze bore into my eyes again and he held my hand a fraction longer than was comfortable. He said something in Portuguese and I looked to Domingo for a translation, but he was struggling to interpret. In the end I nodded and patted both their arms. I think I knew what he was trying to say – be careful, don't try to conquer the sea.

I scrambled into *Sharky* and dragged the rapidly sinking dinghy after me. Manuel had arrived on the harbour wall to offer his goodbyes, together with George and a few others. They waved enthusiastically and shouted for me to return to Sal with my new wife. We'll come back, I thought, when you've got some hot showers installed, but I shouted 'Definitely' as I began my preparations for casting off. I was genuinely sorry to be leaving Palmeira, so much to remember in such a short few days, but busying myself with the boat kept much of my emotion at bay: I would have many days to come when I would be able to look back with fond affection for this isolated spot. Perhaps I would return with my new wife and with my new life – it would be nice to think so. For now though Barbados sounded its distant clarion as I headed *Sharky* out of the harbour and onto a westerly heading. Feeling apprehensive, scared and tense, I gave a last wave back at Sal. The final pieces of my personal jigsaw were lining up to be put in place. My journey of a lifetime was now entering its final and most testing phase.

21 *Conditions on the way to Cape Verde. The gale had eased but it was still lively in a very challenging environment for such a small boat.*

22 *Under storm jib only, Sharky trudged on to the Cape Verde.*

23 (above) Sharky anchored
off in the harbour at Cap
Verde. You can just see her in
the centre of the photo

24 (left) One of the street
in Sal

25 (right) The inside of
the cabin. I could afford
to be untidy as this was
taken in harbour.

26 (left) The shop in Cape Verde where I purchased some final provisions.

27 (below) Antonio made sure I had fresh lobsters every day for breakfast during my stay in Cape Verde.

28 (below) Cape Verde fishermen cleaning the daily catch. They were very generous with the fish before they carted off the best cuts to market.

29 The children were always fascinated to see me in the Cape Verde.

Chapter Fourteen

Farewell to Friends

*The wind held steady at a gentle breeze so I left Maurice
to work his magic.*

ALTHOUGH LEAVING SAL LATER than intended, the delay had
been well worth the sincere farewells from my friends. It was
approaching five o'clock as I sailed from the harbour heading into
a strongish breeze. The green-grey waves capped with white foam
greeted me as I left the lee of the island and reefed the mainsail to
give me more control. Leaving a harbour is always an experience
of conflicting emotions. There is the adrenalin rush of entering deep
water again, and the anticipation of new adventure and challenge.
The senses are revived, the sinews flexed, the body is taut, responding
to the sea surge and anxious to be at one with the boat again. With
all this longing and forward-looking comes the antithesis; the inevitable
retrospective glances as one's more rational side introduces a note
of cautionary calm to counter the rush of blood to the head. Regret,
anxiety, uncertainty, longing and even fear offset the positive feelings,
and so it was again this time as I ventured west on a heading of
260 degrees, the perfect heading across 2,000 miles of solitariness.
The route took me between the islands of Boa Vista to the south

and Sao Nicolau to the north, my gateway to the nightlights shore-side that I hoped would see me safely through the gap. I have long felt an affinity with departures in the evening, a time that, for non-sailors, must seem foolhardy if not downright dangerous. But there is something about the sea at evening, especially if the journey is to the west, as if following the sun to the ends of the earth. To take the ingredients of solitude, the lap of wave against hull, a setting sun and clouds of every hue, and to mix them with a sense of purpose and voyage, is to bake a rich cake of life that cannot be surpassed. Sprinkle a few abiding memories of friendship, and the leaving of safe harbour, and you have a recipe that tingles every part of your being. It's not just some heroic fantasy of the imagination, it's real, raw and infinitely humbling. Leaving Sal astern, the wind picked up as I entered open waters. I could feel oneness with any sailor through history, each with different lives but exactly the same thoughts: thoughts of home and family, thoughts of what lay in store. Past and future inextricably linked in that one present moment. I thought of home and felt closeness with loved ones. I looked into the sun, not quite believing that I was now actually embarking on the final leg, that in a matter of a month or so, God willing, I would be where the sun now was, on the far side of a great and daunting ocean that I would have crossed on my own merit and with my own skill. Looking back to the darkening shadow of Sal was like looking back into my life so far, full of memories crammed into a small span of not yet thirty years. Looking west was literally taking my life into the unknown, borne along by a jumble of wood, metal, rope and fibreglass plucked from the orphanage of a Chesterfield boatyard just a handful of years ago.

There's a fancy tongue-twister of a word to describe the projecting human emotion onto inanimate objects. Anthropomorphism. Well, maybe I was anthropomorphic, and if I was I couldn't have cared less. That jumble had become *Sharky*, no brain, no heart but a heck of a lot of soul. I'd tended to her, stuck by her, left her and returned to her. I'd invested a lot of time, money and much of my soul, so although inanimate she was a living part of me. *Sharky* was definitely 'she' not 'it'. Small and gawky, built for tenacious skirmishing, she had endured and overcome conditions that at times I thought might overwhelm her. *Sharky* had earned the right to be here with me and we complemented each other perfectly. She was a one-man boat that continued to surprise me. Now we would see this adventure through together.

Such were my romantic thoughts as I left Palmeira. Within a few hours I had fully reefed the mainsail, the decks were awash with spray and all notion of noble sentiment had taken a backseat as I battled against increasingly heavy seas. The nightmare of the journey down from Tenerife grabbed at my brain and I prayed to any and every god that was on my wavelength that I wouldn't have to endure the same conditions again. I realised that Maurice was not going to cope well with this weather and resigned myself to the likelihood of a long wet night at the helm. Within an hour of leaving Sal I was feeling very unwell. My stomach griped with pain, which I put down to Manuel's tuna and pig-trotter soup, the very thought of it accentuating the queasy feeling. The seas remained heavy and it proved an uncomfortable night with no sleep. I was in an area frequented by ships and I couldn't afford to nod off in case I ran foul of a hull. Conditions weren't conducive to sleep anyway, and while I managed to maintain a reasonable course it was achieved by much hard work as the sea tried to slew *Sharky* every which way. It would be a lie to say I enjoyed leaving the Cape Verde Islands. Being thrown around with a bad stomach, lashed with spray and with aching arms is not particularly enjoyable, but I didn't find it too unpleasant either. The positive framework of beginning the final leg and the anticipation of a challenging sail bolstered my morale, so I passed the night trying to stave off all feelings of wretchedness, quietly singing songs to myself, thinking of home. Singing, reminiscing and feeling queasy, we seafarers know how to enjoy ourselves!

Fourteen long hours later, I felt confident enough to let go the tiller, take a fix and pass the steering over to Maurice. I was exhausted but feeling much better than I had during the night. The wind was beginning to drop slightly and there was the possibility of a sunny day as light streaked into dawn. I promised myself I would use some of the expensive suntan cream I'd bought in Tenerife, the unopened tube not having seen the light of day since it arrived on the boat. Since leaving Palmeira I'd averaged about three miles an hour, not good but acceptable in these conditions. Today, hopefully, I would be able to let out more sail and increase the speed. For this leg I'd mackled together a running sail from a couple of old jib sheets. Looking like an upside-down kite with a horizontal pole at the base, it replaced the jib to give a larger area of sail. The downside was that as a fixed sail it couldn't be pulled down quickly, plus, it placed a significant strain on the rigging and mast in the event of a sudden squall. I'd designed it to increase my speed but had to be careful to allow sufficient time to dismantle it if the winds picked up. A vital aspect of this leg was a dependency on the trade winds, so-called because of their huge importance to international commerce in the days of sail.

The rest of the day went well, though my stomach still wasn't back to its usual self. I ate sparingly – a few biscuits – and drank copiously. The wind held steady at a gentle breeze so I left Maurice to work his magic. I passed the day easily, reading *Pilgrim's Progress* and listening to music, but I hadn't really got established into a routine as such, experience telling me that I'd need another two or three days yet before I was fully relaxed and settled. My body and mind weren't quite synchronised but I was content enough. Darkness eventually fell, underlining the feeling of aloneness. Strange to think that I knew where I was but nobody else did. Not one single person on the planet had any idea, though I knew a few people would care. I wondered if someone would be thinking of me. I was sure they would, so near in spirit, so far away in person. The only link at that moment was memory, a bunch of electrical and chemical stimuli in my head, fed for the most part on coffee, ciggies and biscuits while storing up life experiences for me to recall. Memory, the only way I could recall that I had friends, family and a life, an amazing part of me probably no bigger than one of my biscuits. The whole concept of life was just simply remarkable. As the wind died away a little more I sat on deck and marvelled again at my good fortune, privileged to be there and grateful to be able to appreciate the opportunity.

Slowly, I established my daily routine on board, which, strangely, consisted of very little routine at all. I adjusted to the cadence of a natural cycle uninterrupted by alarm clocks or civilisation's nine-to-five. I tuned in to my surroundings and tuned out of social trappings. My only regime was the daily noon fix and a write-up of my log every two hours or so. Taking the fix and calculating speed and the day's run was always a big occasion, because it put my journey into perspective. If I lost just fifteen knots a day over thirty days then I would be at sea for at least one more week than planned, crucial for supplies if nothing else. Other than those disciplines I led life as it happened. It takes a while to find this rhythm: the mind worries for a while that it's eight o'clock so it should be breakfast time, it's dark so the body should go to bed. The brain frets incessantly that it hasn't got a plan or a schedule to keep it on track, the ego keeps seeking to impress someone. Many people seem to find difficulty in acquiring this state but once gained it's an incredibly powerful release. As the song goes, the rhythm of life is a powerful beat, and so it is. Imperturbably the strictures instilled by westernised norms melt away, the senses absorb the sounds, smells and sights of nature and a pervading sense of real freedom permeates every pore. Real freedom, where things happen when you want them to for no reason, other than you feel you want them to. There are no external pressures, no one to authorise action or condone behaviour, life just is. If you take nothing else from this book try to make time for a few days to rid your life of any imposed discipline. It's not freaky, or 'touchy-feely', mystical or esoteric, it's not about being spaced out, it's real freedom without stimulants or drug-laden enhancements, but once experienced it leaves you wanting more.

So my tasks became non-routine. If I woke in the night and felt like making a brew and going on deck, then that is what I did. If I wanted to read or sleep I read or slept. In the jargon of the day I chilled out in my own expansive world and began to wish it would never end. Doing what I wanted also included doing what I needed to. The seas stayed heavy with a strong following breeze that added colour to the crest tops but necessitated the occasional adjustments and reefing the mainsail. The fluffy white clouds that were synonymous with the trade winds were nowhere in sight. Days remained cloudy with overcast skies, an occasional appearance of the sun helping to keep my spirit whetted with the hope of warmer times to come. In truth it wasn't too cold out of the blusters and, as I was sailing downwind, the motion was quite comfortable. Within a few days I was easing into the sail and feeling relaxed, enjoying each moment and taking over from Maurice whenever I wanted to commune with the sea through boat and tiller. After the initial fears when leaving Sal I was now beginning to feel like a true ocean traveller, alone in a huge expanse, riding the sea, rolling with the shifting deck, driving down the moderate to large waves, catching the spray. All the components were there – well, would have been, with some sun and fluffy white clouds – but I had the exhilaration of sea fever, I just felt born to it.

There was always plenty to do as jobs on a small boat take forever, mainly because of the motion and the requirement to do things one-handed, the other being used for balance or hanging on to something solid. Getting up, having a shave in lukewarm water followed by a strip wash or cooking a meal could easily take well over an hour. Shaving in particular always seemed to be hysterically lethal, just applying soap without swallowing it or injecting it into my nose or ears was a triumphant start. Using the razor required a cultivated sense of timing and deftness of touch. A semi-crouch resembling a gorilla on a waltzer, an alignment with a mirror clamped to the stove, left hand gripping the bunk for support and the right hand poised for a bristle strike, searching for the minutest moment of calm between wave swells. Half an hour of this malarkey will not give you the closest shave ever or make you desirous to women or mermaids, despite what the adverts promise. Visualise a startling phizog, pockmarked by areas of missed stubble interspersed with blotches of bloodspots, outcrops of congealed soap and an uncanny resemblance to Desperate Dan and you get the idea. It was very tempting to think sod it I'll grow a beard, but the longer the interval between shaves the more difficult to hack your way through to flesh eventually. Besides, a forty-day growth of hair and I might have been greeted in Barbados as someone from the Old Testament. Anyway, I've always liked a challenge. Once shaving was done I'd swap the bristly scum in the bowl for a pint or so of fresh water, then have a strip wash using a flannel, cavorting about with all the finesse of a drunken ballet dancer. Toilet complete, I'd set about breakfast, which, like most meals, consisted of tinned something with rice or fruit, biscuits or whatever came to hand. Hot drinks were always a luxury and a pleasure to be savoured, particularly when over fifty per cent could be drunk not spilled. The simplest act of pouring water into a kettle then transferring it to a mug was hard enough. Taking it from the cabin, through to the cockpit and out on deck required supreme balance, and actually drinking it without too much added sea spray required testing hand-to-mouth coordination. A cigarette was probably the easiest thing I ever put in my mouth.

And so life on board was never dull. Time passed and was occupied. Books were read, the guitar was strummed and tuneless songs sung. Small items of repair were effected, dreams were dreamt and occasional nightmares sweated out. I became part of the bubble that was *Sharky* and me, floating on a bigger bubble that was my endless horizon of sea and sky, a contented perpetual motion purposefully adrift in our own time and space. Ocean sailing has rich rewards as well as real hazards, and at times like these I was reaping the rewards in bucketfuls. Each day was, of course, eventful. This was still a tiny boat in a huge Atlantic and I couldn't afford to be cavalier and dismissive of the elements. Weather, even in the trade-wind zones, is never constant and there were always rogue waves that would crash across the deck or gusts of wind that would catch me unawares. Thus far I'd encountered only a little rain, though it was always possible to spot distant squalls menacing on the horizon. Occasionally these would sweep over *Sharky* at night, she would heel right over scattering any unfixed items, then slowly right herself until the next hammering. Often I'd be dragged from the depths of sleep and have to dash out to drop a sail or take control of the boat and spill the wind. Moments like these were always heart-thumping but never really heart-stopping. Earlier experiences had taught me how *Sharky* would respond to wind and swell, and I had slowly acquired a built-in sense of what was likely to happen. Instinctive and reactive sailing, the best and safest form there is, a true understanding of the marine environment and learnt skills attuned to its many moods.

I was not entirely alone in those first few days. There was a constant strong breeze creating large waves and foaming the crests into a whipped white froth. *Sharky* was climbing the walls and sliding down into the troughs when on my port side, not more than a few feet away, loomed a massive jelly fish, well over two feet across. It just appeared, a pulsating umbrella-shaped blob that provoked a primeval jolt of adrenalin in me. It appeared at eye-level then rose higher in the swell as *Sharky* dived into an adjacent trough. Semi-transparent with vicious-looking tentacles I feared it might be thrown on deck, but it passed serenely by. I had heard of lion's mane jellyfish, which could grow up to three feet across, and wondered whether this specimen had been such, and as I had also heard their venom could be fatal I was glad we hadn't been introduced. Occasionally the sea would throw up tiny flying fish, which landed on deck scattering in all directions. Only about an inch long, I couldn't even consider them as lunch. Other, larger flying fish would fly arrow-like in the middle-distance, but never near enough to get a good look. Finally one skimmed through the waves close to starboard, a thin streak of blue-silver with wing-like fins, a magical sight vanishing in a rising swell. After that first close encounter others appeared at random, often *Sharky* being the catalyst that startled them into flight. Zipping through the waves as an iridescent blur they seemed more bird than fish. I could have watched them for hours.

Running with the wind is elating but it has its drawbacks in big seas. Large waves can threaten to swamp a boat and it can get pretty scary in gales when cascades of water flood the deck and cockpit. On this part of the voyage I was fortunate not to be in such severe conditions, even if they were breakers. *Sharky* would normally lift and ride the waves, more so as the days went on and she became lighter in the water. For the most part the swell would come from astern and roll under the boat, though if I veered off more to broadside then we would certainly get slapped about a bit. Riding the sea this way is invigorating, a bit like riding a bucking horse, but after a while the body adapts and harmonises with the motion. Being swamped or hit by a breaker is like someone momentarily jamming car brakes on when you don't expect it. Rhythm and speed are killed together just as the equivalent of several buckets of water is thrown powerfully at your back. Unpleasant and decidedly wet, but the focus has to be on getting the boat's rhythm back again.

After five days or so, I decided to take stock of my provisions and ascertain the state of the equipment. The trip so far had been generally very enjoyable, though I had spent quite some time latterly cooped up in the cabin trying to keep dry. The notion of freedom I'd described earlier didn't mean that everything was hunky-dory all of the time. I was taking each day as it came but couldn't stifle the emotional changes and moods that made up my being. In some ways being at sea was no different to being anywhere else, environment and incidents affected emotions. What was different was the length of time on my own, much of which I enjoyed, some of which got me down. Small incidents magnified the reaction, a rogue wave that dowsed me unexpectedly, a line from a book or a song that brought on feelings of melancholy, trivial on their own but overblown if I let the inconveniences get to me.

When I first started sailing it worried me that these emotional highs and lows were character faults. By talking to other sailors and reading books, I had realised that these were necessary evils on long voyages. These mood swings were not new to me, I'd experienced them on every leg of this voyage, but sometimes they got in the way of my heightened expectation of a perfect finale. As on previous occasions I just had to accept them as part and parcel of each and every day. On the fifth day out I'd just downed a lunch of chicken and rice when two large swells broke over *Sharky* and soaked the cockpit, the suddenness of it playing hell with my digestive system. I felt frustration well up inside me for no rational reason, but sternly refused to allow the moodiness to overwhelm me. It was on that basis therefore I decided to do a stock-take and see what was what. At first glance some things were clearly not up to the mark. The cheap batteries I'd bought in Espargos, as expected, weren't lasting, and I was using up the packs fast. The ship's clock was now defunct, the batteries in my hand compass dying before my eyes. My wristwatch, which had semi-exploded in Tenerife when I'd spilt petrol over it, was held together with fraying insulation tape, so I taped it over the ship's clock and hoped it would hold out. The main battery for the lights had gone flat after leaving Tenerife, and it had been impossible to recharge it in Sal. Other than my Walkman and torch batteries, which I only intended to use in extremis, I was essentially running out of power, but frankly wasn't much bothered. If my wristwatch could tell me when to take the daily noon fix, that was all I needed. I also noticed that the boat needed bailing every day, though where the leak was remained a mystery. It was more inconvenient than critical, though I kept a wary eye on the situation. As for provisions, I reckoned I should be okay for my predicted sail time. Water supplies seemed to be holding up, though I decided to limit myself carefully until I was well over halfway across. Coffee however was fast running low. Of equal critical concern were the remaining six teabags, which I intended to conserve for anything I determined would constitute a special treat. The fresh fruit and vegetables, which had only a short lifespan, would be gone within a matter of days, leaving only oranges and onions, an interesting combination. Short of catching edible fish, which was a fanciful notion, I would be down to the remaining packets and tins.

Other than the irritating daily bailout, *Sharky* was looking ship-shape and positively Barbadian-bound. Maurice was performing well up to expectations and the repaired tiller and gooseneck were also holding up. Earlier in the day I'd been taking down the running sails when the pole had snapped clean in two. After the initial damn-and-blast reaction I reckoned it had probably been a blessing in disguise, as any excessive strain on the boat and rigging out there could have left me with real problems. I stowed the sails and pole bits and put up the mainsail again, *Sharky* responding without any noticeable loss of speed, and seemingly more comfortable. So, I rounded off my checklist with a tick in most boxes. Provision levels acceptable, *Sharky* and components performing well. All I needed to keep an eye on was me. I gave myself a nine out of ten for physical condition, but hesitated about my mental state. I eventually agreed to give myself ten out of ten for when I was feeling very positive, and when I wasn't I wouldn't bother with stupid and pointless marking systems.

Dark. Absolute, overwhelming darkness. Deep mine-black, impenetrable blindness when it's difficult to know whether your eyes are open or shut. Until I'd started sailing I'd never appreciated that there were different shades of dark, and never more so than at sea away from any landfall. On many nights when the sky is clear and moon or stars are visible, there is a celestial darkness that lifts the spirit and gladdens the heart. On nights when the sea is up the boiling phosphoresce casts a magical glow around the boat, but when the sea is calmer and no heavenly light is cast then darkness can be very black indeed.

It's a strange sensation when the mind can play tricks. There's an unnerving feeling that someone or something is just over your shoulder, compelling you to abandon all rational thought and quickly glance around – just in case, just to be prepared. It's also a time when aloneness can turn to loneliness, when the mind hits that patch of uncertainty that saps the confidence. A time for self-questioning, listening for peculiar sounds, waiting for the unexpected, a time for the bogeyman. With no visible point of reference, sometimes not even the hand in front of your face, such darkness can be very unsettling indeed. At the latitude at which I was sailing I was encountering about eleven or twelve hours of darkness every twenty-four. Needing only about six or seven for sleeping at night, fewer if I'd been dozing throughout the day, I'd frequently wake in the early hours and feel the urge to make a brew and sit out on deck. With my major battery now defunct, this inevitably meant making a drink by torchlight, then going out on deck to sit in some level of darkness. The sort of darkness seemed to affect or reflect my thoughts. A vast starry night would bring on feelings of wonderment, philosophical meanderings about life and thoughts of home and loved ones. Phosphorescent seas required more attention to sailing and practical activity, but the spooky nights were the longest. With nothing to see, drinking by touch alone and with the endless peering into an absolute nothingness, it wasn't long before imagination took over. On one such occasion, for no reason at all, the notion entered my head that I was going to sail into rocks. Totally irrational but nevertheless real: I physically braced myself and waited for an impact. The fact that one never came merely heightened the expectation as I peered expectantly towards the bow. Daft, completely stupid, but very, very real. I physically had to stand up and talk to myself to snap out of the belief. It doesn't take long for the mind to play tricks, so I quickly finished my coffee and went below, to sleep and await the comforting sight of daybreak.

My log for the 8th March read: 'Did a bit of washing today, tomorrow I shall wear clean underpants.' I suppose I wrote that just to remind myself that the life of a transatlantic yachtsman is not all glamour and adrenalin! Since leaving Sal the weather had remained mainly cloudy with masses of cumulus building up each day. The wind had fluctuated between force four and six, moderate through to strong breezes, which had fair pushed *Sharky* along. That, if it kept up, meant I would be making land sometime around the 25th. I'd encountered a squall or two most days, which added interest to an already lively sea, and in a way I began to look forward to the challenge as they formed up on the horizon. I'd now relaxed into the sail but was by no means complacent, the middle of the Atlantic being no place to lose alertness. My stomach had settled down and I was turning out some cracking meals on the two-ring cooker. The exaggerated motion of the boat required extreme caution when cooking, as I had no desire to add burns to the list of bumps, scratches, bruises, chafes and sores that populated my body. I had only one main meal a day, any time between eleven o'clock in the morning and five in the evening. Preparing the meal was a pleasant and much looked-forward-to ritual. I'd chop an onion and a couple of cloves of garlic into the frying pan, add a tin of meat or fish then cook a huge dollop of rice or pasta, Spaghetti Bolognese, pasta shells with chilli and chicken with rice being three of my favourites. Good, hearty and substantial meals, which I always looked forward to with enthusiasm, often over-eating until my stomach cried enough. A craving for my favourite foods depleted the provisions quite quickly, but I was always ravenous and had little willpower to resist adding another chunk of food to the pan. In the same way that small negative incidents seemed to be magnified at sea, so of course did the positive ones. Mealtimes, washing and shaving were such pleasurable events, but the greatest moments to delight in were doubtless concerned with digestive biscuits. It's a strange sort of person, you'd think, who would admit to getting excited about digestive biscuits but, taking the principle of small incidents magnifying frustration or pleasure, digestive biscuits were my all-time sensuous fetish. Every day I would allow myself two or three, a just reward as evening fell, a congratulatory gift to myself for coping with the day. As the tea brewed I'd carefully extract the biscuits from the packet, anticipating then slowly savouring every sweet crumb, the taste lingering on the buds then subsumed with a swallow of tea, a delicious end-of-the-day treat to which I always looked forward. Active life in the open air has always made me hungry, digestive biscuits have always made me salivate. Cast away on a desert island they would be my immediate choice for the one allowed luxury item. Perhaps my tombstone should read: 'Don't mind where I've gone so long as there's a supply of digie biscuits.'

One week out from Sal I'd covered a third of the distance, and was well pleased with the way things were going. I'd been averaging around 100 miles a day, I'd reconciled myself to the usual discomforts of any long voyage and I'd got clean underpants. I still had the chafing caused by sitting down for long periods of time, aggravated by the salt water that caused a constant damp itching and always worse in the more sensitive parts of my anatomy. Other than that, life couldn't get any better (well, a dry sleeping bag would have been nice, a few more teabags wouldn't have come amiss, a bit of a cuddle with the missus-to-be wouldn't have been rejected). A bit of sun and fluffy white clouds would have been welcome, a gentle breeze would have made a nice change, but I wasn't complaining. There was no one listening anyway.

CHAPTER FIFTEEN

Lazy Days

Every tick meant I gained and lost - that's the paradox of life. For everything I gained something else was lost, the bitter-sweetness of passing time.

WITH ONE WEEK ALREADY gone it occurred to me that at this rate it wouldn't be too long before I'd be in Barbados. Every day on *Sharky* was a day less on my adventure. What had started as a distant dream would soon be over. I was being caught in the trap of wanting to complete the sail and achieve my ambition while reluctant to let it end. It wasn't so much the uncertainty of knowing what would happen to my life afterwards – I was confident something would turn up – it was the great gaping hole that this exploit would leave behind. For several years the idea of sailing the Atlantic had consumed my waking hours and occupied my dreams. It had left me perilously short of money and deliriously high on a meaningful purpose. It had contextualised the necessity but relative unimportance of a working life and the potential for a lifetime with the sea. Sailing had given me an escape route from 'normality' and heightened my awareness of a spiritual aspect to life that I felt had made me a more rounded person. Not spiritual in a religious sense, more an appreciation of being human rather than a human being. I'd tested myself physically, mentally, emotionally, and learnt much. I'd grown close to the natural world and felt my soul uplifted. I'd experienced great joy and great distress, and learning to sail had been a major contributory factor. Wanting to sail the Atlantic had been the lighthouse beam that had focused my energies far into the future, the great goal that I'd set my heart on. Now I was getting to the furthermost edge of that beam. Looking back I could see clearly where I had been. Looking forward beyond Barbados, things were decidedly dim. Did I need another sailing challenge? Was I destined to return to 'normality'? I'd started out a single person and would return engaged to be married. Could I combine a passion for sailing with earning an income? Did I have it in me to abandon normality and roam the world in a carefree state? Too many questions that were beginning to intrude into the simple pleasure of riding the waves, but questions I knew would have to be answered quite soon. I resolved to take each moment as it came and enjoy it to the full, but a clock had started ticking. Every tick meant I gained and lost – that's the paradox of life. For everything I gained something else was lost, the bitter-sweetness of passing time.

Things had pretty much settled into a good sailing lifestyle, the skies cloudy, the wind remaining steadily breezy, with a fair amount of spray being hurled on deck. I'd noticed that the swells tended to drop late each afternoon for a few hours, though I reduced the sails again before turning in, as the seas frequently became lumpy as the nights drew in. I'd finally opened the sun-cream tube a few days earlier when the sun broke through, but was still looking forward to more sunshine as a change from the cloudy pall that greeted me most mornings. I opted for a shave and strip wash in seawater by way of a change, which was refreshing to say the least, but not something I was going to do on a regular basis, as I soon developed a very sore neck rash. My recurring back pain continued to give me gyp, exacerbated by the dampness of my sleeping bag and the constant motion of the sea. I was still using my hot water bottle as often as I could to ease the discomfort, but more often than not it was just a background niggle that wouldn't go away. I probably dreamt of a lingering, steaming hot shower every night. If pain was nature's way of reminding me I was alive, then it was doing a great job!

Sharky was also ploughing doggedly on, getting stuck in to the task in hand. Her only complaint manifested itself as a constant creaking, caused by the yawing motion. A boat in water can go in different directions and planes all at once, because it is subjected to forces from different elements as well as the opposing reaction to those forces. Not only will a boat go up and down, it will also go forwards and, particularly going downwind, side-to-side. A boat, and therefore anybody on the boat, can go forwards, up or down and side-to-side all at the same time, making for interesting fine tuning of the balancing function inside the brain. It takes the body a while to adjust to these various movements – recall how you respond on a train when standing and attempting to walk down the corridor, and that's just going forward and sideways a little bit. A boat cannot compensate as the mind can, it just goes where the greatest force pushes it before reacting to the effect of that force or another one. Put simply, it goes where it's told. Part of the physics involves yawing. As a boat goes forwards and up and down it also swings to the left of the forward point about forty-five degrees, before being pushed back and to the right about forty-five degrees, thereby completing a continuous arc of eighty to ninety degrees. Given all the various conflicting pressures, it was no wonder that *Sharky* felt she had the right to complain – hence the constant creaking. *Sharky's* creak from the yawing was a soothing part of the sailing experience, as comforting as the reassuring creak from a familiar trodden stair. It was always there, sometimes buried so deep in my subconscious I scarcely heard it. Sometimes it brought itself back to my attention, a little reminder that it was part and parcel of my existence. Sometimes it was lost in the background scream of a frenzied sea, other times it was all that could be heard, as mellow as leaves rustling on a summer's evening. A friendly noise, evocative and redolent. A noise familiar down countless centuries, whenever and wherever man meets sail and sea.

I don't know whether it was the yawing effect or the general wear and tear of sailing but I'd noticed *Sharky* was again leaking water in the rudder housing. The repair I'd made in Palmeira should ideally have been done out of water and given time to dry out, but there hadn't been the facilities. Now it was leaking again, probably with the constant use of the rudder, the water beginning to invade the whole boat, not just the rudder housing. It was more of a troublesome concern than a major worry, and just warranted an eye keeping on it. One morning I'd bailed out five or six gallons when a large wave crashed over the stern filling up the hatch yet again. I was wearing only underpants in anticipation of getting a little wet, but this dousing was more invigorating than I'd expected – nothing like an ocean power shower to create that all-over tingling sensation. Life on a long sail is full of constant and continuing makeshift repairs, not surprising given the rigours of the environment. Leaks, squeaks and snaps. Repairs helped pass the time by providing opportunities for practical activity and a chance to stand back and admire my handiwork, the inherent pride of cobbling something together from what's available. I had finally managed to stop the mast from creaking by wedging a screwdriver under the mast step and hammering in small wooden wedges. Such a simple remedy, but one with which I was dead chuffed. I kept admiring it on occasion as though it was some major engineering miracle. Like a kid with a new toy, but it kept me happy. I was also delighted with a further repair to one of Maurice's running lines that had snapped again, just after I'd retired to my sleeping bag one night. I'd heard the mainsail flapping and went on deck to discover the line had broken and was trailing aft of the boat. Grabbing some spare line, I harnessed myself up, slung a torch round my neck and leant way out beyond the stern to drag in the old line and install the new. In pitch dark with a torch waving around in all directions and with breakers washing over me it made for an interesting quarter of an hour, but I was pleased to have done it without panic. Other than a nasty scrape on my arm from one of Maurice's bolts, it was just another repair that had to be done quickly. I just hoped my knots would hold out until daybreak, when I could run a more thorough check.

What a difference a day makes. I woke up to find a distinct improvement in the weather, still breezy but warmer and with cumulus clouds billowing up, much nicer than the rather staid stratus stuff that had been hanging about. I was fixed on a heading of 270 degrees, still making about ninety miles a day under a fully reefed mainsail, racking up an average four knots an hour, and looking forward to the day when I could turn the chart over and see the final section in all its anticipated glory. Such a simple act, the turning of a chart, but it would represent a significant achievement for me. My chart had been folded in such a way that when the eastern Atlantic, covering Africa and Europe, was all visible on one side, the western side covering North and South America and the Caribbean was face down. As my daily fix-point crosses were added, the pencil line stretched ever further west towards the all-important crease in the chart. When I reached that point in the ocean that coincided with the crease I would turn over the chart, my destination would now be permanently and constantly visible on the chart table, the lure that would guide me to my final harbour. On that day Barbados would become a real and tangible goal, the prize (albeit not my original port) I had wanted for so long. However, the chart had not yet turned, there was plenty of sailing left, plenty of reading time, plenty of bailing-out time by the looks of it, and plenty of horizon-gazing – a sort of dreamtime when I turned introspective and let my thoughts flow unimpeded wherever they ran: past, present, future, a precious time to let go and just be.

I spent a lot of time thinking about Elaine and wishing she was with me, our future together taking up quite a bit of my horizon-gazing moments. I was intending to phone her when I reached land and arrange for her to fly out so we could share a holiday together – the perfect end to my journey. The human condition is never constant and sometimes I wished I was nearer to finishing, so that I could see her as soon as possible. At other times I wanted to stay on the ocean forever. The nights were the loneliest, each day a visual world waning with the light as my imagination waxed in the dark. Nights could still be long and scary, the roar of the unseen swells chasing *Sharky*'s stern, followed by the hiss of the water when they broke and crowded the cockpit before draining away, the absolute wrap-around blackness all-pervading. Ten days out from Sal, I awoke feeling not quite right, nothing physical, just a feeling. I'd spent another night locked in a series of vivid dreams, which seemed very real, and on waking it was with some disquiet. I'd regularly had disturbing dreams when in a deep sleep, often waking in a sweat, but they'd never affected me afterwards. No, it was something else, a little cog not quite meshing in my head. The feeling lasted most of the day, but I just couldn't put my finger on it. I rounded off the evening with a hearty meal of rice and tuna steak and had just brewed my evening mug of tea when the penny dropped and the niggle was swept away. The disquiet melted and I knew in an instant clarity that I didn't want to do another long ocean sail. I wasn't depressed, miserable or particularly wanting this adventure to finish quickly. I just thought, 'I don't want to do this again. I don't want to spend my life or even a few months sailing solo. I'm not a Moitessier or a Shane Acton.' My earlier thoughts of a life at sea were merely wishful thinking. What I had really wanted to do was *live* the dream of sailing the Atlantic. Somewhere along the line I'd confused living the dream with dreaming about a life at sea. I sat and pondered, and somehow felt better and much relieved. I'd reached another crossroads in my life. I hadn't said I didn't want to sail again, I'd decided I couldn't give my life to it. There was a finality to the thought that I knew wasn't influenced by my current or past moods. I could now look forward to the rest of this journey with a bit more contentment, still not knowing what life had in store for me after it had ended, but knowing that one option was not for me. Sailing was going to remain in my blood but I wasn't going to be driven by it.

Daily life assumed an air of relative predictability but not routine, little incidents adding points of interest when least expected. Reading in my cabin I heard what sounded like high-pitched squeaks and went out to investigate, finding a school of bottlenose dolphins cavorting about the boat. This was the first time I'd seen them so close since Chris and I had sailed from Falmouth on the first leg, and once again I was entranced by their grace and sleekness, lively eyes scanning *Sharky* with curiosity. They dived under and about the boat, their tail flukes providing powerful thrusts to propel them along. I counted eight or nine, each about two to three metres long as they flashed past, sharp interlocking peg teeth grinning in what seemed sheer delight. I'd read that these warm-blooded mammals could empty and re-fill their lungs in less than a fifth of a second, expelling air through their blowholes at speeds in excess of 100 miles an hour. Delightful to look at, these animals were superbly adapted to the sea, and after a few minutes they were gone, lost to sight in the oceanic expanse: it felt a little lonely for a while after they'd disappeared, a bit like close friends who'd dropped in for a quick 'hello' but couldn't stay long. The cabin however was now looking as though several friends had stopped over and overstayed their welcome. It was damp and becoming dirty but I had little enthusiasm for cleaning it, not because I was getting sloppy but because the constant rolling motion was just not conducive to anything more than a desultory attempt at the bare minimum. Most days I determined to improve appearances but never quite got round to it. I was also getting considerably bruised and cut, the ingress of salt water not helping the healing process. The noon fixes continued to be a daily highlight, and although progress was good the little crosses I was marking on the chart each day seemed to be painfully close together. With journey's end estimated to be about a fortnight away, I was beginning to feel restless, with a need for some home comforts, an easing of body pain, a dry bed and a decent shower again, proof I suppose that despite being surrounded by stunning seascapes and having an experience granted only a relatively few, there comes a point when the human spirit has had enough wonderment and just wants something a bit more mundane.

I spent the morning of 8th March making some repairs to the mast, getting a mild touch of sunstroke into the bargain. I hadn't touched the rudder housing or the bilges for a couple of days so had to bail out about ten gallons of water, about seventy-five pounds of deadweight I was glad to lose. As the afternoon wore on the barometer dropped a couple of points and the wind increased to a very strong breeze. The waves heaped up, then bore down on *Sharky*'s back, pushing her forward in a series of smooth surges or raining down even more sea onto her deck. By noon the next day I expected to be about halfway across the Atlantic, and within five or six days of that would come the all-important event, the turning of the chart for the inward run. Large storm clouds began to gather from the east and I felt my mood change with the impending bad weather, which duly arrived in the late evening. I spent the night enduring severe squalls, strong gusts and heavy driving rain, feeling miserable and wanting the whole thing over and done with. I felt at the end of my tether, wishing I were having a few pints with my friends. The increased rolling had upset my stomach, making me feel quite ill and increasing my anxiety levels, though as conditions had become far too rough to cook it didn't really matter about food. By daylight, much to my relief, the squalls were beginning to blow over and by mid-morning we had returned to a steady fresh breeze accompanied by the return of an overcast sky, the sea remaining its usual energetic self, washing the decks with spray and a regular dousing of salt water.

The great solace I had on board was reading. Hardly a day went by without finding my nose buried in a book. It took a while to adjust to small print while being tossed about like salad in a colander, but once in among the pages I was transported and mesmerised, my boat world banished to the edges of my consciousness. I probably spent as much of my voyage in the wastes of Antarctica, the deserts of Arabia, the Himalayan peaks or other exotic locations as I did in the Atlantic. I read avidly and widely, fact and fiction, superficially and profoundly. I covered religion, politics, adventure, philosophy, humour, history and geography in equal measure. I absorbed the written word and spent time considering the thinking behind the writer's intentions. I learnt as much about people as I did their assorted subjects. I became intrigued, horrified, saddened and gladdened at the world about me. I marvelled at the generosity of mankind and in equal measure dismayed by its pitiless cruelty. I began to understand how different writers told their tales and what attracted me to the telling. I soaked up their stories as avidly as the sea soaked into my clothes. At home as I was preparing for the long haul I'd asked my close friends and family each to buy me a book, anything that they thought I might enjoy. I'd made no requests or suggestions, they had complete control over what they gave. What had surprised and delighted me was the huge diversity of my accumulation, even including two fictional horror stories, as if I was not going to encounter sufficient myself! With some additions of my own choosing, I eventually left Buxton with forty books to look forward to. The real pleasure though was not the fact that I had learnt to enjoy them but that I could read them at all. I've mentioned before that my early days of schooling had not been without their problems, not helped by a disrupted childhood involving parental divorce, living with elderly relatives then moving back with Mum and Norman, the new man in her life. The disjointedness of change confused and unsettled me. Moving homes meant moving schools and I can barely remember a thing about my primary education, few teachers or pupils' names, lessons or incidents. Actually that's not strictly correct. I was sent home from my first school one day because I wet myself in class. That's it. One of only two vivid recollections of the most formative years of education the system has provided me with was that I didn't make it to the toilet in time. The other memory was moving into Peak Dale when we went to live with Mum and Norman. It meant another change and I joined the village primary school where my class teacher, Mr Oliver, took me under his wing. Tall, slender and with a deep booming voice, his rendition of assembly hymns would resonate about the high windowed walls. I remember Mrs Potts too but more for the effect on my stomach than my learning. As a school cook she was the best I had encountered in my limited experience and the endurance of schooldays was more for her homemade dinners and puddings than the singular inconsequence of the lessons before and after lunch. I recall regularly watching a BBC schools television programme called *Picture Box* in a room with only a few other children and, puzzled, asking my mum why all the children didn't watch it.

'Must be because you're very important,' she'd say.

I didn't feel very important as in most lessons I seemed to be struggling to keep up with my peers. Particularly with reading and writing, the letters seemed to jump about the page and I just couldn't understand things. After the unexpected transition to a restored stable family, I felt secure in my home life, but in school I was insecure and ill at ease. It was several years before anyone understood that I was severely dyslexic. Going through secondary education and particularly under more personal tuition in the Arabian Gulf, I improved slowly but, by way of compensation, realised I had a talent for arithmetic and mathematics. Throughout my adult life words and figures have been the yin and yang of my skills. Reading has become both a real delight and a daily opportunity to improve my English skills, but it has often been a turgid struggle. Figures have always come more easily. I may not be the best written communicator of all time but give me a boat, a chart and some angles and I can plot where I am and where I'm going, using the full deployment of trigonometry, geometry and mental arithmetic. I find it a peculiar polarity that grammar and spelling can be so taxing to me yet calculations both in business and leisure are second nature. But what a useful second nature they proved to be when sailing.

For general chart work I would use dividers, parallel rule and a square protractor. Calculating speed and distance while taking into account the effect of tides, weather and currents involved no more than basic arithmetic, while taking a sight with a sextant using the sun, moon or stars involved simple trigonometry. I say simple but it was perhaps more complex than complicated. Acquiring the angle of the heavenly body with the sextant then involved using a book with the wonderful title of *The Reeds Nautical Almanac*, full of interpolation and correction tables. I also had a copy of *The Sight Reduction Tables for Marine Navigation* – a weighty tome produced by the Royal Navy hydrographer. By working in a bit of declination, refraction and increments to the figures in the tables and assuming (a vital assumption) that my sextant reading and time taken were correct, then it was a case of lots of addition and subtraction to determine my location and mark it on the chart. I must admit though that the whole process of determining a precise location can be daunting and does require some confidence in one's abilities. Tiredness and carelessness can cause major mistakes, so a disciplined approach is necessary. The first time I used a sextant and tables to plot my position I found myself just south of Iceland, and the fact that I was actually in the Solent at the time with not an iceberg in sight convinced me for all time of the importance of accuracy in measurement and calculation. Twenty-first-century sailors have the advantage of very sophisticated GPS, which takes much of the mental out of the arithmetic but are still fallible: when the battery fails your best friends may yet be a pencil and your brain.

I celebrated the halfway crossing in spectacular if inadvertent fashion. Sound asleep I awoke to the blast of an explosion, a combined crack and whoosh that had my befuddled mind fearing the worst. At first I thought *Sharky* had hit something, then I wondered if someone was firing at me. I sat bolt upright, cracking my head on the cabin roof. The detonation was followed by a gentle rain of sweet-tasting mist that drifted over me, a mist suspiciously reminiscent of Coke. I'd bought a four-pack way back in Tenerife, and the constant motion combined with saltwater corrosion had finally been enough to blow one of them up. I found it hysterically funny, the timing being absolutely perfect. Not only was it the day I had sailed halfway across the Atlantic, it was also Elaine's birthday. A one-can sticky Coke salute was just too delicious for words. I made a brew with my one remaining teabag and raised my mug in a long-distance toast to Elaine. I'd made arrangements, as on previous birthdays when I'd been away, for a bouquet of flowers to be delivered to her. No doubt she'd be out celebrating that evening, which made me momentarily jealous, but I wasn't too put out. Why on earth would I want to be anywhere else than in a damp, rolling cabin in the darkness of the Atlantic, surrounded by my own private arsenal?

As daylight streaked out from the east a majestic azure sky unfolded above me, the sea's colour reacting in similar vein. A huge red sun rose majestically as if offering its own congratulations on my voyage, and a few white clouds formed and reformed in the rising warmth. Good weather stirs the spirits and that, plus the combined occasion of halfway, Elaine's birthday, and the fizzy absurdity of the previous night, found me in good humour. The wind dropped to no more than a light breeze and by mid-morning the clouds had disappeared altogether and the temperature was getting very hot. The previous day's chart position had revealed I'd been making too much northing so I'd altered course by about ten degrees. The light winds sometimes weren't strong enough to get *Sharky* back on course as she snaked downwind, so I'd drifted about a bit too much. Occasional bouts of helming helped counter the accidental gybes but Maurice, coupled with the preventer, generally held us in the right direction overall. Tempting as it was to absorb the sun's rays, I pulled on my jogging bottoms and long-sleeved shirt to cover as much flesh as possible – I had no intention of spoiling today of all days with the effects of sunstroke. A glance at the barometer as I took the noon fix showed pressure was beginning to drop despite the sunny disposition, and I wondered if this was the calm before the storm. I fervently hoped not. I'd endured too many bad days stuck in the cabin. Now I wanted more of the sun and a wider horizon than a curbed fibreglass bowl.

I lunched at about two o'clock, a fairly sorry affair of pasta shells, chilli and a few onions. A few days earlier I thought I had plenty of food, but stocks seemed to be going down quite quickly. What little I had left of the fruit and vegetables was looking rank and grim and my tinned stuff seemed to consist of tuna, sardines, corned beef, chicken and peaches. I threw the rotting fruit and vegetables over the side, leaving me with two semi-respectable onions. I was stuck with the tinned food but for some reason I wasn't too keen to open the chicken. I was still getting a deck full of stranded flying fish most days, sometimes as many as twenty or so, but more sprat-like than anything, all of them being under two inches in length, hardly an edible supplement to their tinned cousins. Water and cigarettes were in plentiful supply, I'd just have to eke out the food and accept I'd be a little more hungry each day than I'd been used to.

That night marked the longest time I had been continually at sea, a day over two weeks. I felt I'd handled it well overall and had got used to the emotional ups and downs. Mostly I'd hated the enforced confinement in the cabin when bad weather had prevailed, dashing out only when the calls of nature made it absolutely essential. I'd suffered physically and mentally but been equally buoyed up by the sea's hypnotic appeal, the beauty of the natural world about me and by the exhilaration of sailing solo. Now I had the endgame in my sights and once more wanted to savour what journey time was left. I lay in my bunk thinking of the finality of adventures, that I probably wouldn't do this again and that the memories might soon fade. I wondered about writing a book some day while the experience was still fresh, a tangible look back for my old age and a family story for my kids and grandchildren.

'Flipping 'eck,' I grinned, 'I'm only thirty, not yet married and here's me worrying about old age, grandkids and a place in history.'

To confirm the decision I wrote in my log, 'I shall make a serious effort to write my own book. I WILL do it!'

I didn't feel tired, couldn't sleep, so went out on deck and watched the moon. The wind died away totally for about fifteen minutes, a short, eerie calm that settled and contented me. I must have sat in a reverie for a long time, recalling only as dawn broke that the big bank of black cloud in front and to the sides of me might be the storm I'd been expecting. The weather remained quite weird throughout the day, hot and sultry, though the barometric pressure continued to fall. The wind fell away to almost nothing, yet it felt as though a strong blow might rush in at any minute. The oppressive air forced a throbbing headache and I almost wished for a storm to freshen everything up. At the noon fix I had sailed 1,056 miles from Sal with just over 900 to go, Barbados still seeming a long way off but, strangely, also pretty close. I really fancied a coffee but my supplies were now very low and as I'd restricted myself to one morning cup each day it took all my willpower to resist the urge. To make matters worse I lost my best bucket overboard, a petty, trivial accident I magnified out of all proportion. It was my favourite bucket, used for just about every possible mentionable and unmentionable function. I watched it bob away from the boat in dismay and futile frustration. I'd just been reading *Tornado Down* by John Nichol and John Peters, recalling how they'd coped with solitary confinement and how vital inconsequential routines and items had been to retaining their sanity. While I was in no way making a comparison with the horrors they endured, I could empathise with their feelings of being alone. I missed my yellow bucket, I really did.

The wind wafted with a vague indifference and I made little headway. The sultry conditions eased only slightly as night fell and the cloud base got thicker, but still no rain. I'd never seen clouds like those before, a foreboding pale yellow mixed with dark streaks. Combined with the quietness of my surroundings it all felt very threatening and menacing, I was exceedingly negative and bowed under by an unseen weight pressing me down. I spent a restless night alternating between sleepless sweating and vivid, terrifying dreams of wars and killings. As morning filtered through the cabin I could stand it no more. I got up, had a strip wash, a cigarette and a cup of coffee. The sea was still calm and I was making no more than a couple of knots an hour. It looked like another long, slow day ahead with my headache mulishly refusing to go away. Foolishly I sunbathed, read, ate lunch and gazed into the distance with no real agenda – just gazed and stared. Lunch consisted of a drab tasteless mush of corned beef and rice and I fantasised about what I would eat when I made land. My head filled with the prospect of bacon butties, ice cream and chocolate, ice-cold beers, large scotch whiskies, fresh fruit, juicy steak and chips and delicious freshly baked bread. I'd had enough of Spartan living. I gave myself full permission for a celebratory blow-out. All I needed was a decent wind to blow me headlong into a land of restaurants – and to hell with the calories!

Chapter Sixteen

A Perfect Moment

A deep calm fell upon me. I had the world to myself, an unrestricted horizon, a beautiful boat and an inner peace.

WHILE THE RESPITE FROM bad weather was a welcome change, the torpid conditions were in some ways just as bad. I'd reckoned on an average of ninety miles a day, but for the past few days I'd slipped further and further behind my schedule. The relaxed informal cadence of the first week was starting to be replaced with an anxiety fuelled by calculating time, by distance travelled and miles to accomplish. The sailing was still balmy, but slow, oh so slow. The winds remained un-trade like, fluky in manner with no pattern to their being. Clouds also had little constant structure, changing from high, wispy cirrus overhead to lower scattered altocumulus further north, provocatively promising rain but to no avail. I could feel the cooler air drawn in by these cumulus clouds but it made no impact on my speed. The anticipation of turning over the chart had turned to a desperation bordering on the 'if' rather than the 'when'. The weather was great, I wasn't really complaining but it was rather like floating on a giant sunbed when what I really wanted was the thrill of riding the waves. Sailing is about challenge, of pitting human skills against a formidable force. It's about wind and sea, exhilaration and fear. I wanted to go back to being a real seafarer, not mimicking a bloody tourist lounging about sipping absurd cocktails. I was ploughing through books like crazy, taking my time and savouring their tales, but I was reading for longer periods of time in the absence of much else happening. I'd stop and try to busy myself with washing clothes or pointless pottering, but I was soon back into the more exciting and imaginative worlds that were happening between the pages. It was crazy. Given all the bad weather and gales I'd endured on every part of my quest, I should have been eternally grateful to the gods for the opportunity to bask in these temperate climes, but, like all spoilt sailors, I wanted the perfect conditions, not too cold, not too warm, not too smooth, not too rough.

What I got of course was what I got. I welcomed my seventeenth morning with a few exercises from a book on Tai Chi I'd recently started, wondering whether the exercises and thought processes would ease the exasperation. By afternoon I sensed the approach of freshening wind with all the eagerness of a child expecting sweets, and sure enough it picked up to a moderate breeze, but only for an hour or so before dying away, *Sharky* barely moving again, a sluggish, lethargic trail more befitting a snail than a sloop. By nightfall the wind increased but only slightly. A bright moon bursting through from its prison of clouds turned the scene almost as bright as day, its glow casting shards of silver across the ocean as far as I could see. A leisurely breeze held throughout the night and I was grateful for small mercies, consistency was infinitely preferable to stop-start conditions. As the next morning progressed, the wind picked up again as the clouds thickened, blowing some apologetic odd spots of rain against my face, and then, predictably, dropping again as the sun burst through the rapidly scattering clouds. I was back to stop-start and again beginning to think it was time to get the trip over and done with.

I spent a lot of the day when the sun came out cooped up in the cabin, not through choice but commonsense. Whenever possible I tried to cover up and use as little suntan cream as possible – the last thing I needed was more burnt skin to add to the rubbing salt chafes that were part of daily life. Having gawped at water for so long, it was getting difficult to remember what green fields and hills looked like. My favourite pursuit, apart from sailing, was walking the hills and dales of Derbyshire with my dog. I'd sort of inherited Whisky from mum, and I used to take him for long walks whenever I needed a break from work. Whisky was a West Highland terrier, full of bounce, who could match me for stamina on long walks. He was bright-eyed and full of energy, with an endearing way of looking at me, head cocked to one side, ears pricked up as if he understood everything I was saying. Being cooped up on *Sharky* without the benefit of really stretching or exercising my legs, I reckoned the dog would probably be fitter than me when I returned. Sitting in the cabin, thoughts inevitably turned to returning home, a prospect now tantalisingly near. I wondered how I'd adjust back to normality: would it be easy having completed my challenge, or would the wanderlust hang about, enticing me back with the promise of high adventure, bad times conveniently erased from my memory? I had no idea: I just wanted to finish with a bang not a whimper. I wanted to hail into Barbados with sails unfurled, with a sailor's wind at my back, sitting at the helm and riding a surging sea. I wanted to finish in style and with panache, a satisfying ending as befitted a lone seafarer. I didn't want a triumphal, self-congratulatory end but perhaps something that might inspire any future children or grandchildren, a Caribbean salty dog endearing and enduring with beguiling tales to tell. At the current rate of progress any children were not going to be that impressed – a sore-arsed, starving and crusty fella limping in on a dead sea or being towed in by a fisherman was probably going to be nearer the truth. I hoped not though, I really did want to finish as I'd started, well and in good spirits. A little bit more wind, please – not much to ask after having come so far, was it?

The light breeze would just not pick up, which was unsettling. It was worse than being fully becalmed. In truth I was covering some distance each day, but not as much I'd anticipated. Relatively, therefore, everything seemed to slow down. I was also living a twenty-four-hour day, unbroken by organised chunks of activity, which had the effect of dragging out time (I'd long lost the natural cadences and was back to my westernised anxieties of material time). The slow, pedantic crawl was akin to creeping in traffic at rush hour. Becalming was understandable but dawdling was agonising. I'd lost over a day's mileage and felt like screaming in frustration. There was less and less to do to fill the days and nights, and much as I loved reading it couldn't be a full-time occupation. My senses were always tuned to the slightest hint of a breeze, and what little there was pushed me a tad too far north of the latitude I wanted for Barbados. Another gybe was required to get back on the course I needed. I realised I was getting through my food supplies more quickly than I'd anticipated, and marvelled that my last onion was now thirty-seven days old and still as firm as when I'd bought it. The tinned supplies were going down because, once opened and in the heat, I had to eat the full contents rather than leave half for another day's meal. I found myself therefore in the interesting position of gorging myself in order to starve! To round off the day's excitement fully, I saw my first ship since leaving the west coast of Africa. My initial thought was that it was another yacht but, two miles astern, it turned out to be a large fishing vessel. I had little chance of getting out of its way, with no headway to speak of, and was quite relieved when it altered course and came no nearer. Although still a long way out for a fishing boat it might have meant that I was in a fishing area, entailing a better watch at night to avoid being part of a catch.

With only the swells providing real momentum, I continued to fret about progress, or rather the lack of it. With a dark sense of irony, my remaining books were horror stories by Stephen King, great for reinforcing my imagination as the black nights rolled in. With such a vast expanse of unlimited horizon it was quite weird to see night approach from such a distance. In a town, night creeps in almost without notice, the distractions of urbanity and the closeness of buildings assuming the greater focus for people's lives. But out here in the ocean, with a heightened feeling of insignificance living at wave-level, the falling of night was something I couldn't escape. Alongside the beauty and wonder of the sky's changing colour and hues, there was often a menacing side to the event. A blue sky would slowly, steadily deepen and darken with a thin band of cloud often sneaking up from the east. The temperature would drop with the sun, and if the cloud bank was storm-dark it was as though a huge stifling blanket was gradually being pulled over me, like a claustrophobic shell from which I couldn't escape. On slow days I often felt a morbid sense of gloomy foreboding as evening and night fell. There was a real sense of understanding that another day of my life was over, never to return, causing me to muse over how I'd spent it – fruitfully or wastefully. Such experiences fascinated, rather than dejected me, a salient reminder of how precious the gift of life was, a gift not to be taken lightly or for granted. Alongside these esoteric musings was the more practical consideration that I would shortly be down to a ration of dried porridge oats. What remaining pasta and tins of tuna I had could be eked out for three or four days at most (I'd chomped my way enthusiastically through the ancient onion a couple of days earlier) but then the vaguely gourmet lifestyle would be over. I'd always looked forward to mealtimes – I just wondered what motivation I'd need to drag up enthusiasm for endless bowls of grey sludge. Nourishing though it is, porridge lacks a certain flair in the presentation stakes, and scores a resounding 'nul point' in the 'yummy tastes' category. Ah well, I reasoned, at least no more deliberating about what to cook for dinner.

Twenty days out and I had my first visitor on board. I'm discounting the tiny flying fish that had earlier crash landed on deck. *Sharky* was quietly bobbing along in the twilight when I was disturbed by a swishing sound. I glanced up to see an elegant dark-grey bird with webbed feet and a three-inch beak looking down on me as it circled the masthead. I think we just stared at each other until I remembered my manners and called out a welcoming 'hello'. The bird merely stared back unblinking as if this sort of thing happened all the time, then flew down to the prow of the boat, tucked one leg under its body and settled down for the night. I had no idea from whence it had come or indeed what sort of bird it was, but it had clearly spotted *Sharky* as a convenient floating motel. It stayed on the deck all night, leaving with a leisurely flapping of wings at daybreak. I also had my best night's sleep for over a week. The relative inactivity of sitting, fretting, reading normally meant I was never tired enough to grab some deep meaningful rest. That night however I slept soundly for over seven hours. Perhaps my itinerant avian friend had calmed me down. It didn't last long though. The blood pressure was up again the following morning as a few high clouds that I thought might bring stronger winds infuriatingly melted away as the sun bore down. Twenty-one days now of which ten had been bloody frustrating periods of turgid meandering getting me nowhere fast. I half-wondered whether it would have been quicker to tie a rope round my waist and swim with *Sharky* in tow. The dawdling is unexplainable. From one perspective you might wonder what on earth there was to be moaning about, total freedom, no work pressure, warm, sunny weather, but ten days of it! There was no change to the monotony, no let-up to the ponderous lethargy. It was like sitting on a train going nowhere with nothing to do other than stare out of the windows. Time, if not standing still, loitered like a recalcitrant child. I was stranded in a slothful warp where day followed night, night followed day, and that was about as exciting as it got. I'd have wept with joy at the prospect of a storm. Even the noon fixes lost their appeal, as the daily mileage was pitiful, down to under forty miles, much of that gleaned from the current. I'd been excited by the prospect of sailing in the trade winds but they seemed to have upped sticks and emigrated. Not for the first time I wrote in my log, 'Come on, wind, blow, please, pretty, please!!'

I'd given up reading for long periods as my eyes quickly started to water and my headaches had returned, whether from the bright water, sun reflections off the page, the strain from concentrating on small text or the oppressive humidity. I therefore had even longer to spend doing nothing but think, especially worrying about my loved ones, who might now be wondering whether I was close to land. I was sure they'd be getting anxious as each day passed, even though I'd overestimated my likely sail time. I tried not to agonise about something totally out of my control, but that was easier said than done. It was somehow quite peculiar to realise that while I bobbed about feeling aggrieved, I knew there'd be plenty of times in the future when I'd look back on this period of inactivity and just wish I could relive it all again. Funny thing the human mind, we always want what we haven't got, then having got it, we don't want it.

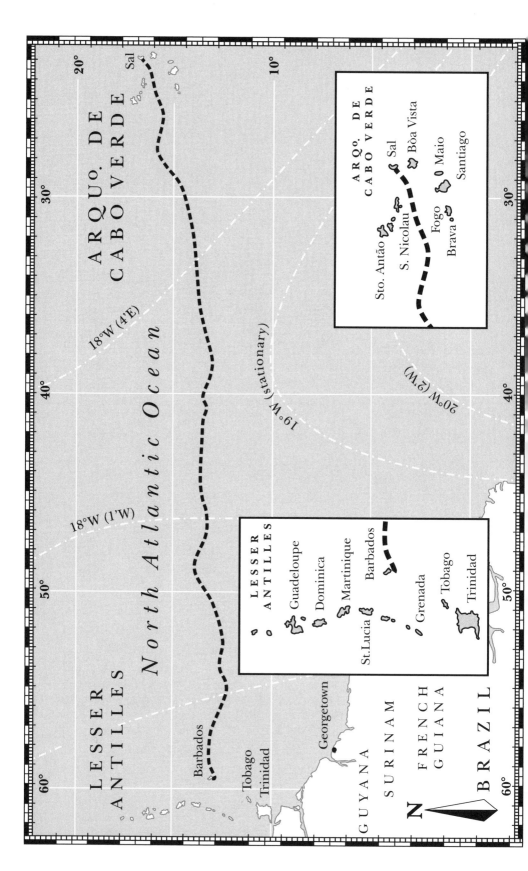

After three weeks of writing petulant comments in my log I awoke on the Monday morning to a small but substantial increase in the wind. Not much more than a gentle breeze, but *Sharky* picked up on it and in the relative scheme of things it felt we were beginning to cut through the water again, the mainsail filling well rather than the morose flapping about I'd got used to. As the day progressed I entered waters full of fish, spotting what I initially thought were sharks, but which I then reckoned were dorados – large ugly-faced golden fish with beautiful blue-green backs covered in blue spots, their pectoral fins a riveting electric blue. They would swim about *Sharky*, then suddenly disappear in search of the numerous flying fish that darted through the air in great shoals. I desperately wanted a decent photo of them but my reaction was always too slow, my camera never pointing in the right direction at the right time. That day I felt good about everything. The sun was again very hot but the wind remained steady. Sighting and watching the fish was absorbing and most enjoyable. I was engaged again, involved in what was going on about me, becoming reacquainted with my situation. In short, I had something to do and something to watch. I said that I felt good about everything, everything of course except lunch, which consisted of porridge. Never mind, I wasn't particularly hungry, and even the grey lumps couldn't detract from an inner feeling of quiet contentment. If this breeze continued and I was careful with my food, and especially the water supplies, I might be able to think cautiously about an estimated time of arrival in Barbados, something I hadn't contemplated for a long time.

And that day got better. About four or five o'clock in the afternoon I went on deck and made my way to the bow. I sat with my legs outstretched, lit a cigarette and lay with my back against the mast. The sun was still hot but the stifling heat of noon had faded. The sky was azure, the ocean reflecting indigo, with the odd flash of light, as a wavelet here and there sparkled in the sunlight. There was a peculiar intensity about the light, vivid, vibrant, dramatic, stark, like a painting bright with rich colours but offering little by way of subtleness. The world was calm and quiet, the wind scarcely ruffling the water, *Sharky*'s hull making the only sound as it hissed quietly through the water. On previous days like this I'd been irritated and restless, not noticing the beauty of my surroundings. But today was different; today I *felt* different. The wind, fish, something, had restored an equilibrium. A deep calm fell upon me. I had the world to myself, an unrestricted horizon, a beautiful boat and an inner peace. There were no external or extraneous interruptions, no engine, electrics or mechanical devices. I had stumbled upon a sensation I hadn't been looking for and I wondered whether this was the sort of experience gurus, monks and so forth spent a lifetime trying to attain. Once again I felt at one with nature, an integral component of the pleasure of being. For maybe thirty minutes or so, I just *was*. Since learning to sail I had enjoyed many instances similar to that extraordinary half-hour, but on reflection this time it was somehow more humbling and special, an indefinably little bit different from previous such moments, and one I don't know whether I shall ever experience again. Whenever I think back to my Atlantic voyage it is that abiding memory that is first and foremost in my mind. I haven't encountered such a profound moment since, and know there is no point in trying to manufacture one. I am certain though it requires the natural elements and solitude. Moments like that don't happen in a frenzied lifestyle. I sincerely hope my children get to experience and wonder at it for themselves. Second-hand words are a poor substitute for living the intense pleasure such occasions bring.

The moment passed and I felt spiritually and physically refreshed. It seemed like another milestone, almost a farewell memory, nature's way of saying thanks for doing the trip and appreciating the beauty about you. In itself it would have made a good ending but I still had another 300 miles to go, endless meals of porridge to look forward to and several days of cramp, raw skin, backache and rotting clothes. That's the problem of touching a higher level of consciousness – it's a damn big drop back to reality! As if to rub it in, the wind dropped back to the light breeze of before, reducing my speed considerably. It was difficult to gauge how many more days at sea there'd be but I reckoned on at least five. A quick check of my water levels revealed about twenty litres suitable for drinking, probably enough without serious rationing, but with the winds back to their fluky state I couldn't afford to be lavish. The prospect of eating dried porridge oats was also a powerful incentive to economise. The day after my 'moment' the weather began to turn a little cloudy and a moderate breeze sprang up. The swells began to bunch together, short intervals that slammed into *Sharky* creating a slapping sound against the hull. With precious little left in the boat she was riding high in the water, exacerbating the jerky movement that came with the swells. Nevertheless it was progress of a sort, accompanied by a change in the colour of the water. The blues of recent days had been replaced by a murky brown, caused by millions of tiny weeds that floated as a huge mat and clung to the hull. The surface film looked distinctly unattractive and was certainly not conducive to swilling in my cooking pans and dishes. The remains of porridge were bad enough without scooping up these weird-looking organisms as well. Two hundred miles to go on the noon fix and I gybed to ease back on a course that overnight had taken me a little too far south. The breeze dipped and picked up in unequal measure, and there was still no reliable consistency. The small course change had to a large extent stopped much of the hull slapping, and *Sharky* rode well, high and buoyant, through the light swells. It was hard to recall the terrors of earlier days when the surges had been so powerful I had literally feared for my life, hard to recall the mix of dread and adrenalin rush as we'd been thrown and thrust about like irrelevant flotsam.

Those days seemed part of a different voyage altogether, a world removed from the reluctant semi-tranquillity I was now in. The sea colour changed again to a monotonic dark green-brown, which, with the cloudy skies, felt like I was sailing in sepia. I was now low on water, coffee, cigarettes, food, wind and spirit. Being so close to finishing, I felt as though I was prematurely winding down, the same effect as watching sprinters approaching the finishing line, a slight slowing down when they should really be speeding up or maintaining momentum, as if the mental will was ahead of the body and beginning to accept it was over before it was: a false finish. With the end figuratively if not visibly in sight I was getting ahead of myself. I wanted to get in touch with home, have a decent shower, sleep, eat some food, and enjoy a surface that remained horizontal when I stepped on it. It wasn't meant to end this way. I still wanted a sort of dashing buccaneer landing, but I was conscious of a great tiredness creeping over me, not helped by a battered and aching body: low in spirit at that time maybe, but still with a determination to finish as best I could. I wasn't going to let a temporary spate of melancholy ruin a great adventure. I recognised I wanted it to end, but on my terms as much as possible.

Cue another bird to lift my heart, a similar one to my erstwhile companion of a few days before. A lazy circling, then a landing on the cabin roof with a perfunctory glance about before settling down to enjoy the view and take a breather. No meeting of the minds, no meaningful conversation, just a lonely sailor sufficiently deranged to speak to another of God's creatures. Clearly it felt offended by the triteness of my chitchat. The bird suffered my presence for a while, its eyes fixed warily on me fearing the worst, then, having had enough, it shivered its feathers in preparation for flight and disappeared. Lucky sod, should have asked it for a tow: better still, I thought viciously, perhaps I should have cooked it.

Thursday 23rd March. I was down to three or four spoonfuls of coffee and about a pint of the water I used for personal hygiene. I had two books left to read, a pack of cigarettes and what seemed like an inexhaustible supply of porridge. Clay Blair's *Survive* was the book in which I was currently engrossed, his account of the Andean plane-crash survivors who had turned to cannibalism – a frighteningly real dilemma I hoped I'd never have to face. A huge bang in the cockpit startled me out of the pages, whereupon I found a stunned flying fish about four or five inches long. I gently picked it up and flipped it back over the side. By way of reward the wind picked up significantly to about a force four, the strongest it had been for ages, and remained at this level overnight and up to the next day's noon fix. I was ecstatic. The combination of a moderate breeze and the short swells breathed some life back into the sailing and put the colour back into the cheeks of the sea, the white crested waves providing a welcome tint to the dark waters. My enthusiasm for a grand finale bubbled up and I felt as boisterous as the sea. Maurice was having trouble with the short swells and I should have reefed the mainsail, but I chose to experience a bit of exhilaration. I was in a hurry, now was not the time to apply the brakes. At the noon fix, under grey skies, spots of rain and gusting winds, I calculated just under 150 miles to the longed-for island of Barbados. I got goose bumps just thinking about it. Two and half days left. Two and a half days to my first Caribbean cold beer, followed very quickly, I had no doubt, by many, many more.

The weather remained cloudy with increasing gusts, Maurice still finding it difficult to cope with the short swells. With the strong southerly current I'd found myself too far north again, requiring some gybing and a course change, until I steadied back on 270 degrees, which would hopefully bring me to the southern tip of Barbados. Any lingering thoughts about the magnitude of my voyage, and the fact that it was nearly over, were banished from my mind as I concentrated on the techniques of sailing. The here and now was focused on reading the sea and the wind while seeking the new position I wanted. This was now just another day at sea, doing what I loved, feeling at one with *Sharky*, feeling the spray and seizing the moment. On a whim I went to the cabin and switched on the radio, half-expecting the batteries to have packed in. I got the surprise of my life. I heard a human voice for the first time in nearly four weeks, a rich Barbadian drawl describing the forthcoming weekend events all over the island. Wow, I thought. WOW! The voice had me transfixed for several minutes while I took pleasure from simply hearing another human being. The voice faded out to be replaced with typical Caribbean ska music, and I did an involuntary jig as I passed through the cockpit, a sort of doubled-up wobble really, taking into account my numerous aching bones.

I switched off the radio and returned to the helm. If the batteries survived, listening in again was going to be something to savour in a few hours' time, wow! I'd covered about 150 miles over the last two days and reckoned I would make landfall some time late on Sunday evening or early Monday morning. As evening fell I realised that this might be my last night at sea on *Sharky*. All being well I hoped to make Carlisle Bay, the only natural anchorage on the southwestern coast, by Sunday nightfall. I lowered the jib about nine o'clock that evening and gybed to change course to 290 degrees. As I turned in for the night a vicious squall erupted from nowhere, a strong breeze that had me hastily reefing the mainsail. For a full half-hour *Sharky* was lashed with rain as the waves increased in size, then, as quickly as it came, the squall passed over and we carried on as if nothing had happened. I couldn't really complain. I'd wanted an eventful ending. The wind began to drop off a little but the gusts remained strong, suddenly blowing over with little warning and surprising force. Huge thunder-black clouds threw more short-lived but vicious squalls over *Sharky*, who nonchalantly shrugged them off as if sensing she had but a few miles to go. These conditions lasted throughout the night, not fading away until the early hours of the morning. Eighty miles to go and I'd been pleased with the previous couple of days' runs, the squalls having given me an opportunity to catch up a little: but they'd now passed over and calm conditions settled over again, barely a flutter on the millpond of a sea. Sunday's early dawn came with miserable grey cloud and little prospect of the wind reappearing. This really was a case of so near and yet so far – so, so frustrating. Morning slipped in and the skies brightened. I stuck my head out of the hatch to find a twenty-five-foot fishing boat no more than fifty yards away. The guy on board was lazily fishing in the now blue sea and I smiled and waved.

'Barbados?' I enquired, pointing forward.

'Yeah, man,' he replied. From his demeanour I could tell he was wondering where the hell I'd sprung up from. For my part I felt a little resentful that someone else was occupying my ocean – cheeky bugger! At least the exchange confirmed I was in the right place and I felt quietly pleased with my navigational skills. Now I would have to deploy all my sailing abilities if I was going to round the southern point and get to Carlisle Bay. At twenty past ten that morning, Sunday 26th March 1994, as the cloud lifted, I glimpsed a dark smudge on the horizon. My heart skipped a beat. Barbados. I couldn't help it, my eyes glistened as a million thoughts and emotions rushed and tumbled through my mind. I was in sight of landfall, of journey's end, of the fulfilment of a crazy dream. The end was literally in sight and I couldn't really comprehend what I'd done, didn't know how to react. I just stared at the smudge, just stared, seeing and unseeing, looking forward, thinking back.

Finding Barbados was one thing, getting there another. I'd noticed that the current was pushing me a little too far south again, probably necessitating another gybe. I decided to leave it awhile before taking this action, as I knew there were some rocks just to the southern point of the island, and I'd no intention of finishing the trip ignominiously shipwrecked, to my eternal embarrassment. Twenty-two miles to go at the noon fix. The weather was sunny but within a couple of hours dark rain clouds reappeared, though there was little wind to speak of. The weather forecast on my still functioning radio gave the westerly wind speed as about six miles an hour, just not enough for my liking. I decided I'd spend the time getting *Sharky* ready for her anchorage, give myself a meagre strip wash using my drinking water, and try to make myself as presentable as possible. As I busied myself I was interrupted by frequent short squalls, which spotted us with rain then raced off. Each time we encountered a squall I'd break off from what I was doing and take the helm, trying to keep *Sharky* on course and pinch as much mileage as possible. Progress was still painfully slow however, and the light fluky winds seemed not to help at all. Barbados remained agonisingly distant as the humidity rose. I remained at the helm all day trying to squeeze every yard from the featherweight winds. In the skies a steady stream of large aircraft droned on their final approaches to the Grantley-Adams International Airport. I wondered whether all the incoming tourists would glance out of their windows and envy the small yacht lazily on her own final approach. I didn't envy them their closeted tin can, but boy was I jealous of their speed.

Slowly, imperceptibly, Barbados edged nearer, but so did the darkening night skies as I rounded the southern tip and sailed north to my intended harbour, the earlier emotional sense of achievement now pushed to the back of my mind. It had been a long, hot, tiring day and I ached with the physical effort and mental turmoil. I had no sense of satisfaction, I just wanted to get near the shoreline and sleep. About eleven o'clock at night I limped into Carlisle Bay, desperately tacking all the time to try to get closer in to shore.

Eventually I got to within a hundred yards or so and dropped anchor in shallow water. I felt safe, not particularly hungry, but overwhelmingly exhausted with the effort of continuous helming. I remember feeling upset that it was all over but also relieved, like a soldier who has been told to stand down after a long spell on duty. I took in all the sail, then tidied up a bit. The noise and smells from the shore were overpowering. The roar of traffic blended with the stench of exhaust fumes and spicy aromas. What was weird was the sound of so many unseen voices, a constant murmur spiked with occasional raised shouts and laughs. It felt threatening and intimidating; for an instant I felt like lifting the anchor and returning to the ocean, but I couldn't, and anyway, there was no wind. It seemed as though I was perched on a meridian, a dividing line between human culture and the natural world. In front of me a new experience, behind me a great adventure that would be now nothing more than a lasting memory. In front stretched a strident waterfront, behind me a vast, quiet ocean patiently lapping at the shore, tempting those who would turn their back on cosmopolitan pleasures to seek solitude and personal challenges. I had dared to dream, dared to turn that dream into reality. The burning ambition that had focused my energies for so long had now been realised.

I knew there'd be some heartache and wistful longing for a short while until something new came along, but I had the memories of a rich experience that would last forever. I took a last glance at the shore, a long lingering look out to the dark sea, then patted my boat affectionately on the cabin roof as I went below.

This challenge was over. The rest of my life was next. Back home. An ocean away.

Epilogue

...I committed the greatest act of treason in my life.

AFTER COMPLETING MY ATLANTIC voyage I stayed in Barbados for six weeks, doing very little other than relaxing and getting the tensions and tiredness out of my system. For the first four weeks I soaked up the atmosphere, watching the island at work and play, talking to the locals and other sailors. I palled up with Yens, a German inhabitant who generously helped me out with money and food, and in return I looked after his children from time to time. My initial fears about Barbados being noisy and dingy were gradually tempered as I got to know the island and its people better. There was (and still is) great poverty but there was also a dignity and self-respect among Barbadians, even the chattels, their 'pick up and go' rickety wooden shacks were more often than not fiercely well looked after despite appearing to defy gravity and remain in one piece. The population gave out an air of warmth and friendliness and were frequently curious about my journey. A couple of local reporters turned up to interview me about my trip and I became a very minor celebrity for a day or so. By an amazing coincidence, one of them, Norman Faria, had actually interviewed Shane Acton many years earlier. Remarkably, I'd dropped anchor in virtually the same spot as he had. The island's natural beauty was wondrous and I recall many pleasant hours viewing tropical gardens, deserted beaches, sugarcane plantations, and diving and snorkelling in the clear blue waters. In between time I spent odd hours cleaning *Sharky* and gradually getting her back to a sleek, shipshape condition. I had no real plans in mind, I'd considered sailing on and through the Panama Canal to the Pacific, but I wasn't sure whether that might feature too highly in the future Mrs Clarke's plans.

After four weeks Elaine and Mum flew out to join me and we holidayed for a further fortnight before returning home to the UK. Yet again I was forced to say goodbye to *Sharky*, leaving her in the good hands of the Barbados Cruising Club, who slipped her up on the beach to await a later decision from me.

Several months later, in the November of 1994, I was asked by an Italian family to skipper their luxury fifty-foot yacht to the Caribbean and then around the world in a yacht rally. I took them on a similar route to the one I'd taken, but after a short time my heart wasn't in it. It wasn't sailing. I couldn't feel the wind or spray and I was several metres higher than the ocean. There was no 'feel', I might as well have been driving a car. Everything was electronic and kitted out with flush toilets, showers, fridges and other home comforts. We berthed in the Caribbean where Elaine joined me, then set off again. Within a month we'd had enough and decided to jump ship. The owner hired another skipper and Elaine and I returned to Barbados where I committed the greatest act of treason in my life. As expected the likelihood of a Pacific sail received a positive negative, in any case I just didn't have the finances to consider it realistically. We wanted to extend our time in the Caribbean by a further three months, then travel to America for a further month before settling down at home. The only option was to sell *Sharky*. In some ways it was an easy decision, but I hated doing it. That little lump of wood and fibreglass had been a home, a friend and a soul mate. I sold her and walked away feeling intensely guilty. Writing this book is some sort of catharsis of that guilt. If ever I meet up with *Sharky* again I can at least look her in the mast and say I've tried to immortalise her. I wonder where she is now.

On my return to the UK I spent three frantic days on the phone trying to find employment, and started with a government training agency drawing upon my previous experience in the retail trade. I eventually formed my own training company, Positive Outcomes, in late 1996. I remain the Managing Director and proud to be head of a thriving company staffed with well-motivated people.

Elaine and I were married near Macclesfield in September 1997. Our photographs and a small feature were included in *The Times*, staff of which contacted us out of the blue. They were desperately looking for a good-news story, as our wedding coincided with the funeral of Princess Diana, a sad day for much of the world but a gloriously happy one for us.

I still keep in touch with Chris, Simon and Maurice (the person, not the self-steering gear!). I hope they feel I have correctly related their involvement in my story. We remain good friends, though meetings are increasingly rare as our separate lives pull us in different directions.

I now live with my wife and two feisty sons, Bradley and Joel, in the North of England, not too far from where I spent much of my childhood. I still wander the countryside with Whisky, my Highland terrier. I've discovered mountain climbing and hill walking as the perfect anecdotes to the onset of my mid-life crisis.

I occasionally drive by Thornheyes, where I spent so much of my formative years. The ghosts of the past rise up to greet me as I approach, and I cannot pass without a lump forming in my throat. In truth a part of me has never really left.

The reasons for writing this book are twofold. Firstly the challenge made a huge mark on my life. It caused real sacrifice through my single-mindedness and forced me to examine my motives and self-belief constantly. There were times when I could easily have given up, but determination and stubbornness, traits I'd rather define as objectivity (!), kept me steadfast. I had many emotional highs and lows, particularly on the open ocean, but through them I gained a deeper insight into my being. Sailing is so much more than going to sea in a boat. The senses become razor sharp and I defy anyone not to experience a particular thrill. The adventure also reaffirmed my abiding love of nature and the outdoors – the home of real freedom and inner peace.

The second reason for writing the book was to relive my adventure and perhaps offer some inspiration to people who likewise have a dream but stop short of fulfilling it — perhaps you're one of them. 'Nothing ventured, nothing gained' is accurate as a truism, and personal sacrifices are an unavoidable reality. I'm not suggesting you immediately set out to emulate my voyage. *Your* dream is *your* dream, at whatever level you wish it to be. I didn't write this book as an exercise in self-glorification. I wrote it because it was another ambition I wanted to attain. In life we all need a Maurice, our own personal self-steering gear, keeping us true to our intended course despite inevitable setbacks and hardships. I'm not extraordinary or heroic, or even brave. I took a decision and followed it through. I hope you might be inspired to do the same. *Carpe diem*, seize the day. Life is too precious to sit and merely dream.

Since realising my Atlantic voyage I have never again sailed solo in a small boat. Sometimes as I sit by the ocean, the sound of the waves and the wind pull me back to a jumble of joyful aching recollections and an ever-distancing longing. I met so many wonderful people, visited so many interesting places and found myself into the bargain. I am, without doubt, a billionaire of rich memories.

I have also rediscovered my love for porridge.

Dave Clarke, 2007